Arnold Arthurs

Through Persia by Caravan

Arnold Arthurs

Through Persia by Caravan

ISBN/EAN: 9783744646338

Printed in Europe, USA, Canada, Australia, Japan

Cover: Foto ©Andreas Hilbeck / pixelio.de

More available books at **www.hansebooks.com**

CONTENTS

OF

THE SECOND VOLUME.

CHAPTER I.

The Zil-i-Sultan—Order about the school—Not responsible for murder—Telegraph to Tehran—Reports and rumours—Excitement in Djulfa—Closing the British School—Relapse of fever—Letter from the Prince—Persian compliments—Prescriptions by telegraphs—A Persian doctor—Persian medical treatment—Persian leeches—The Prince's Hakim—His letter of introduction—His newspaper and autobiography—The Prince and the province—A son of a moollah—"The sticks"—How punishment is given—A snow torture—A Persian dinner party—Before dinner—An Englishman's legs—A great khan—The first course—Les pièces de résistance—Going home   pp. 1—21

CHAPTER II.

Ispahan—Zil-i-Sultan and the British school—Church Missionary Society—The "Crown of Islam"—A ride through Ispahan—The Meidan—Runaway horses in bazaar—"Ambassador Lilies"—New Year's Eve—Severe cold—Sufferings of the poor

—A supper in Ispahan—Kerbela and Nedjif—Houssein and Ali—Imām Juma's Court—Confiscation of Christians' property—Bāb and Bābis—Execution of Bāb—Attempted assassination of the Shah—Punishment of the conspirators—Revenge of the Koran—Bāb and Behar—The followers of Behar

pp. 22—35

CHAPTER III.

Getting out of Persia—Northern and southern roads—Advantage of Russia—Russian goods in Persia—English interests in Persia——Mr. Mackenzie's plan—Navigation of the Karun river—From Ispahan to Shuster—A subsidy required—Price of wheat—East India Company's survey—Letter to Lord Derby—Baron Reuter's concession—Traffic in Persia—Mules and railways—Difficulties of construction—Intercourse between towns—Estimates of population—Travelling in Persia—Mountain scenery—Plains covered with snow—Persia and the " Arabian Nights"—No old men—The lady and the house—The greatest power in Persia . . . . pp. 36—50

CHAPTER IV.

Leaving Ispahan—The "Farewell" Hill—Opium manufacture—The Telegraph superintendent—Punishing a servant—Khadji Josef's tea-party—Marg—Kum-i-Shah—The baggage lost—Neither Ispahan nor Shiraz—Ahminabad—English doctor robbed—Doubt and danger—Yezdikhast—A vaulted chamber—A black vault—Telegram from Shiraz—The Abadeh Istikbal—A travelling pipe—Display of horsemanship—Abadeh—The Governor's present—Bread from Tehran—Letter from Abadeh—An ill-looking escort—Khanikora—Miserable lodging—

Soldiers refuse to march—Up the mountains—Houssein Khan
—Dehbid—Shooting foxes—Khanikergan—Meshed-i-Murghaub—Robbers about—Persian justice—Tofanghees

pp. 51—81

CHAPTER V.

Classic Persia—The Tomb of Cyrus—Date of the ruins—Passar-
gardæ—Columns of Cyrus' Tomb—Colour of Ruins—Neglected
by Persians—Kawamabad—Takht-i rawan in danger—Houssein
Khan and the Sheep—Village of Sidoon—Ruins of Istakr—
Situation of Persepolis—Araxes or Bendemeer—Staircase at
Persepolis—Darius and Xerxes—Cuneiform inscriptions—Study
of Cuneiform—Chronology of Assyria—Great Hall of Xerxes—
The Persepolitan lion—Hall of a Hundred Columns—Pro-
fessor Rawlinson on the ruins—Tomb of Darius—"The Great
God Ormazd"—The bringer of evil—Divs and Devils—
Errors in religion and art—Pedigree of architecture—Persians,
Medes, and Greeks—Origin of Ionic architecture—Leaving
Persepolis—Plain of Mervdasht . . . . pp. 82—108

CHAPTER VI.

Kinara—A family house—A troublesome cat—Houssein Khan and
the sheep—Soldiers and their debtors—Zergan—Persian
scenery—A Persian funeral—Zergan to Shiraz—Pass of Allahu
Akbar—Snow-storm at Shiraz—The English doctor—Gate of
Shiraz—A good Persian house—A present from Firman Firma
—Letter from his Excellency—A dervish at the gate—Meidan
of Shiraz—Visit to Firman Firma—Widow of Teki Khan—
Firman Firma's character—Poverty of Persia—Passion play in
Mohurrem—Bazaar of Shiraz—Tomb of Hafiz—Odes inscribed
on tomb—Translation of Hafiz—The new garden—Tea in an
imaret . . . . pp. 109—133

CONTENTS OF THE SECOND VOLUME.

CHAPTER VII.

Literature of Persia—Hafiz and Sa'di—Contemporary of Dante—Mr. Bicknell's translation of Hafiz—Consulting Hafiz as an oracle—Nadir Shah and Hafiz—Hafiz' fragments—"Tetrastichs" of Hafiz—Sa'di's "Bustan"—Sa'di's "Gulistan"—Extracts from "Gulistan"—Sa'di's wit and wisdom—Gardens of Shiraz—Slaves and slave-brokers—English surgeons and Persian patients—Influence of Russia—Mr. Thomson and Mr. Bruce—Indo-Persian telegraph—Major Champain's reports—A view of the neighbours—Persian homes—Government of Shiraz—Eeliats in Fars—Attack on a caravan—A vengeful Government—Cruel Execution of robbers—Firman Firma superseded—Taxation in Persia—The Shah and Shiraz

pp. 134—159

CHAPTER VIII.

The road to Bushire—Yahia Khan's portrait—To Cinerada—Last view of Shiraz—Difficult travelling—Khan-i-Zenoon—A caravan in trouble—A cold caravanserai—Murder of Sergeant Collins—Death of Sergeant MacLeod—Advantage of an escort—Dashtiarjan—"Eaten a bullet"—Plain of Dashtiarjan—Ghooloo-Kojeh pass—A lion in the path—Mr. Blanford's "Interview"—Up a tree—A wounded horse—Kaleh Mushír—Mount Perizan—Kotul Perizan—A solitary rock—View of Mian-kotul

pp. 160—179

CHAPTER IX.

Mian-kotul Caravanserai—Tofanghees on guard—Feuds between villagers—Kotul Dochter—Travelling on the Kotul—The Mushir-el-Mulk—Lake Famoor—Encampment of Eeliats—Ruins of ancient Persia—Plain of Kazeroon—Songs of Persian

CONTENTS OF THE SECOND VOLUME. ix

soldiers—Kazeroon—Anniversary of Houssein's death—"Ah! Houssein!"—Fanatical exercises—Orange gardens—The Sheik of Kazeroon—Plain of Kazeroon—Attack on Major Napier's caravan—Village of Kamaridj—Plain of Khan-i-Takhte—Hospitality in Persia—Kotul Maloo—A difficult path—Daliki river—Arabs in Persia—Palm-leaf huts—A loopholed bedroom—Petroleum at Daliki—Barasjoon—Rifle practice—Indian officers in Persia—Functions of Political Resident—Sowars from Bushire—Caravanserai at Ahmedy—Arrival of Captain Fraser—The Mashillah—A wet day's ride—Bushire . . . pp. 180—205

CHAPTER X.

Bushire—The Residency—Arab towers and wooden "guns"—Government in Persian Gulf—The Arabian shore—Arabs and Arabs—The Sultan's power in Arabia—Oman and the Ibadhis—Pilgrims to Mecca—Destiny of rotten steam-ships—Pilgrims' coffins—Six hundred Arabs drowned—Persian land revenue—Collecting customs' duties—Trade and population—Commerce of Bushire—Cultivation of opium—Opium and cereals—Export of opium—British expedition in 1857—Occupation of Persia—Persian army in 1857—Interests of England—The Indo-European telegraph—Persia ripe for conquest—Persia and India . . . . pp. 206—225

CHAPTER XI.

The Province of Fars—Memorandum by Colonel Ross—Boundaries of Fars—Government of Fars—Six first-class Governments—The districts of Bushire—Karagash River—Eeliats—Nomad tribes of Fars—Numbers of the tribes—Eel-Khanee and Eel-Begee—Chief routes in Fars—Taxation and revenue—A revenue survey . . . . pp. 226—235

CHAPTER XII.

British India Steam Navigation Company—Crew of the *Euphrates*—Pilgrims in difficulty—Streets of Bushire—German Archæological Expedition—Sermons in bricks—Leaving Bushire—Slavery in Persian Gulf—Fugitive Slave Circulars—The Parsee engineer's evidence—Ships searched for slaves—Pearl fisheries of Bahrein—Anglo-Turkish ideas—Lingah in Laristan—Bunder Abbas—Landing at Cape Jahsk—" Pegs" and pale clerks—A master mariner's grievance—The end of Persia—Coast of Beloochistan—Shooting sleeping turtles—Harbour of Kurrachee — Kurrachee boat-wallahs— The orthodox Scinde hat— Faults of Indian society—English ladies in India—Intercourse with natives—Unmannerly Englishmen—Exceptional behaviour

pp. 236—256

CHAPTER XIII.

Bombay—The *Serapis* in harbour—Suburbs of Bombay—Parsee dead—Towers of Silence—Hindoo cremation ground—Cotton manufacture in India—Report of Indian commission—Neglect of Indian Government—A Bombay cotton factory—Hours of factory labour—Seven weeks' work—Natives of India—Expenditure of Indian Government—The great absentee landlord—Grievance of cultivators—Their enemies, the money-lenders—English and native equity—The Suez Canal—Landing at Ismailia—English at the Pyramids—Alexandria—" Cleopatra's Needle"—Proposed removal to England—Condition of the Obelisk—Recent excavation—Captain Methven's plan—Removal in an iron vessel—Cost of removal—Egypt and the Khedive—Preparing for Mr. Cave—Sham civilisation—The horse trampling ceremony—English *en voyage*—Egypt and Persia—Customs' officers at Alexandria—Egypt and Turkey

pp. 257—277

CHAPTER XIV.

"From the Levant"—Sunnis and Shi'ahs—Turkish Government and Turkish debt—Fuad and Midhat Pashas—Not a "sick man"—"Best police of the Bosphorus"—Religious sanction for decrees—The Council of State—" Qui est-ce qu'on trompe ?"— Murad and Hamid—Error of the West—Precepts of the Cheri —Authority of the Sultan—Non-Mussulman population—Abdul-Hamid's Hatt—A foreign garrison—Hatt-y-Houmayoun of 1856—Failure of promises—Fetva of Sheik-ul-Islam—Non-Mussulmans and the army—Firman of December, 1875—Sir Henry Elliot and the Porte—Conscription in Turkey

pp. 278—295

CHAPTER XV.

Islam in Persia—Mahommedans of India—Ali of the Shi'ahs— —Abu-Bekr, successor of Mahommed—Imāms of the Shi'ahs— Reza and Mehdee—Religion in the East—Mahommed as a soldier—War with infidels—Christianity of Middle Ages— Stretching the Koran—Mahommed's marriage law—Status of Mahommedan women—Women and civilisation—Special privilege of Mahommed—Mormonism and Mahommedanism— Consequences of polygamy—Protection of polygamy—Mahommed and Ayesha—Scandal silenced by the Koran—Mahommed's domestic difficulty—Law for men and women— Women in Mahommed's heaven—The Mahommedan paradise —Mahommed and the Jews—Birth of Christ in the Koran— Miracles of Christ—English leaning to Islam—Mahommedanism and Christianity—Christians of the East—Moslem intemperance—Wine and the Koran—Superiority of Christianity

pp. 296—325

THROUGH PERSIA BY CARAVAN.

CHAPTER I.

The Zil-i-Sultan—Order about the school—Not responsibl for murder—Telegraph to Tehran—Reports and rumours—Excitement in Djulfa—Closing the British school—Relapse of fever—Letter from the Prince—Persian compliments—Prescriptions by telegraphs—A Persian doctor—Persian medical treatment—Persian leeches—The Prince's Hakim—His letter of introduction—His newspaper and autobiography—The Prince and the province—A son of a moollah—"The sticks"—How punishment is given—A snow torture—A Persian dinner party—Before dinner—An Englishman's legs—A great khan—The first course—Les pièces de résistance—Going home.

MRS. ARNOLD had such painful experience of the Zil-i-Sultan's carriage, that we hoped she would not return in it, and had sent a servant to bring up the takht-i-rawan; but, as we afterwards learnt, the mules were not easily found, and we had to leave as we arrived, with my wife in the carriage. Mr. Bruce joined us in about twenty minutes. I was anxious to know the cause of the missionary's detention. He was evidently very much disturbed. He told us that after I had left the room, the Zil-i-Sultan had said to him, in presence of the moollah and the vakeel, and indeed of all who remained, that his school had caused much complaint, and that it must be closed at once. Mr. Bruce asked the reason for this sudden order. Then the Prince began a rambling statement made up of the accusations he had heard from all sides: the missionary had boasted of having converted a Mussulman; there were Mussulman children in the school; the teachers were not good men; he or they had said that the Virgin Mary was just like other women; the Armenian priests had said the school was doing harm in Djulfa; in short, the Zil i-Sultan would not have it; the school must be closed. His Highness concluded by turning to the officer who had charge of his relations with aliens in religion and allegiance, and saying: "You see that this is done, or I'll cut your ears off." This officer, whose place is an established one in the Imperial system of Persia, bowed, and Mr. Bruce endeavoured to excuse his school. "It is quite free," he said; "no one is constrained to attend, and to the people of Djulfa it is a very great benefit." "Free!" shouted the Zil-i-Sultan, with a show of the native Kajar tiger. "Free! No one is free except my father and me. If I please that the people shall not go to school, and grow up barbarians, that is my affair." He would hear no more. But Mr. Bruce is a persevering man, and still he argued that his school ought not to be closed, and intimated that he could not obey the order. "If you are murdered," replied the Prince—with cruelly thoughtless exposure of this good man's life to the fanaticism of all who heard him, and all to whom his words were to be reported—" I shall not be responsible."

And so the interview ended; the fanaticism of Ispahan encouraged to attack and murder the British missionary, and his school to be closed. It was a dangerous position, not only for Mr. Bruce but in a less degree for ourselves. The American mission schools in Tehran and Tabriz have never been molested by the Shah's Government, and the missionary naturally felt most unwilling to close this, the only British school in Persia. We agreed that it would be best not to close the school until there was further pressure, amounting to force, from the Prince, and Mr. Bruce determined that the pupils should be received next day as usual. We had just settled this when the takht-i-rawan came in sight, and on the Zayinderud bridge, after enduring the pavement of the avenue, we dismissed the carriage, having first satisfied the clamour of its five attendants for "pish-kish."

On arriving at Mr. Bruce's house, we immediately arranged a long telegram to the British Minister in Tehran, informing Mr. Thomson of the Prince's order and of his invitation to murder, requesting that immediate steps might be taken to secure Mr. Bruce's personal safety and to enable him to continue the useful work of his school. We had not long to wait for evidence that the Zil-i-Sultan's rash speech was known throughout all Ispahan. Next morning an Armenian came in full of the news. A report, and a very accurate report of the Prince's words, was circulating in Djulfa, with embellishments of Persian flavour. This man said he had heard that the Roman Catholic "padre," the Armenian bishop, and the chief sheik of Ispahan, had given the Prince two hundred tomans as the price of the order for the closing of the school, and that Mr. Bruce, who is popularly regarded as a rich man because he aided very largely in obtaining and distributing the Persian Famine Relief Fund, had since capped their bribe by the larger one of six hundred tomans, for which sum the Zil-i-Sultan had agreed to put three of the missionary's enemies to death.

Throughout the day, many of the pupils were absent from the school, and by evening, the order of the Prince and his threat of "the sticks" to the parents of those who disobeyed, were known to all. The school was nearly deserted; and the Christian people of Djulfa very fearful of outrage by the Mussulmans. The excitement was intense, and in the circumstances, Mr. Bruce thought it his duty, for the preservation of peace and order to close the school. In the ordinary course of events, the Christmas holidays would have commenced in ten days, and on closing the school, he affixed a notice upon the doors announcing that the vacation would begin ten days earlier than usual.

Unfortunately I was at this time in bed suffering a serious relapse of fever, accompanied with the most agonizing rheumatic pains. For a fortnight I could not put my feet to the ground. I fell ill within a few hours after leaving the palace. The Zil-i-Sultan had quitted Ispahan for his favourite hunting grounds at Marg, a chapar-khanah in the mountains, about twelve miles distant. On the day after our interview, the controller of his palace arrived at Mr. Bruce's house followed by two slaves who carried a large antelope tied to a pole, the ends of which rested on their shoulders. It was the first fruit of the Prince's sporting expedition, very kindly sent to me as a present. With the venison, the Prince Governor sent a letter, in Persian, which is a very interesting specimen of polite letter-writing in a country where it is a breach of good manners not to employ compliments, and of good sense to take them for more than mere words. I am quite sure his Royal Highness would not object to see his letter in English print:—

"EXALTED IN DIGNITY, COMPANION OF HONOUR, MR. ARNOLD !—In the first place I write to inquire after your health, and am extremely desirous that your time should be spent happily, and that you should enjoy good health and peace, especially during your sojourn in Ispahan. You should, without fail, visit the ancient buildings of this place, which are the memorials of mighty kings who had their wars, their cares, and pleasures in this world, and against their wills left this earth and have passed away. Now, here are we remaining behind, and what Allah may decree concerning us ——.

"It would have given me much pleasure to have remained in the city that I might fully enjoy your society, for you appeared to me to be a perfect man and well-informed. I shall return on Saturday.

"I should be delighted if you could come to these hunting-grounds and see with what difficulty and courage Persian horsemen strike this kind of game, for without doubt it is a sight well worth seeing. The chase in Persia is attended with much hardship, and is not as it is in Europe.

"I send you by my servant an antelope which I have shot with my own hand. I hope you will eat it in company of friends.

"SULTAN MAZŪD MIRZA, KAJAR,

"ZIL-I-султан."

The least acquaintance with Persian habits of speech reduces such extravagant expressions as are met with in the above letter to their proper meaning, which is simply that of a mere flourish of the pen. To say in Persian that Mr. So-and-so is "exalted" and "perfect" means nothing more than, or nothing very different from, the words in which any Englishman, refusing the prayer of a humble correspondent, assures that suppliant for favour that he (the great man) remains the "faithful servant" or the "most obedient, humble servant" of the disappointed place-hunter.

In thanking the Prince for his letter and present, I did not feel able to allude to his arbitrary decree concerning the school, and soon I became much too ill to leave my bed. There was no English doctor nearer than Tehran on one side and Shiraz on the other, a ride of a week for any one who "chapared" hard either way. We sent an account of my condition by telegraph to Dr. Baker, the medical superintendent of the Indo-Persian Telegraph, and with prompt kindness he prescribed by "wire." As for medicine, there was fortunately a small supply of that he recommended, at the Telegraph Office in Ispahan, but he also ordered immediate application of leeches, and accordingly we despatched Kazem in search of those live lancets which seem common to all countries. There had been a heavy fall of snow in the night, which lay white and deep about the doors and windows of my bedroom. Kazem returned with tidings of a man renowned for the application of leeches, who was to follow him. Presently the *hakim* himself arrived with his box of leeches, an old man with a long beard dyed a most fiery red, his eyes deeply sunken, his head covered with the drab skull-cap of the country; his outer garment of sheepskin, fitting loosely over a long tunic of blue cotton; the lower part of his legs was bare, and almost as dark in colour as the woven socks which covered his feet. His shoes were of course left outside the door, and his tread was noiseless as that of a cat.

The ideas of a Persian doctor are few. He relies most conspicuously upon the aid of. Allah, whom he invokes every minute, and at every step in his proceedings. He has a decided tendency to blood-letting, and a delight in strong medicines. In a morning's walk through the streets of Ispahan, we have often seen the snow blood-stained as if slaughter had been done in these public places. Sometimes we saw in passing the actual operation, a patient extending his bare arm in the street for the barber's lancet. We inquired of several, why they were thus bled? One replied that he had a cold, another that he had a pain in his stomach, a third that his head ached and so on. Perhaps it may be said without error, that such drastic treatment, whether purgative or phlebotomic, will remove, in ninety-nine cases out of a hundred, the particular sensation which led the patient to the doctor. It is not for us to assess the amount of subsequent injury or physical deterioration. The probability is of itself alone sufficient to account for the high esteem in which ignorant people hold strong treatment, a regard always exhibited with inverse ratio to the education and enlightenment of people. In a country like Persia, every Englishman is tempted to play the doctor; to Persians the mere sight of a European seems to suggest a cry of "*dvor!*" "*dvor!*" (medicine! medicine!) We have met with sufferers from ophthalmia who shouted the word as they laid fingers on their eyes, and who turned away with disgust when we recommended a plentiful application of water, the neglect of which is half the cause of that terrible and disabling disease.

My Persian had something of the manner of an English medical man, though with a gravity which does not belong to Europe. "He had seen worse cases," and "Inshallah!" (God willing!) he would make me better. I felt interested in seeing what there would be of novelty in his simple work. He prescribed a hot bran mash to be used as a vapour bath, and before applying the leeches, provided himself with a quantity of the tinder of burnt linen, in which he placed the utmost faith for stopping undue bleeding from the leech bites. He did his work well, came on three consecutive days to see how it was progressing, and when asked to name his own remuneration, mentioned three krans, about two shillings and sixpence, with evident doubt as to whether he was not making an exorbitant demand.

But we were to receive a far greater medicine man. The news of my illness reached the ears of the Zil-i-Sultan, who sent the following letter, in Persian, by the hands of his own "hakim," a man of great renown in Southern Persia, not only for medical skill, but for literary acquirements. There was commotion at his arrival with a train of royal servants. He was a bright-eyed, pleasant-looking man, about six-and-thirty years of age, dressed in military uniform, of European cut, with the high black hat of the Persians. He had a sword at his side and a cigarette in his mouth. Throwing off his shoes at the door, he approached my couch with a low bow, and presented the Prince's letter, which upon translation into English ran thus:—

"EXALTED IN DIGNITY, COMPANION OF HONOUR, MR. ARNOLD!—God knows that on hearing continually of your illness I have been greatly distressed, for two reasons. First, because I saw you were a good and perfect man; and it is a sad thing that such a man as you should be ill without any apparent cause.

"Secondly, I could not in any wise be happy that

you should not pass your time pleasantly while you are in my province; and, with all lowliness of mind, do I pray and beseech the blessed and most high God, and those near His presence, to give you complete restoration to health, that you may leave my Government in great happiness.

"I send my chief doctor, Mirza Tagi Khan, Colonel, a man who has travelled, and who is skilled in home and foreign sciences, to look to your health. If you will consult him, he will have much pleasure in prescribing for you. This is that distinguished individual who cured my hand when it was so bad that I had no hopes that any one in the Empire of Persia could heal it. He made that perfect cure which you have seen, and, Inshallah! he will work as wonderfully in future. It was with that very hand I shot the deer I sent you.

"I long to hear of your recovery and to enjoy your society. As soon as you are well I hope I shall have the pleasure of a talk with you.

"SULTAN MAZŪD MIRZA, KAJAR,
"ZIL-I-SULTAN."

Tagi Khan could talk more French than any Persian we had met with, and we made no objection to his very simple prescription of quassia, which he subsequently sent in a queer-shaped bottle "corked" with cotton-wool. The Persians are badly off for bottles and have no corks. The bottles they make of very brittle glass, have small mouths, and the cotton-wool used for stopping, is, when necessary, secured with sealing-wax.

Tagi Khan willingly turned the conversation from my illness to his own accomplishments. While attending the Zil-i-Sultan, when the Prince was Governor of Shiraz, he had edited a newspaper, of which twelve copies had been published. These he had bound into a volume, of which he kindly proposed to send us a copy. He had also written an autobiography, of which he would send us a copy containing his photograph. Both arrived in the evening. The newspaper is a curiosity, in size equal to two pages of the *Echo* in its first and most prosperous days. Its pages contain, together with a few telegrams and extracts from foreign letters translated from European journals, nothing but accounts of the movements of the Shah and of the Imperial family. It is, however, much better than nothing at all; and when Tagi Khan came again to see us, we pressed him to continue in Ispahan the work he had begun in Shiraz. The copy of his autobiography is a beautiful manuscript, a mode of publication which, having passed away from Europe, survives in the more ancient countries of Asia.

The Zil-i-Sultan is worth looking at again if only because he is a fair type of a Persian ruler. It is impossible to be insensible to his good qualities or blind to his faults. Perhaps it may be said that while the former are natural, the latter result from defective education and from the unbridled exercise of despotic authority. With the tastes of a hunter, with no idea of government but that of force, with no shadow of doubt as to the absolute right of his father and himself to dispose, at their pleasure, of the liberties and lives, the property and relationships of every one in Ispahan; controlled only by fear of exciting a fanaticism which would rise in a body stronger than his authority, and taught from infancy to regard the people as existing only to make wealth for the monarch and his officers—why should we look for good results from the absolute rule of such a man? To me, the Prince seemed a wayward, passionate youth, moved by strong impulses, alternately good and very bad. Disliking, yet fearing the priests of Islam; utterly untaught as to the higher principles of morality, such a man's standard of right is never erect. I can quite believe that the writer of those gracious, kindly letters I have quoted, is at other moments the ferocious tyrant he is said to be by the people of Ispahan.

Shortly before our arrival, the Zil-i-Sultan had displayed some energy in opposing the domination of the priesthood; had sent soldiers to force a criminal from sanctuary, and had banished a sheik-priest who, in his capacity of judge in the Court of the Imām-

Juma, had been guilty of horrible oppression. When we were riding into Ispahan, we met this ecclesiastic on his way into exile, seated upon a white donkey, and attended by three moollahs. But before he reached the first stage out from Ispahan, he had been fetched back, and reinstated by the Prince, who had thus quickly given way to ecclesiastical influence, and perhaps menace. There lived in Ispahan a man, the son of a moollah, well known for the liberality, as we should say, of his religious opinions—one who had been treated in a friendly manner by the Zil-i-Sultan, who is known to share his theological views. To the horror of the sheik-priest, this man wore clothes which did not indicate that his parents belonged to the sacred order, and frequent complaint of this impropriety was lodged at the palace. It was during my illness that the Prince sent for this man, and bade him change his clothing, which his Highness said was offensive upon one of his descent to the Sheik-ul-Islam. The man, eager to obey the wish of his illustrious friend, departed, and quickly reappeared in orthodox costume. "Go," said the gratified Prince, "to the sheik, and show him how quickly you have at my request conformed to his desire." The man went; but immediately upon reaching the presence of the religious authority, he was seized and ordered to be beaten with "one hundred sticks." We were told of this in a street of Ispahan, and at once made close inquiry into the truth of the story. We found that no exaggeration had been made, and that the sufferer had been so cruelly punished that for weeks he would be unable to put his feet to the ground.

In Persia, death or "the sticks" is the commonest punishment. The man, in the latter case, is laid on the ground, and after his shoes and stockings are removed, his ankles are passed through leather loops fastened to a beam, which is held by two men at nearly the length of his legs from the ground, and by them is turned until his ankles are so tightly secured that no writhing of his back can unplace them. Near him are laid the precise number of sticks to which he is sentenced. These are lithe switches, five or six feet long and rather more than half an inch thick in the centre. Two experts—who usually wear scarlet coats bound with black, which is the uniform of the Shah's executioners—then take their places near the beam, each armed with a stick, with which they in turn belabour the soles of the feet until the stick is broken too short for use. In the case above referred to, the beating was continued until the hundred sticks were reduced to this condition. The Prince was annoyed at the severe punishment of his friend, but his Highness had to bear it; for in Persia, unless stirred to unwonted effort, the Shah's Government is far less powerful than the chief priests of Islam.

A European doctor, to his shame be it said, talking

one day with the Zil-i-Sultan upon the interesting topic of torture, suggested an ancient method which, we were told, at once struck the Prince as applicable in the snowy region of Ispahan. To draw the teeth of Jews who refused gifts to the Government, was the practice in days when the civilisation of England was no more advanced than that of Persia; but I never heard before of stuffing a man's trousers with snow and ice as an efficient way of combating his refusal to pay a large demand in the season when the thermometer stands—as it does in Central Persia—for months below zero. We were told that one day when the Prince was returning from hunting, he met two dervishes on the road, who did not recognise or make way for him. The Zil-i-Sultan at once snatched his gun from a servant, and wounded the unhappy dervishes—a story to which it would be easy to add many others of similar import.

I was invited to a dinner which was to be thoroughly Persian. It was a bitterly cold evening and the guests arrived mostly on mules, and all wrapped from head to foot in furs. At first, it does strike one as odd, to be received upon an occasion of ceremony, in a room without chairs or table, indeed with nothing but a carpet. The room was high, the ceiling domed and painted, and upon it there was a good deal of gilding and stalactite ornament such as is seen in the Crystal Palace revival of the colouring of the

Alhambra. There were hung on the walls several pictures of women such as are exhibited for view in the Palais Royal, and there were also one or two familiar prints from the *Illustrated London News*. At a lower level, there were some pictures painted in Persian style, that is, crowded with figures, no regard being had to perspective or to gradation of colour. One represented the miraculous procession of birds and beasts into Noah's Ark, the rear brought up by Noah himself, whose beard, colossal and black as a raven's wing, drew attention to the far background.

The shoes of all the guests who were not European were outside the door; their overcoats thrown in a corner of the apartment, which was at once reception and dining-room. In a rectangular recess, three musicians, sitting on the floor, discoursed strange song and music. One had a wiry instrument, resembling a small guitar; another produced short screams from a sort of flageolet; and the third, who also contributed the chief part of the vocal entertainment, had a small drum. In the centre of the room, there was a Persian carpet of many and beautiful colours; round the sides were felts, nearly half an inch thick, and five feet wide, upon which most of the guests sat or reclined.

It is not considered good manners in the East to display much of one's legs upon the carpet. Mahommed, the founder of Islam, has been praised by his biographer because he never projected his legs or his feet before company; and we are told that the Prophet showed his humility of spirit in never suffering his knees to stand out beyond those of the person with whom he was conversing. But an Englishman at a Persian dinner wishes in vain for the power of fulfilling the rigorous demands of etiquette. To sit on one's heels, as camels and Persians do, requires the training of a lifetime. No one can assume the fashion for the first time in manhood. I found my legs appearing so awkward that I was glad to hide the exhibition with a shawl. The imposing dignity with which my neighbour, a man of splendid apparel and appearance, managed his naked extremities, fondling now and then his toes with his hands, made my legs and booted feet so very obvious a nuisance. This man wore a robe of honour, of cashmere, which had been given him by the Shah, and underneath this garment, upon the junction of his green tunic and loose trousers of black satin, his waist was bound with a magnificent scarf. He seemed a man of immense strength; his face, full of power, was bounded on the top by his black hat, and beneath by a dense beard, dyed with the same colour. He had but one tone of voice, and that the loudest in the room. He had, it was said, amassed great wealth from farming the Customs in all the south of Persia. I had already heard of this person, and had met with some account of his transactions in official reports. For the privilege of collecting as much as he could obtain under the name of Customs in the port of Bushire, the principal port of Persia, in the year 1873, this Khan paid 32,000 tomans, or about 12,800*l*. None but his dependents are employed in obtaining the revenue; there is no interference of any sort by employés of the Government, and no returns or reports are required of any of his transactions. In these circumstances, surely it was mild language which the British Resident at Bushire used in reference to this monstrous abuse of fiscal authority, when he wrote to the Indian Government, that "the system is felt to be inconvenient by traders."

Having disposed of my intrusive limbs, I asked my neighbour on the other side something more about this man, and he told me it was notorious he had began life as a robber, and that his greatest success in that line had been in connexion with a royal caravan. "But," said he, "the Khan has bad times. I met him the other day coming from Tehran, and he looked so 'miserable, that I at once believed I had heard a correct account of his visit to the capital. He is obliged to pay so much every year to the Imperial revenue, but occasional contributions are forced at Tehran by threats of loss of office or of the sticks."

The Khan was roaring, the singers twanging, piping, drumming, and shouting monotonous love-songs, when the first "dish" was served. A servant walked round the room carrying a large bottle of arrack in one hand, and wine in the other. The Khan took half a tumbler of the fiery spirit, and drank it off without winking; most of the guests preferred arrack. Another servant followed with a plate, in which was laid about half of a sheet of Persian bread, thin, tough, and flabby. Upon the bread was a heap of kababs, pieces of meat about an inch square, well cooked, and covered with the remainder of the bread, which was turned over them. Each guest raised the bread flap, took a kabab with his fingers, added a piece of the flap, or wiped his fingers upon it, as he pleased. For three hours this was the form of the entertainment; the talk and the music went on while the kababs, the arrack, and the wine circulated. About ten o'clock the real dinner began. A table was brought in, a cloth spread; bowls of sherbet, piles of boiled rice, other piles of pillau, a mixture of rice and stewed fowls, were introduced. In one huge dish was placed a lamb, roasted whole, presenting a horribly sacrificial appearance. I watched the Khan, curious to see if it was possible that appetite for boiled rice remained after he had drank about a pint of raw alcohol, intermixed with kababs. His attendants—the servants of every guest share in the work on these occasions—drew a couch towards the table, upon which the Khan lifted himself; then he pointed with a loud laugh to the soup tureen, from which the British Agent, an Armenian, was helping himself. "That's what makes you such a little fellow," he said. "I like pillau." He bared his huge arm to the elbow to vindicate his preference, and for the better handling of the rice. Plunging his fingers into a pile, he kneaded a huge bolus of the greasy rice at a single pinch, and pressed it into his mouth; another and another followed, until he had made a great hole in the heap of pillau. For nearly an hour there was little talk, much eating and drinking; then some coffee, and after that the guests were hoisted on to the high saddles of their steady, patient mules, and jogged homewards through the narrow streets, lighted only by the lanterns of their attendants.

CHAPTER II.

Ispahan—Zil-i-Sultan and the British school—Church Missionary Society—The "Crown of Islam"—A ride through Ispahan—The Meidan—Runaway horses in bazaar—"Ambassador Lilies"—New Year's Eve—Severe cold—Sufferings of the poor—A supper in Ispahan—Kerbela and Nedjif—Houssein and Ali—Imām Juma's Court—Confiscation of Christians' property—Bāb and Bābis—Execution of Bāb—Attempted assassination of the Shah—Punishment of the conspirators—Revenge of the Koran—Bāb and Behar—The followers of Behar.

AS soon as I was able to leave my bed, I desired the British Agent to ask the Zil-i-Sultan for an audience, that I might offer some remarks upon the closing of the British school. The Prince appeared glad to see me, and at once cleared his room that we might talk more freely. I suggested that possibly he was not aware of the character of the school, which I explained was not, as many Persians supposed, maintained by the missionary, but by a great society (the Church Missionary Society), to which hundreds of thousands of English men and women, including the Queen, subscribed. The English people would not, I said, contend that they had a right to establish schools in Persia. I could not question the authority of his Royal Highness to close the school, but I ventured to add that this arbitrary proceeding would be regarded by England as a very unkindly act, and would do much, when it became generally known, to destroy all the good feeling which the liberal professions of the Shah during his stay in England had caused to prevail towards the Government of Persia; that the English people were not ambitious of changing the established religion of Persia was, I urged, evident from the fact that the Church Missionary Society, with an income of about 175,000*l.* a year, expended no more than a few hundreds in the Persian Empire, and confined all that expenditure to Ispahan.

I did not refrain from adding that his Highness's order appeared the more unjust because the Armenian Orthodox, and the Roman Catholic schools in Djulfa were not molested; and because in Tehran and in Tabriz, the schools of American missionaries had been long established and were prospering under the immediate government of the Shah and of the Crown Prince.

The Zil-i-Sultan appeared somewhat moved by these arguments, and said he was very anxious to explain the circumstances under which he had felt bound to issue the order for closing Mr. Bruce's school. "The Shah, my father, and I," he said," are friends of education. You must do us the justice to admit that. I am no fanatic. I mean to ask my father to allow my children to be educated in Europe; that will show you I am not a bigot. But Ispahan is Ispahan. They call it the 'Crown of Islam,' and the moollahs are very strong here. I closed the school to preserve the peace of the town. The Armenian bishop came to me; the Roman Catholic priest came to me; the moollahs complained; they came here and cried; tears ran down their faces. What could I do? They said that Mr. Bruce had converted a moollah; that he had spoken in the streets of the Virgin Mary as being not different from other women; they stirred up the people, and I was obliged to close the school. But I give you my word it shall be opened again—at the proper time. I will see Mr. Bruce. He thinks I am not a friend to him, but I am his friend. I will show him how to act so as not to excite the moollahs."

After taking leave of the Prince, I rode for some hours about the streets and bazaars of Ispahan. There are literally miles of ruins in and about the city, and of ruins that are never picturesque nor in any way attractive. Along the side of the river there is nothing but ruin. Thick walls of mud bricks which have not lost their original colour by exposure to the sun (the only baking that Persian bricks ever get), are broken into heaps of dusty ruin, and have remained untouched, the home of birds and lizards. Some of the bazaars are well built, with lofty, vaulted roofs of stone, but of these not a few are deserted. I rode through these sombre, cold, deserted places, the way encumbered by stones fallen from the overhanging roof, in momentary danger of another fall. Decay, dilapidation, and ruin are never out of sight. In the largest open place, the Meidan, which is about five hundred yards in length and two hundred broad, there is the best view of the life of the city. Caravans of camels or mules carrying travellers, pilgrims, merchandise, or supplies of fuel and vegetables, are always there. At one end is the Musjid-i-Juma, the great mosque of Ispahan, the dome and minarets adorned with coloured bricks and tiles. In the centre of the Meidan is a small, circular mound, built of brick, about as big as half a dozen wagon wheels piled together, and where the axle would be, is reared a ragged pole. This is the execution ground, and the pole at times bears the head of a criminal.

Some of the bazaars which we entered from the Meidan are full of life and interest, crowded the whole day long. It is perhaps as difficult to ride as to walk through the bazaars. A passing donkey with a load of wood is a dangerous neighbour for the knee on horseback, and on foot the jagged sticks may strike one in some tender and vital place. And then a horse may be frightened and run into a hundred dangers of this sort. On one occasion, I dismounted in a bazaar of Ispahan to buy a fur coat, and while I was trying it on, with the assistance of a crowd of idlers attracted by the sight of a foreigner, my horse broke away from my servant, and with a loud neigh flung up his heels, rushed at the servant's horse, threw himself upon it, bit it in the neck till it screamed with pain and, breaking loose, started away down the narrow bazaar, my horse in furious pursuit. I was in great fear as to the result. Such a rout I never saw. Steady-going camels roared and groaned with fright; purchasers bounded on to the stalls for safety; several people were knocked down. Fortunately no damage was done, and nobody much hurt. The runaways were caught before they got outside the bazaars, but they would not be held, and it was only by remounting that we could control them.

Ispahan would look its best in April or May, when the dark violet lilies—called "*celchee soosun*," or "ambassador lilies," because they are the first to blossom—appear, and when the mud colour of the town is relieved by the tender green of the young leaves of the plane trees. Then, as at all times, the charm is not in the buildings of the city, but in its exquisite situation, with immensely expanded views of plain begirt with mountains. The view of Ispahan from the Djulfa side of the river is not easily effaced from the memory. No doubt the great name of the city has something to do with the impression which the prospect plants upon the mind. But the real glory of the scene is the ever-varying colour of the many-shaped mountains, and the indescribable, yet not less real sense of freedom which is imparted by the aspect of the plain.

It is difficult to enter any Mahommedan city without treading on the graves of departed citizens. Main roads in the East often cross burial-grounds. Indeed, no place of sepulture is more desired than that in which there are most travellers. Fences there are none, and the tombs afford the only sign of burial. As with us, the grave is sometimes marked with a horizontal stone and sometimes with a perpendicular slab. A translation of an epitaph not uncommon in the graveyards about Ispahan runs thus:—

"The Lord of earth and sky is our helper.
The eyes of all are fixed on the Prophet.
We need not fear the light of the searching sun of the resurrection,
While the protection of Murteza Ali surrounds and covers us."

On the last day of 1875, we rode out of Djulfa to the great cemeteries on the edge of the plain. An icy wind blew over the frozen snow in which most of the gravestones were buried; only on the slopes which lay exposed to the southern sun could the brown earth be seen. One or two peasants, miserably clad in cotton, covered with a ragged sheepskin, were trying to get a handful of fuel by uprooting the camel-thorns from the desert. In the far distance, some black dots upon the snow indicated a caravan of mules approaching the city. The sun was dimmed with clouds, and where its rays did not shine, there all remained hardbound with frost.

Anywhere in the world, for those who have money in a city full of people, cold is more endurable than heat. One is not prostrated by cold as by heat, and one recovers more quickly from its effects. Frostbite is better than sunstroke, and to be chilled to the bone less painful than fever. For my part, I would rather endure an attack by robbers than be perpetually the prey of vermin; but in the extreme cold of the Persian winter there is less danger of either pest. Both hybernate in the season of frost and snow. And do not the warmth and the pleasant blaze of a wood fire make amends for the cold, while for the heat which has fevered one's brain into sleepless misery, there is sometimes no relief.

But as we turn homewards from our ride on New Year's Eve and pass though the walled, and narrow, and deadly cold streets, the deep mud frozen into hard rocks over which our horses roll and stumble, we are forced to remember how little the poor of Persia are armed against cold more intense than is ever felt in London. In Persia, the poor have no firing, few clothes, and little food. Of a group comprising half a dozen huddled round a handful of live ashes in an earthenware dish, not one had any covering on the legs between the ankle and the knee. Among the poorest of Persia, frostbite is not uncommon. They walk barefooted or in miserable shoes in the snow; then ride perhaps for hours, their feet covered with halfmelted snow; upon these the frost fixes with fatal grip, and the poor wretches ignorantly seeking relief from their tortures at the first fire they approach, lose sometimes their toes and sometimes their feet.

Happy are those who are not forced to endure extremes of climate; theirs is the most pitiable condition who sustain both severe heat and extreme cold, as do the Persians. "*Tre mese invierno; nove mese inferno*" ("three months winter and nine months hell") is the saying of Spaniards concerning the climate of Madrid. But the poor of Persia suffer in a magnified degree the miseries of poverty in Madrid.

For me, there was organised a supper, to which every person in Ispahan who could speak even a few words of any European language was invited, and the Roman Catholic priest had lent a bell, which being suspended upon a temporary stand of poles, was to be made to resound the witching hour of midnight by the servants of our entertainer. In the motley company assembled in his rooms, Armenian was perhaps the predominating element, and the Armenians are not a jovial people. The entertainment was a failure, by reason of the cold. Only one room had a fireplace, and in that a few damp logs fizzled but refused to burn continuously, and warmth could not be obtained by drinking cold thin wine of Shiraz, or egg cups of lukewarm coffee. Hot punch would have relieved the iciness of the supper; but warmth was conspicuously absent from the feast. And there was a mechanical failure. When we were trying to make merry with cold meats and colder wine, news was brought that the bell had fallen from its perch, and we were therefore left to form our own ideas as to the moment of midnight. When no doubt remained as to that having passed, we lighted our lanterns and began the work of the new year, by groping our way home through the unlighted streets of Djulfa-Ispahan, disturbing no one but the wolfish dogs which prowled in piteous hunger upon the snow.

While we were in Ispahan, a report was spread that Kerbela, where Houssein was buried, and Nedjif, where rest the remains of his father Ali, were to be ceded to the Shah. This, which would naturally delight the hearts of all true Shi'ahs, was reported in two ways. First it was said that the Sultan would give up these sacred towns to Persia as the price of an alliance, offensive and defensive, against Russia; and again it was said, that Kerbela and Nedjif were to be purchased by the Shah from the Porte for a million of tomans. One day, I showed a sketch of

Kerbela to our servants, and to a knot of bystanders, telling them what it represented. Immediately the picture was in danger. All wished to kiss it; to press it to their foreheads, and cried "Ah! Houssein!" with an expression of deep regret, more true and tender in the ardour of sincerity than one expects to find uttered over a grave which has been closed for twelve centuries.

There is but little expression of dissent in Persia; and in Ispahan orthodoxy is practically enforced by the Court of the Imām Juma. Armenians in Djulfa have actually been robbed of their property by authority of this Court, upon the representation of a renegade member of their family who had joined the community of Islam. Mr. Bruce assured us, that after he had purchased a piece of ground from an Armenian, he was cited to appear in the Imām Juma's Court, to answer the complaint of a Mahommedan, who alleged that the property did not belong to the vendor, but had passed to him, a member of the family, who had adopted the faith of Islam. The English missionary declined to acknowledge the authority of the Court. But this defiance, which was not dangerous in the case of a well-known British subject, is quite beyond the power of his poorer Christian neighbours, who are naturally fearful of the courts of law, which are strictly governed by the language of the Koran, and presided over by priests as fanatical and cruel as any Inquisitor of that European period which is well described as the Dark Ages.

The measure of injustice and oppression which these courts of the Koran inflict upon the Christians may seem mild, in comparison with the treatment by which they suppress nonconformity within the pale of their own community. We have seen an example in the sentence of "a hundred sticks," which the incautious expression of liberal views brought upon the friend of the Zil-i-Sultan, who added to free speech the wickedness of wearing trousers of European cut. There is, however, in Ispahan a surviving heresy, the most notable in Persia, which, when proved against a man, is almost a death warrant.

Early in the present century, a boy was born at Shiraz, the son of a grocer, whose name has not been preserved. Arrived at manhood, this grocer's son expounded his idea of a religion even more indulgent than that of Mahommed. He is known by the name of Bāb (the gate), and his followers are called Bābis. In 1850, Bāb had established some reputation as a prophet, and was surrounded by followers as ready to shed their blood in his defence as any who formed the body-guard of Mahommed in those early days at Medina, when he had gained no fame in battle, and had not conceived the plan of the

Koran. Bāb was attacked as an enemy of God and man, and at last taken prisoner by the Persian Government, and sentenced to death. He was to be shot. Tied to a stake in Tabriz, he confronted the firing party and awaited death. The report of the muskets was heard, and Bāb felt himself wounded, but at liberty. He was not seriously hurt, and the bullets had cut the cord which bound him. Clouds of smoke hung about the spot where he stood, and probably he felt a gleam of hope that he might escape when he rushed from the stake into a neighbouring guardhouse. He had a great reputation, and very little was necessary to make soldiers and people believe that his life had been spared by a genuine miracle. Half the population of Persia would perhaps have become Bābis, had that guardhouse contained the entrance to a safe hiding place. But there was nothing of the sort. The poor wretch was only a man, and the soldiers saw he had no supernatural powers whatever. He was dragged again to the firing place and killed. But dissent is not to be suppressed by punishment, and of course Bābism did not die with him. Two years afterwards, when the present Shah was enjoying his favourite sport, and was somewhat in advance of his followers, three men rushed upon his Majesty and wounded him in an attempted assassination. The life of Nazr-ed-deen Shah, Kajar, was saved by his own quickness and by the arrival of his followers, who made prisoners of the assassins. They declared themselves Bābis, and gloried in their attempt to avenge the death of their leader and to propagate their doctrines by the murder of the Shah. The baffled criminals were put to death with the cruelty which the offences of this sect always meet with. Lighted candles were inserted in slits cut in their living bodies, and, after lingering long in agony, their tortured frames were hewn in pieces with hatchets.

In most countries, the theory of punishment is, that the State, on behalf of the community, must take vengeance upon the offender. But in Persia it is otherwise. There, in accordance with the teaching of the Koran, the theory and basis of punishment is, that the relations of the victim must take revenge upon the actual or would-be murderers. In conformity with this idea, the Shah's chamberlain executed on his Majesty's behalf, and with his own hand, one of the conspirators. Yet the Bābis remain the terror and trouble of the Government of Ispahan, where the sect is reputed to number more followers than anywhere else in Persia. But many of them have, in the present day, transferred their allegiance from Bāb to Behar, a man who was lately, and may be at present, imprisoned at Acca, in Arabia, by the Turkish Government. Behar represents himself as God the Father in human form, and declares that

Bāb occupies the same position, in regard to himself, that John the Baptist held to Jesus Christ. We were assured that there are respectable families in Ispahan who worship this imprisoned fanatic, who endanger their property and their lives by a secret devotion, which, if known, would bring them to destitution, and probably to a cruel death.

CHAPTER III.

Getting out of Persia—Northern and southern roads—Advantage of Russia—Russian goods in Persia—English interests in Persia—Mr. Mackenzie's plan—Navigation of the Karun river—From Ispahan to Shuster—A subsidy required—Price of wheat—East India Company's survey—Letter to Lord Derby—Baron Reuter's concession—Traffic in Persia—Mules and railways—Difficulties of construction—Intercourse between towns—Estimates of population—Travelling in Persia—Mountain scenery—Plains covered with snow—Persia and the "Arabian Nights"—No old men—The lady and the house—The greatest power in Persia.

THE ways and means of getting out of Persia, are especially forced upon the mind of the traveller from Europe, when he is in Ispahan, the central city of the Empire. If he is fatigued or not in good health, one fact will weigh upon his mind—he must ride, or be carried in a takht-i-rawan, for five hundred miles before he can be clear of the dominions of the Shah, or obtain any more easy conveyance.

It is far less difficult to ride northwards to the Caspian Sea than southwards to the Persian Gulf. And as it is with travellers so it is with goods. Nothing in the way of merchandise can arrive in Ispahan except on the backs of mules, or horses, or camels. The consequence is, owing to the easier access from the north and to the proximity of Russia, that Russian imports are pressing southwards to the exclusion of English manufactures from the markets of Persia.

The entry of English goods to Persia and the export of corn, cattle, wool, and other products of that country, have been rendered much more easy by the construction of the Suez Canal, but as regards the market for our manufactures, we shall be beaten back to the coast by Russia, unless some better road is opened for the conveyance of goods to Ispahan. Russia has a great advantage over us in this respect from the north, and the bazaars of Tehran are chiefly supplied with Russian manufactures. The proposal, which was noised as being the first large work to be undertaken upon the concession to Baron Reuter, to construct a railway from Resht to Tehran, would, if carried out, have facilitated most obviously the entry of Russian goods, and have enabled Russia to command the trade, not of Tehran only, but of Ispahan, and probably of Shiraz.

Of all the Powers, Russia is the most ungenerous and unenlightened in her tariffs. She forces her wretched hardware and inferior cottons upon her subjects and her near neighbours of the semi-barbarous sort, to the complete exclusion of the superior goods which England could furnish; the north gate of Persia is absolutely in her keeping, and the proposal to carry her commerce to the chief towns of

Persia by a railway, to be constructed with English gold, implied either great ignorance of the nature and consequences of the work, or an astounding confidence in the unselfish disposition of British capitalists. Moreover, we have never been able, in passing over the ground, to see what security could be obtained for expenditure in this direction. There can be no doubt that Russia would be grateful to any foreign capitalists who would make a railway from the Caspian Sea to Tehran and Ispahan, but this would hardly diminish any desire she may have to possess the rich northern provinces of Persia; and it is undeniable that she may take them at any moment she pleases to put forth her hand; there is nothing but the Persian army to withstand her, and the railway, besides promoting her commerce, would render the military occupation of northern Persia less costly and much more secure.

For English interests it is very necessary to improve the means of communication in the south; and the best scheme I have met with, is that which was pressed in January last, though without any success, upon the Shah's Government by Mr. George Mackenzie, a British merchant, of the firm of Gray, Mackenzie and Co., resident at Bagdad. The united waters of the Tigris and the Euphrates flow past the Turkish town of Bussorah into the Persian Gulf. This confluence of the two rivers is called the Shat-el-Arab. At right angles to this great stream, and nearly opposite the town of Bussorah, the Persian river Karun contributes its flow, the junction being at the town of Mahommerah, the taking of which was the only considerable achievement of the British Expedition under the command of Sir James Outram in 1856. At Shuster, nearly half way between Mahommerah and Ispahan, the Karun is navigable by steamboats drawing four feet of water, and Mr. Mackenzie, who has lately been over the whole route, has reported that the passage of mules from Ispahan to Shuster, would be far more easy than upon the difficult path between Shiraz and Bushire. The path by which English manufactures must be carried on mules, camels, or donkeys from Bushire to Ispahan, is very little less than five hundred miles in length, whereas from Shuster to the central city of Persia, the distance would be not more than two hundred and seventy miles.

Mr. Mackenzie, probably the first Englishman who has passed over this little known region of Persia, found the Bakhtiari tribes by whom it is inhabited, better than their reputation, which is that of marauding gipsies. He states that they are hospitable, obliging, and free from caste prejudices. Mr. Mackenzie says of the tribes between Ispahan and Shuster:—" They evinced no objection to eat out of the same dish with me, smoking the kalian too at all times after me." He found the Bakhtiari people " ignorant of the division of time or of distances."

"Generally," he says, "they know of two other nations only; the Farangi [a term equivalent to 'Gentiles,' but generally employed in describing the English] and the Russ. To the latter, they appear to give precedence, as I was at more than one place asked whether the Emperor of Russia was not the Shah-in-Shah. They are a happy and contented people, entirely under the control of one chief, the Eel-khanie, whose authority alone they acknowledge." Mr. Mackenzie's proposal was that the Shah's Government should concede to his firm—which is in close relations with that of Messrs. Gray, Dawes and Co., of London—permission to put steam-vessels on the Karun, and these gentlemen have informed Lord Derby that if the British Government would give them a subsidy of 4000*l* a year they would undertake to run a steamer monthly from Shuster to Mahommerah and back. From the latter town, the vessels of the British India Steam Navigation Company, of which the firm above-mentioned are agents, run to Bushire and Bombay, and, by the Suez Canal, to London.

I have no means of judging whether the subsidy is justly calculated; but 'I know that the Russian Government gives a large subsidy, nominally for carrying the mails, to the line of steamers belonging to the Caucasus and Mercury Company—a purely Russian undertaking—which call at all the Persian landing places on the Caspian; that the British Government adopts a similar policy with regard to the British India Company; and it is obvious that in both cases this is done with a view of promoting influence and trade in Persia. But English trade is being beaten out of Persia for want of a letter entry than by the terrible road from Bushire to Shiraz; and Persia would benefit immensely by having a more ready outlet for her surplus produce. In villages not distant from the Karun, a quarter of wheat may be bought for about four shillings; so that Persia might hope, if this river were made available, to reduce the adverse balance of trade, which, in its constant augmentation, threatens the country with ruin. I am not acquainted with the precise language in which the refusal of the concession was conveyed; but I have no doubt that the negotiation failed because some Persians in high official position wanted to be paid, and largely paid, for allowing Englishmen to confer gratuitous benefit upon their country.

In 1842, when Lieutenant Selby ascended the Karun river by direction of the East India Company, he concluded his report with the words—" I feel sure the day is not far distant when these rivers will be as well known and traversed as the Indus and the Ganges." As to the present condition of British, in competition with Russian trade, Messrs. Gray, Dawes and Co., than whom probably no persons are more competent to form a trustworthy opinion, have written to Lord Derby as follows:—

"Ispahan, the centre of the Persian trade, may fairly be taken to be the common ground where Russian and British commerce meet, and until recently the expense of transporting goods to and produce from that point, by the northern and southern routes, was nearly the same. Of late years, however, the Russian Government has so far improved the northern facilities, that by degrees, various articles of commerce (for instance, copper, iron, refined sugar, manufactured hardware, candles, &c.), have been closed to us; and their trade is extending further south; and, in some instances, we are beaten even at the coast ports. The facilities provided are; frequent, cheap, and direct communication to the Caspian, abolition of the transit duties through the Caucusus on goods, viâ Poti and Tiflis, and a resolute insisting upon a prompt settlement of the claims which their traders have against the Persian authorities."

"To compensate for these growing disadvantages, we would respectfully urge upon your Lordship's consideration the necessity of adopting some protective measures for our trade in the south; and we would suggest; first, that a British Consul should be placed at Ispahan; and, secondly, that the Shah's Government should concede to us the privilege of placing steamers on the river Karún, to run from Mahommerah and Shuster, in connexion with the steamers from Bombay and London."

"About fifteen years ago, in the interests of trade the Government subsidised river steamers to ply between Bussorah and Bagdad; this has resulted in a very large and still increasing trade; the subsidy, we believe, was 4000*l.* per annum. For the same subsidy, we would be prepared to place a steamer on the Karún, and maintain a monthly service between Shuster and Mahommerah, connecting at Mahommerah with the mail steamers from Bombay, Kurrachee, and London."

Baron Reuter has not yet abandoned Persia, and is still engaged, I believe, in projecting railways, having turned his attention from north to south. If it were possible to obtain money for the construction of a railway in Persia, there can be no doubt that British interests would benefit most by a line from Yezd, through Ispahan, to Shuster, to run in connexion with steamboats on the Karun. But I cannot believe that a railway would be profitable in any part of Persia. The passengers would be but very few, and it would be extremely difficult to take the goods traffic from the backs of mules at profitable rates. We have sometimes ridden for eight hours between Tehran and Ispahan without meeting a traveller of whom it might reasonably be supposed that he would have paid to go by rail. For the ten or twelve mules and horses we required, we paid little more than the value of a shilling a day for each—a sum which included the attendance of muleteers as well as the feeding and stabling of the animals. In his report to Baron Reuter upon improved communications in Persia, Captain St. John, R.E., made the following statement:—

COST	Miles a day.	PER TON PER MILE.		
		Maximum.	Minimum.	Average.
By mules, average speed	22	15d.	3d.	3d.
By camels or asses, average speed	12	9d.	2d.	4d.

These are low rates, and the muleteers' trade in Persia is one that would die hard. The charvodars, and all of their men, are accustomed to enormous fatigues, and the class is certainly one of the most honest and worthy in Persia. In the towns, many of the wealthiest people have invested money in mules; and these, too, would look with unfriendly eyes upon the new mode of travelling.

But such interested objections, of course, wear out. The real question is whether the concession of power to construct and work a railway would be respected, and whether the traffic is, or is likely to become, sufficient to render the undertaking profitable. From all that we have seen during five months in Persia, I am inclined to think that no sufficient security could be given to justify confidence that the concession would be respected, especially if the railway were successful; and that there is nowhere in Persia—one of the most sparsely inhabited countries of the world—sufficient traffic to render a railway profitable. As to the cost of construction, although in the plains the work would be very inexpensive, yet it must be remembered that no two towns can be connected without overcoming great engineering difficulties. Between the chief towns of Persia, there are mountains which must be crossed at a height of 6000 or 8000 feet, and which are without exception rocky, some of them composed of the hardest stone. These, however, are only such obstacles as English engineers delight in surmounting; the real difficulty is in the want of security, and in the unsatisfying prospect of remunerative returns.

There is very little intercourse between the chief towns of Persia. Those doorless hovels of mud-brick, covered with a rude cement of mud and straw, which are placed at distances of twenty to thirty miles apart on the way from Resht, through Tehran and Ispahan to Shiraz, have but the one room, the bala-khanah, elevated above the noisome yard in which horses and mules are enclosed for the night. In a ride of about four and twenty days to Ispahan, we had never found, on arriving at a station, this one room already occupied, which is perhaps the strongest evidence that could be afforded of the scarcity of native or foreign travellers. Perchance some bold speculator will in the next budget of bubbles be prepared to "float" a company for working the Tehran or Ispahan Steam Tramways, Limited, regardless of the fact that it is more than doubtful if a carriage of any sort could make its way through any town in Persia. It is certainly a fact that no carriage can be obtained for hire in either of those places.

As to the population of the towns and of the country generally, there exist no trustworthy figures. The number of the inhabitants of Ispahan is stated to be more than 90,000, but after passing five weeks in the city and becoming well acquainted with nearly every part of it, I am not inclined to believe that more than half that number of people can ever at any one time be found in the " Crown of Islam." The Persians do not seem to retain their senses or their calculating faculties when the numbers rise over one thousand. I have said that the Zil-i-Sultan told me that the Shah had five Persian crores of soldiers (2,500,000 men), but after seeing much more of his father's dominions than he has himself beheld, it would not surprise me to learn that the whole number of men, women, children, and slaves in Persia does not exceed his Royal Highness's estimate of the Persian army. We have never travelled in a country so thinly populated, and in this respect the contrast with India is very striking. Even on the most frequented track in Persia, the mule-path from Tehran to Ispahan, we have ridden eight and twenty miles in daylight without seeing a human habitation or, except the footmarks upon the road, a trace of man.

But the charm of travelling in Persia is utterly lost when one weighs all that is met with in the scale of progress. In Persia, passing from the swift and, on the whole, steady career of Western Europe in the ways of civilisation, there appears to be not only an absence of progress, but rather retrogression. That which is truly interesting in Persia is the extended scenery and the out-door life—for no European sees much of the indoor existence—of the people. Persia is *par excellence* the land of magnificent distances. In summer the mountains, always in sight and in many places strongly coloured with the metallic ores which they contain, glow with wondrous beauty in the roselight of the morning sun, and harden into masses of deep purple and black when the clear and pleasant starlight is substituted for the glare of the blazing sun of Persia. In another season, when looking from the snow-covered mountains, we have seen the plains resembling an Arctic sea, the apparently perfect level covered with a dazzling expanse of untrodden snow; and again when the white hills loomed through the blinding storm like icebergs of Polar regions.

Wherever the people are seen their presence adds to the charm of the landscape. The men are handsome and picturesque in their costumes of blue or white cotton, with here and there one in red or yellow.

In the towns the traveller recognises in the people the characters of the tales in the "Arabian Nights." There is the handsome, stalwart porter, the *hamal*, with panting breast exposed and darkly sunburnt skin, scratching his shaved head, ready for any new summons, including that of the mysterious lady, the mistress of the equally mysterious house, wherein he may be murdered or enriched, killed and buried like a dog, or clad in splendid robes and served by lovely maidens bearing dishes of gold and silver, according to the good pleasure of the genii. There, in the streets or bazaars of Ispahan, is the merchant from Bagdad, wearing the respectable marks of a pilgrim, and saluted in virtue of his journey to Mecca by all men as "Hadji." His green or white turban is spotless and ample; a cloak of fine cloth, gold braided, hangs from his shoulders, and his tunic of purple or green is bound with a costly sash, in which probably the case containing his materials for writing is thrust like a dagger. Everywhere is seen the priest or moollah, riding, with nothing of meekness in his face, a white donkey; his dress proclaiming him to be a member of the caste which is strongest in Persia. There are no old men, for those whose beards are naturally white with age have been transformed into unnatural youth by dyeing the hair bright red with khenna. The hands and feet of such are often coloured with the same preparation, and they sit smoking a talian or reading the Koran upon the front planks of their stall in the cool bazaar, without any more apparent interest in their business than if it were a mere cloak for the supernatural concerns of their active life in such another sphere as that in which moved the genii of those wonderful tales.

Even without aid from the genii there are always present in Persia two mysteries, which no doubt will serve to transmit as long as they exist, the ideas of the "Arabian Nights." These are the veiled lady, and the walled-up house, into which no outside eye can penetrate. No giaour can see even the eyes of a Persian woman of the middle and superior classes. She moves through the streets and bazaars on her white donkey, or on foot, in complete disguise. Even her husband would not recognise her. She is covered —as I described the women of Resht—from head to foot in the loose chudder of indigo, or black-dyed cotton or silk. Over her face there is the long white veil tied across the chudder, where that envelope covers all but the visage. The legs are hidden in loose trousers of cotton or silk of the same colour as the chudder, which are not worn in the house. In all her outdoor life she is a moving mystery. She may be young or old, white or black, fair or ugly, on a mission of sin, or upon an errand of charity; no one knows who she is as she shuffles along upon shoes which are difficult to keep upon her feet, as the upper leather ends far before the heel. She raises at some mud-walled house an iron knocker upon a door like that of a fortification; is admitted; the door is closed, and what goes on within that house, what is the fate of the women, the children, and the slaves, no one outside can know. There is no window from which they can communicate with the outer world—it is a despotism within a despotism. Each one of these walled houses is the seat of a despotic sovereignty, established and confirmed by the greatest power in Persia—that of the Koran.

CHAPTER IV.

Leaving Ispahan—The "Farewell" Hill—Opium manufacture—The Telegraph superintendent—Punishing a servant—Khadji Josef's tea-party— Marg — Kum-i-Shah — The baggage lost—Neither Ispahan nor Shiraz—Ahminabad—English doctor robbed—Doubt and danger - Yezdikhast—A vaulted chamber—A black vault—Telegram from Shiraz—The Abadeh Istikbal—A travelling pipe—Display of horsemanship—Abadeh—The Governor's present—Bread from Tehran—Letter from Abadeh—An ill-looking escort—Khanikora—Miserable lodging—Soldiers refuse to march—Up the mountains—Houssein Khan—Dehbid—Shooting foxes—Khanikergan—Meshed-i-Murghaub—Robbers about—Persian justice —Tofanghees.

OVERLOOKING the rich and extensive "Vega," or Plain of Granada, there is a hill called "El Ultimo Sospiro del Moro" ("The last sigh of the Moor."). It is supposed, or assumed, that the last of the Mahommedans, on quitting the Alhambra and its glorious neighbourhood, cast from this hill "a longing, lingering look behind" at the Spanish city, the name of which is for ever associated with their rule. Near Ispahan, on the way to Shiraz, there is a hill commanding a view as extensive, and it is called "the farewell," or "the good-bye."

It is not every day that travellers set out from

Ispahan for Shiraz, and on the day of our departure all Djulfa was astir. A superintendent of the Persian Telegraph, who was about to make his annual inspection of the line, which ran at all times in the neighbourhood of our path, very kindly arranged his journey so that he and his five servants might join our caravan. We had engaged mules and horses on the recommendation of an Armenian merchant, one Khadji Josef, in whose service our mules had carried opium to Bushire. During our stay, there were always men engaged in the manufacture of opium at Khadji Josef's house. In the process, the opium looked exactly like Menier's chocolate. Each man had a large tin tray before him, under which was a small fire of charcoal. On the tray was a quantity of crude opium, which with sticks the workman always kept in motion, until after much stirring and kneading it was poured into moulds, and came out in the shape of small two-pound cakes, ready for export to England. Most of the Persian opium, it is said, is sent to this country, to be used here, and exported from England to other countries for medicinal purposes, for which it is especially suitable, owing to the large quantity of morphia it contains. Khadji Josef, the opium merchant, had hospitably resolved, that as the thermometer was not below zero—it was very little above freezing-point even in the sun—he would give an *al fresco* entertainment at the "good-bye."

In Persia, where it is common to take one's food upon the desert, the notion of sending out into the wilderness half a dozen servants to make tea and to get pipes ready and in good smoking order, does not appear strange.

Of course hours passed before we were prepared to start. It is always so; the loading of each mule for the first time is a tedious work of art, in which charvodars show great skill. Weights, as nearly as may be equal, must be suspended on each side of the animal. If a trunk is put on one side, and another trunk upon the other side is not so heavy, then in the same slings an iron bedstead, or something else to make up the weight must be placed upon the lighter trunk; then on the top of some bulky goods the small things must be stacked, so that they will not be upset by the motion of the animal, nor injured by collision. While all this was being arranged the cavalcade grew larger: Khadji Josef and his pretty wife, an Armenian girl, with no other enjoyment but that of riding high-spirited horses over the plains of Ispahan, were there; the British Agent; our good friend the missionary; and everybody we had known in the Persian city, all mounted and attended by mounted servants. The Telegraph Superintendent had ten baggage mules, besides the five servants who were mounted on his own horses.

Kazem told me he was glad this Superintendent

was going with us; he would be a good protection against robbers, and certainly it seemed from his armament that robbers we must expect to meet. Every man of his following carried a carbine; one or two had sword and pistol; he himself had a revolver stuck in his belt. But Kazem had another reason; he said that one of the Superintendent's servants was his "brother." I understood him literally, and wondered to see no personal resemblance. It was explained that there was no relationship between them other than that they had vowed affection and called each other by the name of "brother," after a fashion not uncommon in Persia. We were talking of this man when we heard a cry something like a yell, and saw the Superintendent, a strong, thick-set man, standing in his stirrups and with a heavy horsewhip beating the very person. Kazem's "brother" had come up to join the caravan the worse for wine, and his master, waving the terrible thong of his whip over his head, was executing summary punishment in a land where there is no justice. The servant was a good-looking man, with dark and sombre face, over which his high black Persian hat was perched like the shako of a guardsman. He wore a plum-coloured tunic of stuff made of goats' hair, and black trousers. His feet were firmly set in the huge sledge-like stirrups, and though his face was pale with fright, he took his beating as if there was no possibility of resistance or escape. The poor wretch howled like a dog, and when the Superintendent refolded the thong of his whip, the man seemed to be perfectly sober, but without power of steadying himself in the saddle. He paused a minute as if writhing with pain; then touched his horse, which sprang at once into a gallop. The man rocked fearfully in his saddle as he rode off; but he was soon too far from us to appear anything but a vanishing spot upon the plain. We could see, however, that he knew where he was going, and that he had merely preceded upon the road we must follow. It turned out that we ascribed this sudden gallop to the right cause—to his desire to escape from the sight of those who had witnessed his disgraceful punishment.

At last we set off—a band of very irregular cavalry —my wife's takht-i-rawan being the rallying point of the caravan. My horse had those qualities most advantageous for a nineteen days' ride—steadiness and endurance, which however are not showy. Our Persian friends were prancing over the plain, dashing from right to left in true Oriental fashion, while we plodded on up the gentle ascent from Djulfa to the "good-bye." After riding about four miles we reached a small plateau, where Khadji Josef's servants were already expecting us with boiling samovars, and a white cloth spread upon the desert, on which were laid cakes of Persian bread, manna, sweetmeats of many kinds, boxes of sardines, and pots of jam imported from Europe. There were bottles of wine, for which the servants had dug holes in the desert, and arrack for those who preferred that fiery liquor. A heavy spirit duty would not be an evil in Persia. The best quality of this pure alcohol may be bought in Tehran or Ispahan at fifteen shihees (7½d.) a bottle.

We all dismounted and enjoyed not only the tea, but also the view over Djulfa and Ispahan divided by the silver streak of the Zayinderud. It was a perfectly barren place where we stood, and we had passed not a sign of cultivation in the four miles we had ridden. The air was not very cold, though upon the plain there were large patches of snow and the mountains all around were white and glistening. We were sorry to part company from all who had ridden out with us from Ispahan; but more than all with Mr. Bruce, the missionary. Our way lay towards the mountains, which when they obscured the sunlight looked very cold and desolate. The sky too, which had been clear, was gathering in clouds. But we were soon at Marg, and hard at work in the endeavour to make the bala-khanah somewhat windproof for the night, which after sunset was bitterly cold.

Next day about noon, having collected some withered thorns, which are the only vegetation of the desert, the servants made a fire and gave us a hot luncheon of stewed meat and rice, by the side of a stream, the water of which produced in the food something of that chalybeate flavour which Sam Weller identified with the taste of "warm flat irons."

We rested at the chapar-khanah of Mayar on the second night after leaving Ispahan From Mayar to Kum-i-Shah, the third day's march, is a distance of about twenty miles. Kum-i-Shah is the place of a shrine, in ruins of course. We had just come in sight of the green dome, which marked the sacred place, when two men, evidently Europeans, wearing the pith helmets so common in India, appeared on the scene. They were the Telegraph clerk and the inspector resident at Kum-i-Shah, both Scotchmen, and after kindly attending us to our wretched lodging, a mud hovel in a town of still inferior mud hovels, they appeared again in the morning to ride with us part of the way to Mux-al-beg, the next station. The temperature had been falling every day since we left Ispahan. The cold on the plain from Mayar to Mux-al-beg was the most severe we had experienced. For hours we crawled over the plain, for the most part covered with snow, at the rate of three miles an hour, exposed to a wind so keen that my moustache was painfully weighted with pendents of ice which were renewed as often as I melted them by pressing my hand upon my face. I was clad from head to foot in a fur coat I had bought in the bazaars of

Ispahan, a quite invaluable purchase. Externally the coat was of yellow leather, so long that the skirt touched the toes of my boots, and in circumference ample enough to lap over a foot in front. It was secured at the neck with strings of Persian silk, and at the waist with a leather strap. The outside was beautifully worked in patterns with amber silk; inside was the warm, long wool of the Cabul sheep. The sleeves, which reached nearly to the ground, and were at the elbow ample as a bishop's lawn, were almost tight at the wrists, an excellent arrangement for excluding the icy wind of the Persian plains.

The gholams who had charge of our baggage-mules were always lagging behind, so much so that I was afraid they might get cut off by robbers, for whom they would have been an easy prey, and our baggage a rich booty. I called them forward and made them understand that they were to push on before us and get to Mux-al-beg as soon as possible. But they missed the way, and we experienced perhaps the acme of misery as travellers, in waiting for a couple of hours in the cold bala-khanah without seats or furniture of any description. Just as we arrived, snow began to fall heavily, and this added to our anxiety, for the sea does not look more pathless than an Asiatic plain in a snow-storm.

After snow has fallen, the weather is always less cold. But the landscape the next morning when we straggled out about sunrise into the deep snow, was one of the most cheerless I have ever beheld. The sky and the ground were of one whiteness, and there was no sign of the position of the sun. For some time our mules and horses blundered into holes and out of holes until we found the track Through the white gloom, we rode on, and on, over the snow for three hours. Then we reached a ruined caravanserai. From this we could just see in the farthest distance another building which the Telegraph Superintendent told me was a second caravanserai, and "the ground between the two is," he said, "no man's land." This disowned territory lies between the Governments of Ispahan and Shiraz, and although offences have occurred upon it, the two Governments have never decided which is responsible. "At this caravanserai," continued the Superintendent, pointing to the ruined and deserted building, "I was robbed. We were passing, as we are passing now, and a lot of fellows rushed out, armed; they surrounded us, and robbed us of everything." But we passed safely over the neutral ground, and though I was so stiff with cold and rheumatism on arriving at the second caravanserai, that it took me some five minutes to get off my horse, I was able to enjoy a stew of kidneys and rice which Kazem, with the assistance of about fifty ragamuffins who stood round his fire, and interfered on every possible occasion, had prepared. Where those people came from, what they were, what they subsisted upon, I cannot tell. But perhaps a Persian would feel equally puzzled with regard to the hangers-on about the public houses of England, men whose business in life seems to be that of secreting an appetite for gin, by standing outside the licensed doors with their hands in their pockets.

With some difficulty, I hoisted my painful bones into one of the deep arches in the wall of the caravanserai, and the bystanders watched every mouthful with an eager eye to the remainder which I took care should be as large as possible. My wife was taking luncheon in her takht-i-rawan. But her mules would not stand still, and at last she was obliged to set off in advance of the caravan, with no one in attendance but her mule driver and one servant. When I mounted again and rode out of the caravanserai, which was called Ahminabad, I could see that my *yaboo* was tired with trudging through the deep snow. We had yet twelve miles to go before reaching the end of our day's journey at Yezdikhast. Snow began to fall, and I had no indication of the path except the half-covered footmarks of my wife's mules. I urged my horse forward to reach the takht-i-rawan, but could do no more than keep it in sight. I was glad to hear the cheery voice of the Telegraph Superintendent as he galloped up behind me. The ground was for the most part level, but now and then there were gentle undulations which hid the takht-i-rawan, "ups and downs," which he said " were famous places for robbers." "It was about here," he continued, "that Dr. W——, one of our medical staff, was attacked. A band of men sprung out upon him from behind that turn in the road. There they stripped him literally naked and tied him to one of those scrubby trees." "How was he released?" I asked. "Oh," replied the Superintendent, "it was in this way; a foot passenger, a Persian, arrived at the chapar-khanah, from which the Doctor had hired a horse which he was to leave at the next station, and the keeper of the post-house naturally asked him if he had met the Doctor on the road, and when the traveller said 'No,' then they all suspected the truth, and several of the villagers took up their guns and set out to look out for the Doctor, whom they found in a most miserable condition." The Superintendent was full of anecdotes concerning the perils of Englishmen in Persia, and I, interested, took little note of the way. We had found by experience that nothing faster than a walk could be obtained from my horse, and had resigned ourselves too completely to the slow rate of progress. The Superintendent appeared to be suddenly alarmed on looking at his watch. The falling snow and mist hid all but the plain from our view, and I could well understand that to lose our way or to fail in reaching the village before nightfall might mean death. There could be no possibility of keeping in the track after dark, and there was much room to doubt whether we should be alive in the morning, after passing the cold hours of the night, without food, upon the plain. We pushed forward and tried to keep the takht-i-rawan in sight. Our baggage mules and all our servants were far in advance; the greater number had not stayed with us at Ahminabad. The difficulty was that as we were unable to see the mountains, even those who knew, or believed they knew the road, had no indication of our whereabouts. At last, when we were becoming extremely anxious, there loomed in front of us the vague outline of a mountain, which dissolved all doubts and alarms.

Soon afterwards, almost suddenly, we came upon a ravine in which the village of Yezdikhast is most singularly situated, upon an isolated rock, the surface of which is level with the plain. The village seems from a distance to be seated on the level; from the edge of the ravine the site appears extraordinary and picturesque. Nearly a hundred feet from the ground, some of the inhabitants peered at us from the village walls on our arrival. We descended, cold and covered with snow, to the bottom of the ravine, where the caravanserai stood outside the village. The recollection of our apartment at Yezdikhast is almost enough to induce catarrh. To clear away the snow from the steps which led to the roof was no easy matter. Upon the roof, snow lay thick, and the only room on that elevation was as big as a small chapel with a vaulted roof five and twenty feet from the floor, which was like a chalky road with heaps of ashes here and there, the remains of past fires, lighted in the Persian manner in any part of the room. The open doorway was wide; over that we suspended rugs. High over the door was a square hole, almost as large and quite out of reach. The idea of warming such a place was of course absurd. We lighted some logs, had a hasty dinner and got into our beds. Next morning the snow was so deep, and my wife so unwell, that we determined to stay where we were; but not in the bala-khanah. Kazem and I selected the best of the gloomy arches which surrounded the yard, had it swept out, lighted a fire, hung a mat in the doorway; had our furniture moved, and my wife carried down into this brick-vault, which, when the doorway was screened, was utterly without light. After the manner common throughout Persia in such places, the domed roof was covered with a black coating of bitumen, and one of our difficulties was in dealing with the impenetrable darkness. The glow of the fire seemed pressed back into the grate, and the light of our candles to extend no further than the table on which they were placed. All day long we lived in this Cimmerian gloom with our travelling thermometer too near zero. Our strenuous efforts to warm the bricks of this black vault involved a most unusual consumption of firewood, which was regarded by the people as reckless extravagance ; but with us it was really a question of life or death, for my wife had symptoms of inflammation of the lungs, and I could not get the temperature up to 40°. I have seen a more comfortable room at the bottom of a coal-pit than that in which we passed the 13th of January at Yezdikhast. The rough curtain over the door did not exclude the freezing wind, nor the brayings and the shouts from the mules and their drivers, who thronged in the yard, from which this curtain was our only separation. All day long, snow fell fast and thick. We became anxious as to the possibility of crossing the mountains which we should reach after four days' march from Yezdikhast.

When we set out on the morning of the 14th for Shulgistan, the snow was inconveniently deep, so deep that a bivouac at midday, except in the saddle, was out of the question. For eight hours, we toiled through it, meeting no living creature all day, except one small caravan of donkeys from Shiraz. At Abadeh, the next station after Shulgistan, we expected to find an escort, provided by the Governor of Shiraz. At Kum-i-Shah, I had received a telegram from his Excellency; forwarded in translation by the English clerk at Shiraz, saying that he had heard of our approach, and that he wished to place a residence at our disposal during our stay in Shiraz, to which I replied that we had already accepted an invitation from Mr. Odling, the resident medical officer of the Indo-Persian Telegraph, but that I should be obliged if his Excellency would send us a suitable escort of soldiers to accompany our caravan from Abadeh to Shiraz.

At Abadeh, we were to lose the company of the Superintendent and of his servants. I noticed that all the servants were humanely provided with blue spectacles, which are indeed the only means of escaping the torture of inflamed eyes in crossing these snow-covered plains. The all-penetrating dust of summer, and the painful glare of snow in winter, are sufficient to account for the prevalence of sore eyes among the muleteers. Along the way to Abadeh, the Superintendent gave fresh illustrations of brigandage in Persia, and soon after midday he and all his troop trotted off. I sent on the baggage at a quicker pace than was possible for the takht-i-rawan, and soon afterwards I told our own servants to get on and prepare an early dinner. We were left alone on the plain with two muleteers. It was about three o'clock in the afternoon, as we were approaching a ruined village, which lay half a mile to the left of the path, that I saw a number of wild horsemen pouring out from these ruins. They galloped hard towards Kazem, who was perhaps a mile in front of us. I had no doubt that they were robbers. Their place of hiding and mode of attack were precisely such as had been described. To fight forty armed horsemen was impossible, and of escape there was no chance. I saw them gallop up to Kazem, surround him, and bring him back in our direction. Kazem, seated between his saddle-bags, looked as if he were the prisoner of Persian bashi-bazouks. I could see them gesticulating fiercely around him. The appearance of the band was the wildest imaginable. Hair, and clothes, and horses, they were all alike only in this quality of wildness. I placed my horse close beside the takht-i-rawan as we advanced to meet them. I had not a doubt we were about to be robbed, and perhaps ill-treated; and when half a dozen sprang forward, I was intensely surprised, though I am sure I exhibited no astonishment, when, instead of pointing their carbines and lances, they bowed to their saddles, and I heard from their leader, the word, "Hakem." Then I knew in a moment that this wild troop had been sent out to meet us, as a guard of honour, by the "Hakem" or Governor of Abadeh, and that they had been waiting, probably for hours, in the ruined village.*

---

* The troop formed an *istikbal*, which is the Persian word for a welcoming party. The number of men composing the *istikbal* is an affair of great importance with ceremonious Persians. The native Princes of India are extremely ambitious in the matter of gunpowder

They had ridden to Kazem to inquire if we were the expected Ferangis, and this point being settled, they surrounded us. The leader called for the kalian, which is never absent on these occasions of ceremony. Two of the wild horsemen were concerned in producing the ceremonious pipe. One, who was pipe-bearer, carried, dangling at his saddle, far below the belly of his horse, a perforated pot of charcoal, which swung and rattled as he rode, and on the other side, was suspended the water-bowl of the kalian, the stem and fittings of which were carried by the second man. No one stopped while the pipe was being prepared, and when I declined it and the machine was passed on to the leader of the wild horsemen, he supported it on his saddle, while he laboriously inhaled the smoke in which Persians so much delight. Meanwhile, the horsemen commenced a display on their own account. They rode round and round us, shouting and levelling their lances or their guns. Then some dashed away over the snow, in pretended encounter; others dropped their lances, and then galloping at full speed, picked up the weapon without dismounting. In some form or other these exhibi-

---

salutes; the number of guns with which they are welcomed is an indication of rank which they regard with jealous attention; and so it is in Persia with the numbers composing the *istikbal*. Terrible has been the wrath of great men when they were received outside Persian towns with a meagre *istikbal*.

tions were kept up until we reached Abadeh, where the whole population seemed to have turned out in the miserable streets. The Superintendent had kindly promised, as the chapar-khanah had a very bad reputation, to engage for us the best room he could find in the town. But the streets were so narrow, and so encumbered with frozen snow, that it was impossible for the takht-i-rawan to approach the house. To the great delight of the crowd, it was lowered from the mules at some distance; but their curiosity was disappointed when the lady preferred to be locked in her carriage until the room was ready for her reception. The "room" would be called a "shed," and a very insecure shed, in any part of Western Europe. Nothing would induce the door to close within about two inches, and there was a greater defect of the same sort about the shutters which were in the window-holes; the floor was of beaten clay, the walls plastered with mud, and the smoke-dyed beams of the roof were well hung with cobwebs. Upon these beams dried grass had been piled, which projected in dusty festoons.

Kazem and his helpers had hardly completed all the necessary arrangements, when a train of soldiers and slaves arrived from the Governor, a petty potentate subject to the Governor General who ruled at Shiraz, bearing a present, consisting of two plates of sweetmeats, two pots of sweet cream, a large tray covered with cakes of the thin bread of the country, and three live fowls. The Governor's servants said he was very anxious that I should pay him a visit. They were extremely frank about their master's feelings on the subject. They urged that it would be such a humiliation if I did not see him, and that this was the reason why he was so anxious. I had been riding all day, I was very tired, and we were to leave the next morning early; but however I promised to pay his Excellency a visit, and took with me, as a present from Mrs. Arnold to the Governor's wife, a Russian leather pocket-book, which he accepted with great enthusiasm. He had received orders, he said, from the Firman Firma (the title given by the Shah to Yahia Khan, the Governor of Shiraz), that we were to be attended from Abadeh by the captain of the road guard and a troop of his men; and after the usual set out of coffee, pipes, and tea, I returned to our dinner of soup and pillau. But on the way I was stopped by our charvodar, from whose loud lamentations I gathered that one of his gholams had deserted, taking with him a few krans belonging to the charvodar. There could be no doubt that the gholam had engaged to go to Shiraz, and immediately I took steps to have him found, which did not appear to be a work of great difficulty. When the missing gholam was brought forward by the Governor's officers, I led him apart and asked if he was willing to go the whole journey. He said "Yes," and that he had ran away only because of some dispute, which the charvodar was willing to settle. I warned him that on leaving Abadeh to cross the mountains no desertion would be permitted, and that our guard would have orders to look after him. He seemed quite contented, and gave no further trouble.

With a few soldiers for escort we set out again over the snow for Zurmak, a short march of sixteen miles upon a nearly level plain. We had just gone to bed in the customary discomfort of the bala-khanah, when there was noise of tremendous knocking at the outer door of the chapar-khanah, which is always exactly under the bala-khanah. This we learned denoted the arrival of the Legation messenger, on his monthly journey from Tehran to Shiraz, with letters for the Indian mail. To us, he brought a most welcome present—six loaves of good bread from Madame Læssoë. A soldier who travelled with him, and who had orders to add himself to our escort, presented a letter from the Governor of Abadeh addressed to myself, of which the following is a translation :—

"At the service of the exalted, excellent gentleman, the munificent—I forward abundance of well-wishing and congratulation.

"God willing, I trust you have arrived in safety at the stage of Zurmak, and that your time will pass pleasantly. I am exceedingly sorry that I have not been of service to you during your stay here. Because fortune did not assist me the day you left, and proper service was not done by me to you, and because I was not ennobled by being able to help you, I am indeed sad and grieved. I feel certain that the services which should have been done for you have not been accomplished. Forgive me; God is witness, I hoped to be some days in your company, and to show my devotion to you.

"I trust you will let me know of your arrival at Shiraz, that I may be assured of the safety of your noble person. I have no more to say.

"(Seal of)   MAHOMMED REZA."

In Persia, very few persons sign their name—very few perhaps have the power of doing so—but many who can write, prefer to give their letters the greater dignity of their seal. And as we found at Tehran, so throughout all Persia, everybody who has or is likely to have a financial transaction carries a seal. Even the poorest charvodar, with the sorriest troop of mules, produces the engraved stone or brass, which is his seal, and stamps an agreement for a journey. The letter of Mahommed Reza is a fair specimen of the flowery and complimentary style common to all Persian letters of ceremony. His Excellency provided us with an escort, but the captain and the rest of the troop were to join us on the top of the pass at Dehbid. We were approaching the most dangerous part of our travels and the most famous haunts of robbers, in the mountains between Ispahan and Shiraz. In the world it would perhaps hardly be possible to find more ill-looking fellows than our escort. Appearing upon any stage as the villains of a play, they would have had an immense success; and for my own part I felt very little confidence in their protection. A better friend was the cold, which was every day becoming more intense as we ascended towards the pass of Dehbid. To ride at a walking pace for nine hours through a freezing wind involves suffering of which even the recollection is painful; and on the way from Zurmak to Khanikora, I was not able to walk part of the way, because I found that if I took to the saddle again after my boots were covered with snow, there was danger of frostbite from the boot being encrusted with ice. Seeing a brown, bare patch about midday, I got off to take luncheon; but this was worse than any other place, for it was not, as I supposed, cleared of snow by wind, but by the salts in the earth, which melted the snow as it fell into a freezing mixture. Standing in this terribly cold slush, I took from the takht-i-rawan the remainder of a piece of brawn, which had been made for us in Ispahan. But it was frozen into crystals of ice, and had no taste but that of extreme cold.

We have an abiding recollection of the bala-khanah at Khanikora; this was one of the most wretched, and the cold was the most severe we had experienced. From the yard, filled high with frozen snow, the mules, their drivers, and the soldiers crept quickly into the hovels at the side, where all lay down together. The bala-khanah was about eight feet square and seven feet high, black with smoke, and with a hole for doorway or window on every side. We lighted a fire, and the place was at once filled with stifling smoke. We saw that though the thermometer was some degrees below zero, and a frosty wind blowing through the wretched place, it would nôt be possible to have a fire. Having stuffed up the windows and doorways with rugs and stones and sticks and planks, we got through the night, and learned the first thing in the morning that the soldiers refused, on account of the extreme severity of the weather to proceed up the pass to Dehbid, which is seven thousand five hundred feet above the sea. There were two good reasons for pushing onwards: our miserable position at Khanikora, and our firm belief that the intense cold preceded another fall of snow, which would block the pass, and detain us many days in this wretched chapar-khanah without fire and with no supply of food. I sent word to the soldiers by Kazem that we intented to start immediately, and that they could go or remain behind as they pleased.

I knew we should hear no more of their objections; which however, when we got well out upon the frozen snow, and in the full grip of the wind, had, I was compelled to admit, a really terrible foundation. Up the slope we struggled in Indian file for hours, the snow laying in drifts ten, fifteen, and in some places twenty feet deep. One caravan had passed before, and in the footsteps of these pioneers we found security. If a horse or mule missed the track, which zigzagged from side to side, it was at once half buried in the snow. There could be little reason to feel fear of robbers, even in this favourite place of attack, in such weather. My face was skinned and burnt a reddish-black in a few hours by the wind and sun. The snow drifted into my hair, and froze in lumps and icicles about my face. Not a word was heard; none were in the humour for talking. To hide themselves from the biting wind, two of the soldiers and Kazem lay down on their large saddles, and covered themselves over with their goats'-hair cloaks, so that no part of their faces or bodies was visible. At twenty yards distance no one would have supposed that their horses carried men.

At last, in the teeth of this wind, we reached the summit, from which the view was such as I can fancy would much resemble the look-out in Polar regions from the top of some huge iceberg. The apparently limitless, snow-covered plain looked flat as the frozen ocean, and the hills rising from it like the ice-mountains. There was not a tree, nor a house, nor a bare patch to vary the white monotony of the scene; and overhead, the dull sky seemed loaded with snow, which was just beginning to fall. We were still ten miles from Dehbid, when the path began to descend gently. Presently we saw a party of horsemen approaching, whom, from my experience at Abadeh, I presumed to be friends. It was Houssein Khan, the captain of the road guard, who was to conduct us to Shiraz, and a troop of his followers. He was a thin, roguish-looking man, his saddle a perfect armoury of handsomely inlaid weapons. He made his salaam, and in spite of the freezing temperature and the falling snow, his pipe-bearer produced the travelling kalian. But the ceremonies of greeting, which in Persia cannot be disregarded, were scarcely ended when the storm broke. The wind hissed, and the snow fell in blinding clouds. Houssein Khan was vanquished by the weather. He had for a little while adopted our walking pace and placed himself behind me, his men being divided about equally into a front and rear guard. But the snowstorm and the freezing wind made him think only of himself. He had come out with the wind at his back, and had not suffered much. It was now unendurable, and he shuffled past me, then gained a corner of the road, and there he set off at a trot for the shelter of Dehbid. One by one, the rear-guard stole past, and soon we were left alone with our muleteers.

We could not see more than a hundred yards before us, and the track was getting covered up. The wind seemed to pierce my riding-boots as if they had been made of cotton. At last, after nearly two hours of this difficult and solitary progress, we met Mr. Markar, the Armenian clerk of the Telegraph at Dehbid, who had kindly ridden out to look for us. It was at his house we were to pass the night. I was delighted to see him, and he, the inhabitant of one of the most desolate and lonely stations in the world, was evidently glad. But in such a wind and storm it was impossible to talk. We were soon at his fireside, recovering warmth from cups of hot tea. We were rejoiced that we had made the journey and pushed through to Dehbid. Had we given way to our escort and stayed at Khanikora, we should have been imprisoned. It would have been quite impossible to leave that most wretched chapar-khanah for days, perhaps for weeks, after such a storm, which must have filled the defile in many places with impassable depths of snow.

Mr. Markar's house was of the usual kind. A quadrangle of mud-bricks, mud-cemented, with no external opening but through the strongly-barred door; the buildings having a uniform height, like that of four mud boxes placed round the central court. Our apartment had a door, and over that a curtain of Manchester cotton; but when I got out of bed in the morning I found the snow laying in a white drift across the room, having been blown in the night through door and curtain. Mr. Markur was a sportsman, and had outside his wall what he called a fox-trap. This was the remains of a dead mule, near which he posted himself at night, and sometimes shot one or two foxes, which are valuable for their handsome grey fur. No one in Persia seems to understand the proper preparation of fur. The Persians have a means of temporary preservation sufficient to secure the fox skins until they reach a European market. In Ispahan and Shiraz there is a considerable traffic in these skins, which are bought by the merchants at about two krans apiece. They are then sent to England or Russia to be dressed and made up. Although among the higher classes much fur is worn in Persia, none is made up in the country.

Houssein Khan and his men were glad to leave the mountain-tops. They looked blue with cold when we were getting the caravan together to proceed towards Shiraz. We could take the warmest part of the day for leaving Dehbid, as the distance to Khanikergan, the next station, was only twelve miles. For the whole of the way, the ground was covered deep with snow. One caravan had set out before us and marked a track, but we met no one. We were prepared by evil report to find none but most wretched lodging at Khanikergan, yet we had not placed our expectations low enough. The caravanserai was an old stone building, and the surrounding arches were not, as usual, raised above the yard, but were on the same level. We had the best, but it was disagreeably evident that it had been recently occupied by mules; and from the smoke-hole in the centre of the roof melting snow dripped slowly into the hollow which served as a stove when this place had been occupied by animals who cook their food. We could only have a fire at the cost of being stifled with smoke, so we preferred to lay a stone over the hole in the roof, an undertaking which brought down the snow in heaps into the room. Until sunset, the stone walls of this noisome place trickled with cold moisture, which then froze hard in icicles and stalactites. We had no security that some curious mule would not push his head through the flimsy covering of the doorway. But, however, we slept; and when Kazem brought the usual kettle of hot coffee with the first dawn of the morning, we were rejoiced to think that Khanikergan was to be a place of the past.

At Meshed-i-Murghaub, which we reached on the evening of the 21st January, the chapar-khanah was outside the village, which was surrounded with a mud wall. This is one of the most dangerous centres in Persia, and as we rode up, a number of the villagers armed with guns and accompanied by others who had no weapons, came out to meet us, making a great noise, in which I could hear the Persian word for "robbers" frequently mentioned. It appeared that a band of robbers had been seen in the neighbourhood, and these poor people had taken up arms to defend themselves and their property in case of attack. We were looked upon as a valuable reinforcement, and as a possible source of danger, for, according to Persian law, the districts in which robbery occurs have to make good the losses sustained by travellers, and this, though inoperative when Persians are the subject of attack, is, the people well know, not likely to be disregarded when Europeans have been plundered. Not that they believe the proceeds will be conveyed to the plundered party; they have not sufficient conviction of the honesty of their Government for that. But they are shrewd enough to know that the robbery would afford excellent ground for the extortion of money by the officers of the Governor.

A Persian argues with himself that when there is trouble in the country some people will have to pay, with life or property, or both; and it is most likely this will fall upon those in the neighbourhood. The circumstances of his country have never led him to think of justice as an abstract matter, or of justice as pursuing criminality with discrimination or discretion. He knows by experience that the victims of justice are more accidental than those of crime, and when that authority which stands for justice in Persia is abroad, his first thought is to fly away or to hide everything which he possesses. When a European traveller has been robbed or murdered, it has happened that large encampments of Eeliats, and even villages, have been deserted, owing to the universal fear among these people of being selected to suffer punishment for the criminals. On such occasions, somebody must be hanged or tortured to death, and if the criminals are not taken red-handed, Persian justice sees none so likely to be guilty as those nearest to the scene of crime.

In every village, there are a certain number of men accustomed to carry arms; tofanghees (gun-carriers) they are called. More or less these men are under the orders of the Governor. He can require their attendance in any part of the district surrounding their village, either as an escort for travellers, or merchandise, or for the destruction of robber bands. But no one seems to place much confidence in a tofanghee. Generally he is "a man with a gun,"'and nothing more. In the south of Persia, the attentions of the tofanghees to the traveller are frequent and embarrassing. Sometimes they march out with him in the morning, whether he will or no, and when they are tired, when they approach the boundary of the next village, or especially when they think there is a band of robbers at hand, they ask for money and for leave to make their salaam. Surrounded by a dozen wild-looking men, well armed and asking for money in this attitude, a doubt has crossed my mind whether they are so very different from the robbers against whom they pretend to be a protection.

CHAPTER V.

Classic Persia—The Tomb of Cyrus—Date of the ruins—Passargardæ—Columns of Cyrus' Tomb—Colour of ruins—Neglected by Persians—Kawamabad—Takht-i-rawan in danger—Houssein Khan and the sheep—Village of Sidoon—Ruins of Istakr—Situation of Persepolis—Araxes or Bendemeer—Staircase at Persepolis—Darius and Xerxes—Cuneiform inscriptions—Study of Cuneiform—Chronology of Assyria—Great Hall of Xerxes—The Persepolitan lion—Hall of a Hundred Columns—Professor Rawlinson on the ruins—Tomb of Darius—"The Great God Ormazd"—The bringer of evil—Divs and Devils—Errors in religion and art—Pedigree of architecture—Persians, Medes, and Greeks—Origin of Ionic architecture—Leaving Persepolis—Plain of Mervdasht.

AT Murghaub, we approach the grandest relics of the time when Persia was the great Empire of Cyrus, of Darius, and of Xerxes. At three hours' ride from the village, the plain is fringed with low hills, among which stands, close by the path from Ispahan to Shiraz, the Tomb of Cyrus. Near this, we had seen rising from the snow all that remains of his city of Passargardæ, where the inscription "I am Cyrus, the King, the Achæmenian," may be read more than once upon the ruins. It is partly from the proximity of these unquestionably genuine ruins and also from the dignity and obviously funereal character of this massive mausoleum, that it has become accepted as the original resting-place of the body of the great King.

The period which these highly interesting ruins illustrate, is concurrent with that of the Achæmenian dynasty, or to put it in another form, it is the period extending from the accession of Cyrus in 560 B.C. to the death of Alexander in 323 B.C. The reigns specially illustrated are those of Cyrus, of Darius, of Xerxes, and Artaxerxes. We shall fix the time more clearly still in the mind if we remember that the buildings of Persepolis are of about the same date as those of the Acropolis of Athens. We may find many points of curious and interesting comparison between the work of Darius and that of Pericles, and regarding both, we see at once how great a disadvantage the Persians suffered in not having at hand such marble as that of Pentelicus.

It was on this plain of Murghaub, that Cyrus won Persia. I think it is Professor Rawlinson who tells us in his "Five Ancient Monarchies," how King Darius was bound whenever he visited this ancient city of Passargardæ to present to each Persian woman who appeared before him, a sum equal to twenty Attic drachmas, or about sixteen shillings of English money, according to a custom established in commemoration of the services rendered by the sex in the battle wherein Cyrus first repulsed the forces of Astyages.

We dismounted at the Tomb of Cyrus, and walked about in the snow, while Kazem made a fire preparatory to the manufacture of an omelette. As a rule, Oriental monuments owe much to the grandeur of their situation; and this is no exception. They are set in solitude; they have a surrounding of space, which is all their own. When the thought of the traveller is arrested by so vast a retrospect, he becomes more impressed with the natural grandeur of the desert; and there seems to be a hush, a singular silence in the air which moves around these most ancient monuments, as if Nature herself were paying homage at these shrines of departed greatness. For more than two thousand four hundred years this Tomb has defied the levelling hand of Time; and another period of not less duration may apparently be sustained without further injury.

The Tomb was originally surrounded by columns, set probably in a double row, with a covered space between. But none are left standing. Most of the columns have disappeared entirely; some are prostrate, and of only a few is there a broken fragment remaining in position. These columns were not colossal; probably not more than eighteen feet high, and the space enclosed is hardly more than a hundred and fifty feet across. In the centre of this space stands the Tomb, approached by a pyramid of steps, about forty five feet square at the base. These steps, the rise of each being two feet, are composed of large blocks of marble, the colour of which has darkened to a yellowish brown. Upon a platform about eighteen feet from the ground, and twenty feet square, stands the Tomb—a small, solid, unadorned building, composed of a few blocks and huge slabs of marble; the whole being scarcely more than fifteen feet high from the platform to the peak of the marble roof. In shape it exactly resembles a child's "Noah's Ark," with the boat arrangement cut off. At one end, there is a low, massive doorway, through which, if the remains of Cyrus really rested there, they were carried to be deposited upon the floor of this little temple. By all writers, including Professor Rawlinson, this is accepted as the resting-place of the great King; and it is believed that his body was placed here in a golden coffin.

That it is a tomb, or that it is the tomb of some very exalted personage, or that it was constructed about the same date as the neighbouring ruins of Passargardæ, which are unquestionably erections made in the reign of Cyrus, there can be no doubt. Some travellers appear to have thought that the marble has not sufficient aspect of antiquity to warrant this conclusion. But what, then, would they say of the Parthenon? The marble masonry upon the Acropolis of Athens is similar to this upon the plain of Murghaub, in massiveness, in colouring, and in the absence of mortar or cement, of which none was used by the builders in either place. But the Tomb of Cyrus has a less fresh appearance than the walls of the Parthenon. Alas, that no Historic Monuments Bill can apply to the plain of Murghaub! There is nothing to attract the acquisitive powers of an Elgin, for the marbles are utterly without inscription or adornment; and there is nothing to hinder ravage by the Persians. I have never seen in any Mahommedan people an exhibition of the slightest desire for the protection of the great historic monuments of which they have been or are possessed. The Pashas of Stamboul looked on unconcerned while the marbles of ancient Greece were burned to make lime for building cattle sheds; were it in ruins, they would as soon burn the stones of Santa Sophia as the timbers of an old man-of-war; and for the Persians, these great ruins, which should be the pride and most sacred treasure of their country, are nothing more than useless heaps of tumbled stone. If any man needed lime in the neighbourhood, or stone to build a caravanserai, he would probably use the marbles of Cyrus' Tomb, or the columns of the Hall of Darius; and these invaluable records and memorials of a period concerning which very much more than our present knowledge might be gathered by excavation and research upon the spot, are regarded with no more concern or attention than the bones of a dead camel.

From Cyrus' Tomb we rode through a narrow plain for several hours to the village of Kawamabad, a collection of mud huts lying near the mountains. There was no chapar-khanah at Kawamabad, and we were obliged to hire a room in the village, to get at which we had to pass through two cowsheds and into a walled straw yard, where there was a mud-built shed, of which we took possession. The takht-i-rawan could not enter the doorway of this range of buildings, and was, as usual, left outside. But immediately upon its being lowered to the ground, the villagers who stood looking on said that would never do. "Robbers! robbers!" they cried; and pointed to the hills. They were in a state of great excitement. A band of robbers had visited Kawamabad that day; it was feared they would return, and the poor villagers did not want to be responsible for the rifling of our takht-i-rawan. It was impossible for the mules to carry it within the building, so the villagers took the work upon themselves, and with many invocations of "Allah," of "Ali," and "Houssein," and with an amount of force, of which a third, if disciplined, would have been more than sufficient, they lugged the takht-i-rawan into greater safety.

If the band which had visited Kawamabad were disposed to attack our caravan, I expected we should meet them next day during our ride to Sidoon. In addition to Houssein Khan and his soldiers, half a dozen villagers with guns in their hands set out with us in the morning, and by their advice we kept the baggage mules close up, and allowed no straggling on the part of those animals. But Houssein Khan did not seem apprehensive, and when the villagers were tired and returned, he was quite ready to do a little highway robbery, or rather, sheep-stealing, on his own account. We were in a region of moderate fertility; there were a few flocks of sheep and goats upon the plains, each flock tended by one or two herdsmen. Whenever we approached a flock of sheep, Houssein Khan trotted off, as I at first supposed, to consult the herdsman about the security of the road and the position of the rabble musketeers who were supposed to guard the path under his command. Gradually I perceived that these rides had a more strictly personal object. From every one of these visits he returned with a sheep across his saddle, or upon that of one of his men, which was soon afterwards set upon its legs, until there was a small flock of half a dozen following him under the care of one of our own Persian bashi-bazouks. At first I thought Houssein Khan was buying the animals for food; but we were within three days' march of Shiraz, and it was evident that two would have been enough for the whole caravan. I had not sufficient Persian at command to obtain a thorough explanation. But I called Kazem, and made him understand that I thought the herdsmen were being robbed, and told him to let Houssein Khan know at once of my suspicions, to watch what was done with the sheep and to report to me everything. Kazem smiled, as if he thought such concern was extremely prudish; and said something, in which a word sounding like "medocle" occurred. This I knew to be the Persian mode of expressing forced and illicit contributions; and in Sidoon I learnt that the sheep were sold by Houssein Khan at about two-and-sixpence each. The chapar-khanah at Sidoon lay in a terribly cold situation, in the shade of a range of mountains; but we bore the discomforts of the place, with the recollection that on the morrow we should see Persepolis, and in three days end our journey in Shiraz.

The natural formation of the country in the neighbourhood of these illustrious ruins, is picturesque and remarkable. Journeying from Ispahan, the plain, at one end of which stand the remains of Persepolis, is approached through a vast natural gateway in which run the road and the River Pulvar, and of which the pillars are strangely-shaped and many-coloured mountains of the hardest limestone. The table mountain on the right has a very singular contour, and in this entrance, which is too wide to be called a gorge, are found the massive ruins of the city of Istakr, which one has not patience to examine carefully when so near to the far more interesting remains of Persepolis. At Istakr, the road winds to the left round the bold spur of the mountain which forms the back ground of Persepolis.

On approaching the ruins of the halls, and temples, and tombs of Darius and his descendants, the traveller, recalling perhaps to mind, all that he has seen at Baalbec, at Pæstum, and upon the Athenian Acropolis, will surely be struck with a sense of disappointment, because there is here no outline of ancient hall or temple, no realisable structure in which he can place the form of Darius or Xerxes. There is nothing more than remains of the Temples of Jupiter in Athens and in Rome, a few solitary or connected columns, and the massive stones of some part of an ancient hall or propylæum. The distant aspect of the ruins of Persepolis will fall below anticipation as much as the results of careful examination in detail will exceed expectation. In fact, the most interesting ruins in the world, because they are the most richly covered and adorned with eloquent records of the past, these stones are not arranged for a *coup d'œil*.

The mule path passes close to the side of the mountain from which the platform of Persepolis is projected into the Plain of Mervdasht. Through this plain runs the river, which in classic times was called Araxes, afterwards known as Bundamir, or Bendemeer, as Moore has called it in "Lalla Rookh." Standing upon the platform of Persepolis, the view across the river is uninterrupted for more than twenty miles. The extreme height of this platform, where it faces the plain, is about forty-five feet, its length from north to south about fifteen hundred feet, and the average depth from east to west about eight hundred feet.

The grandest work at Persepolis is in connexion with this platform. The masonry of the supporting walls of the platform is irregular; the blocks, mostly of huge size, presenting angles of every degree. The surface of this immense work is true and sound as it was two thousand years ago. But it is not in this that the glory of this platform rests. At its greatest height, the platform is ascended from the plain by a staircase which for the magnificence of its proportions and the beauty of construction, deserves to have been regarded as one of the wonders of the world. The staircase at Persepolis has had no equal in ancient or modern times. Compared with this, a work probably of the time of Darius, the marble stairs which lead to the Parthenon are insignificant, and the Imperial steps in the Roman Colosseum, barbarous. A regiment of cavalry ten abreast, could ride easily up the double flights of the Persepolitan staircase. The steps, which appear to be composed of the hardest syenite, are twenty-two feet wide; each step rises only three-and-a-half inches and has a tread of fifteen inches. In some places, the blocks of the masonry in this staircase are so large that three or four steps have been hewn out from the same piece of stone.

We little thought, when in spite of the cautious counsels of Mr. Erskine, then British Minister at Athens, we passed a day upon the Plain of Marathon, that a few years afterwards we should stand among the ruins of the Hall of Darius, the place to which he probably returned after that unsuccessful expedition against the Greeks, or that when we rested in sight of that splendid landscape, near which

"A king stood on the rocky brow
That looks o'er seagirt Salamis,"

we should afterwards enter the magnificent ruin of the Propylæum of this King—of Xerxes at Persepolis. This is the building which stood at the top of the grand staircase, and the most massive of the ruins upon the platform of Persepolis, are those of this edifice. Upon the piers, there are inscriptions in cuneiform letters which as clearly as the winged bulls above these writings, testify the relationship between the Assyrians of Nineveh and the Medes of Persepolis. The inscription is the same on each pier, and is written in three languages. It has been translated by Sir Henry Rawlinson into the following :—

"The great god, Ahura-mazda; (Ormazd) he it is who has given (made) this world, who has given mankind, who has made Xerxes king, both king of the people and lawgiver of the people. I am Xerxes the king, the great king, the king of kings, the king of the many-peopled countries, the supporter also of the great world, the son of king Darius the Achæmenian. Says Xerxes the king, by the grace of Ormazd I have made this gate of entrance (or this public portal) there is many another nobler work besides (or in) this Persepolis which I have executed and which my father has executed. Whatsoever noble works are to be seen, we have executed all of them by the grace of Ormazd. Says Xerxes the king, may Ormazd protect me and my empire. Both that which has been executed by me and that which has been executed by my father, may Ormazd protect it."

This is repeated twelve times in all, and looking upon the original with Sir Henry's translation in one's mind, it is surprising how so much can be conveyed in so few letters. Very little more than a fourth of the space which would be required for this inscription in English is occupied by the cuneiform letters.

It would be interesting to trace in detail the process by which scholars have acquired the art of deciphering these and similar inscriptions; of forcing the secret of their long-concealed meaning from these strange characters, which no more resemble the Arabic or Persian letters of our day than do the forms of the English alphabet. It is, however, perseverance and acuteness rather than scholarship which are re-

which this particular monarch lived, and the time of his reign appeared to be fixed with unquestionable accuracy when the calculations of astronomers showed that the only total eclipse of the sun falling about the middle of the year, visible in Assyria between B.C. 847 and B.C. 647, which certainly includes the time of the reign of Asshurdamin-il II., was the one which, according to their figures, must have taken place on June 15th, B.C. 763.

With regard to the Propylæum of Xerxes, of the two readings given by Sir Henry Rawlinson, "this public portal" is probably better than "this gate of entrance," because these gates were in all Oriental countries, from the earliest, down to Christian times, places of business as much as of passage. Upon the inner sides of the massive stones of this "public portal" are sculptured in low relief the stalwart forms of winged bulls, some with human, others with bovine heads. The largest of these quadrupeds have the human head, covered with tiara, and on the shoulders, wings, similar in all points to those which Mr. Layard introduced to the world from Nineveh.

Upon the vast platform at Persepolis, there are remains of at least five important buildings, four lying to the right of the Propylæum of Xerxes, and no two of them being precisely upon the same level. The first of these important buildings is the Propylæum, and near that a staircase (as elegant in construction, though much smaller than the grand flights of stairs rising from the plain to the platform) leads to the level of the building known as the Great Hall of Xerxes. This name " Hall," is given in ignorance of its real object or designation. Mr. Fergusson, the distinguished architect, to whose work* I have before alluded, has written upon these ancient stones, and has, in fancy, reconstructed them with remarkable insight, though, like most who have written about them, he has never beheld the ruins of Persepolis. But, had he seen these remains, he could not have described with greater truth and accuracy the real difficulty in forming any supposition apart from the actual evidence afforded by inscriptions and ruins, than he has in the true remark:—" At Persepolis we have pillars, doorways, and windows, but not one vestige of the walls that clothed them, or of the roofs they supported." That the Great Hall and other buildings of Persepolis were roofed, is pretty obvious both from the shape of the capitals of the columns and from the number of the columns, which are not placed, as in Greek buildings, merely at the sides of the structure, but at equal distances over all the floor. We can see that the columns which supported the portico of the Great Hall of Xerxes were of marble. Those which remain are crowned with

---

* Fergusson's " Nineveh and Persepolis."

capitals composed of two bulls' heads, placed neck to neck, forming an excellent rest for the entablature. These columns are fluted, and have upon their pedestals that ornamentation which was so long considered as a Greek invention—the honeysuckle with the bud of the lotus; in fact, the decoration known everywhere as "the Greek honeysuckle." In the north portico of this great Hall, there is yet more striking evidence of the debt which the perfection of architecture in Greece owes to Persia, to Assyria, and possibly to Egypt. In the capitals of these columns there is an elongated or double volute, almost identical in figure with that which is seen upon the later buildings of Greece; while upon the walls of doorways there are sculptures, truly Oriental, of kings on thrones or on foot, attended by slaves holding the parasol of state, or the fly-chaser, equally an emblem of royal dignity. By the Persians this Hall is called "Chehil Minar," or "Forty Columns," which is in fact a common name for any columned buildings of grand dimensions in Persia. The shabby old pavilion at Ispahan with twenty tall columns of wood, set with grimy mirrors, is called "Chehil Minar."

I do not feel at all sure that the columns of the interior of some, if not of all, the great buildings of Persepolis, were not of wood. There can be no doubt that, in those remote days, the lion had the characteristics of strength and supremacy which are still attributed to the "king of beasts." At Persepolis, the angular sides of the staircase, leading to the Great Hall of Xerxes, are filled in with very powerful sculptures in low relief, in which an animal of enormous strength, with much resemblance to a lion, has fixed his teeth and claws into the hind quarters of a bull, which fills the higher angle of the space by rearing and turning its uplifted head in helpless anguish from its devourer. From that time to this there have been lions in the mountainous region round Shiraz; and àpropos of Persian lions, I shall never forget the tone of plaintive envy in which the formidable Zil-i-Sultan spoke of his father the Shah "having killed a lion." In this feat, he seemed to consider lay the real superiority of the Shah over himself.

It is noticeable in the buildings of Persepolis, as compared with the Parthenon, that there is nothing resembling the continuous action displayed in the processions upon the frieze of the Greek building. At Persepolis, upon the sides of the staircases and in other places, there are processions, but as a rule one figure is exactly like the next; there is no connected action. The modern ornamentation of Tehran is like that of Persepolis in this respect; a soldier occupies a panel, another soldier of the same pattern is seen in the next, and so on.

The grandest of the buildings of Persepolis, the ruins of which are known as those of "the Hall of a Hundred Columns," stood behind the Great Hall of Xerxes. The bases of the columns and parts of the outer walls remain. We can trace the regular position of the columns, but cannot decide whether, being of wood they have perished, or of stone have been carried off for the adornment of some mosque or palace. They were certainly not very large. The area covered by this building was considerable, but neither this nor any of the buildings of Persepolis could have had anything like the grand proportions of the Temple of Jupiter at Athens. In reading Professor Rawlinson's careful work, "The History of the Five Ancient Monarchies," one is often reminded of the disadvantage under which an author labours, be he ever so learned and acute, who writes of buildings and of countries he has never beheld. Had Professor Rawlinson seen the buildings of Italy, of Greece, of Egypt, and of Asia, he never would have written of these ruins of Persepolis, and in particular of this "Hall of a Hundred Columns," as "the great pillared halls which constitute the glory of Arian architecture, and which, even in their ruins, provoke the wonder and admiration of modern Europeans, familiar with all the triumphs of Western art, with Grecian temples, Roman baths and amphitheatres, Moorish' palaces, Turkish mosques and Christian cathedrals." This is just the point in which the buildings of Persepolis fail. They are deeply interesting as records of the Achæmenian dynasty; they are illustrated books of priceless value in their inscriptions and sculpture; but for grandeur, and even solidity, they never were comparable to some of the buildings of Athens, nor among modern and Christian buildings, to the church of St. Isaac's in St. Petersburg.

The floor of the Hall of a Hundred Columns is, for the most part, buried deep under rubbish, the washings of ages from the neighbouring mountains. Against the stoutest blocks of the richly-sculptured walls this detritus lies undisturbed, concealing sometimes the legs of a winged bull, at others the lower garments of a king, and how much besides which the passing traveller cannot see nor guess? What new lights for history, what treasures of antiquity, may be lying within two or three feet of the surface in these neglected ruins! In the walls of this Hall there are deep recesses or niches, the likeness of which is invariably met with in every modern Persian house.

That portion of the platform farthest from the great staircase and the Propylæum of Xerxes, is occupied, first, with the Palace of Darius, and last with the Palace of Xerxes; and in the far background, in the side of the mountain, originally approached by steps, is the Tomb of Darius. Above the small doorway, which lets into a cave hewn from the solid rock, the face of the mountain is smoothed and sculptured. In the foreground of this work of ancient art, is the crowned figure of the King, and at the opposite end, on the same level, an altar with fire burning upon it. Above this altar is the round full orb of the sun, and hovering in mid air, between the sun and the monarch, is what Mr. Fergusson calls "his *ferouher* or disembodied spirit." But this is unintelligible. Professor Rawlinson suggests, with greater show of reason, that this figure is the emblematic resemblance of Ahura-mazda, the "good" god of the Medes, the Ormazd of the inscriptions of Xerxes. The figure is that of a man crowned and robed like King Darius, his feet unsupported, his body passed through a ring, which connects a pair of vast wings, and of this Professor Rawlinson says, "the winged circle, with or without the addition of the human figure, which was in Assyria the emblem of the chief Assyrian deity Asshur, became with the Persians the ordinary representation of the Supreme God, Ormazd."

The language of the inscriptions of the time of Darius has been described as an old form of Persian, closely allied to the Vedic Sanscrit of India on the one hand, and to the more modern Zend of Persia on the other; and the religion seems to have been the ancient representative of the faith of the Parsees of to-day. In this Tomb of Darius, the greatest place in

the heavens is given to the sun, and on earth, to the
altar of fire, the terrestrial emblem of the sun. Then
in the heavens again, Ahura-mazda, or Ormazd, is
the god of all good things, prayed to, and revered by
humanity below. We know that, according to the
belief of the time, Ormazd was not all-powerful.
Whatsoever things were good came from him, and to
him all the hopes and fears of mankind under the
sun were addressed. But there was another besides
Ormazd, the spirit of evil, Angro-mainyus, who, for
obvious reasons, does not appear in this sculpture.
He, the bringer of all trouble and pain, was helped
by "divs," bad spirits, whose delight was to thwart
the work of Ormazd. Is it possible that these were
the forerunners of our own familiar Devil, the belief
in whose existence and obnoxious activity is passing
away from this generation like a bad dream? In time
to come, when the orthodox Devil has followed the
"divs" of the time of Darius into the tomb of the
past, there will remain none the less a true and
inexpugnable devil in the world, a sum of evil made
up by individual ignorance and excess, of disregard
of duty towards oneself and one's neighbours, a devil
within ourselves, which, however, will be the more
easily attacked, and the more probably vanquished,
when we shall have recognised that it is no supernatural force which opposes our appreciation of the
enduring pleasures which follow in the train of

those lines of human conduct which we rightly call virtues.

In religion, the people of Western Europe, proud of their civilisation and enlightenment, have been, however, the victims of an error now grown inveterate. In daily contemplation of the doctrines of Christ as the oracles of God, they have been surprised to learn that the germs at least of that which is most ennobling and sublime in these doctrines had been long present in the world before the birth of Christ. And instead of feeling strengthened in their faith, and in acceptance of these doctrines, by this larger and fuller evidence of their truth and their title to the allegiance of mankind, they have been prone,—not to abandon these doctrines, for that is beyond their power, but to feel, as it were, disappointed, in learning that ideas which they cherished as supernatural revelation, are not less honoured as the transmitted experience of humanity.

A like error has been made in the lesser sphere of Art. To many generations past, the Greeks have been in Art, a people endowed with capacity for leaping at once into the highest realms of knowledge, gifted with genius unapproachable by later peoples; the men who from nothing, and with no previous light, gave to Athens her gorgeous temples, and to Rome all that she has known of Art. But now a truer conception is passing into the mind of the world. Such supernatural ability as has been in past times ascribed to the Greeks is seen not to be the monopoly, much less the sole invention of any people. The roots of the tree of knowledge, it is now perceived, may be hidden, but must exist, and it is understood that the magnificence of Ionic and Corinthian architecture could not spring fully clothed even from the rich soil of Greece, but that, like every good thing in the possession of mankind, these must be the results of long and laborious growth, of transmission or transplantation from one scene to another in the life of the universe.

Highest in the records of history stands the foundation of the Egyptian monarchy; and it is probable that the oldest buildings upon the soil of the earth—the Pyramids of Ghizeh—were erected about seven centuries after that date, in 3200 B.C. We know that Assyria was a country of renown two thousand years before that birth occurred at Bethlehem, in the lower lands of those wonderful valleys of the Tigris and Euphrates, from which all Europe, except Turkey, reckons the beginning of time. We can trace in the sculptures of Nineveh, and in those of Persepolis, a substantial resemblance. We know from the names inscribed, and from other evidence, that the latter is the descendant of the former, though probably with an interval of a thousand or fifteen hundred years. The winged bull of Nineveh has its ancestors in Egypt, and its successors in the same image and likeness at Persepolis. The bulbous columns of Egypt and of Nineveh have, in the later work of Persepolis, given birth to columns containing features which had not then appeared in Greece, but which were soon to be seen there improved and refashioned, if not reproduced, by the most artistic people of the world. The historical connexion is link by link in the mind of many a schoolboy.

The most illustrious epoch in the history of the country we have been treading, shows us, first, the victorious Cyrus; then the victor of the Nile, Cambyses, the master of Egypt; then, of the same dynasty, the great Darius, who carried his legions to Greece, and met defeat upon the plain of Marathon. Again, another association of the Greeks with the Medes and Persians, occurs through the ambition of Xerxes, whose name stands imperishably upon the roll of fame —not for his successes, not for his works at Persepolis and elsewhere, but for his defeats at Thermopylæ and Salamis. Of that period, Persepolis is the illustration in stone; and, looking upon the ruins, I am quite disposed to concur in the opinion so confidently expressed by Mr. Fergusson, that "all that is Ionic in the arts of Greece is derived from the valleys of the Tigris and the Euphrates." The volute, that distinctive feature of Ionic architecture, suggested perhaps by the use of bulls' heads or rams' heads in couples for the capitals of columns, was in use at Persepolis before it passed to Greece; whilst in Greece there was as yet only to be seen the massive simplicity of Doric architecture. At Persepolis, we have witnessed not only the origin of the volute, but also the "Greek honeysuckle," before that decoration had passed into Greece; and there too, upon the Palace of Darius are those well-known rosettes, so often repeated upon Ionic doorways; the same which may be seen upon the Erectheum of Athens, and which are faithfully copied upon a thousand edifices, including the well-known church in the Euston Road of modern London. Greek art brought out in stronger and more perfect form the members of Eastern architecture. The sculptors of Persepolis did not attempt to carve their columns in human form, and to lay the burdens of architecture upon the heads of slaves. The Caryatides are essentially a Greek production; but is it possible to concede to them all the merit of perfect originality when one sees vast stones piled upon the human heads of these winged bulls, which in part present to us a form very like that of man?

It was only in obedience to the setting sun, the god of the builders of Persepolis, that we reluctantly turned our backs upon the Tomb of Darius, and descended by the grand staircase to the plain. May the sun shine upon that, the noblest work of Persepolis, in all its present completeness, until it shall be in the East as it is in the West, and there shall be no more fear of ignorance accomplishing the ruin of the finest ascent ever made by human hands! It is recorded in the Second Book of Chronicles, of the Queen of Sheba, that when her Majesty went into Solomon's house, and saw "the ascent by which he went up into the house of the Lord, there was no more spirit in her;" she could contain her admiration of his works no longer, and her heart poured over with delight in the words, "It *was* a true report which I heard in mine own land of thine acts." It is hardly possible to doubt that had she been received by King Xerxes at Persepolis, her amazement and rapture would have been far greater. It is probable too that then the plain across which we rode towards the stream of the river Araxes or Bendemir, was not treeless, arid, and waste as at present. We have indeed good evidence that there, as in so many other places, Persia has gone backwards in production. Chardin, the French traveller, to whom the world has been so much indebted for its knowledge of Persia, says of this plain of Mervdasht, that it is "fertile, riche, abondante, belle et délicieuse." When we passed over it in the present year, it produced nothing but a few scrubby thorns, nibbled by the goats of the village of Kinara, to which our steps were directed.

CHAPTER VI.

Kinara—A family house—A troublesome cat—Houssein Khan and the sheep—Soldiers and their debtors—Zergan—Persian scenery—A Persian funeral—Zergun to Shiraz—Pass of Allahu Akbar—Snow-storm at Shiraz—The English doctor—Gate of Shiraz—A good Persian house—A present from Firman Firma—Letter from his Excellency—A dervish at the gate—Meidan of Shiraz—Visit to Firman Firma—Widow of Teki Khan—Firman Firma's character—Poverty of Persia—Passion play in Mohurrem—Bazaar of Shiraz—Tomb of Hafiz—Odes inscribed on tomb—Translation of Hafiz—The new garden—Tea in an imaret.

OUTSIDE the village of Kinara, there was a hole in the mud wall through which we might have passed the takht-i-rawan; but had we done so, the narrowness of the streets would have prevented its approach to the house in which a room had been secured for us. We halted therefore in a field of young wheat, at a place where rubbish had been flung out from the houses of the village and over the wall in such quantity, that now it was frozen hard and innoxious as rock, we could walk up the slope and over the wall into the village.

The mode of access prepared us for the characteristics of Kinara. The family in whose house we were to lodge, was much disturbed by our sudden arrival. We had struggled through the dirty snow in the narrow street and entered the low door in the mud wall of the house. In the yard, deep in filth, much of which was happily frozen, were two mules and a donkey, and about their legs a legion of fowls, of which one lay headless at the requisition of Kazem, whose imperious airs in a Persian village were sometimes very amusing. Up a narrow passage, past a stable in which two donkeys were eating straw, there were some mud-plastered steps leading to the roof of the buildings surrounding the yard. Upon this roof was the shed which it was the delight of the family to let to us for the night, with the prospect of some payment in the morning.

Like the roof, our apartment was of mud. In the hole which was the door, there was a shutter of wood which could not be made close by half a dozen inches, and in the hole at the further end which served as a window, there was nothing to keep out the frosty wind until we stuffed a saddle bag into the refrigerating aperture. The roof was extensive, and in another place there was a second shed in which the family hay and melons were preserved, and into which the contents of our apartment, previous to our occupation, were hurriedly thrust by the retreating inhabitants, some of whom sat on the roof, while some stood among the other animals in the yard, contemplating with avid interest, every one of our movements. Upon any pretence and sometimes without pretext, one of them would appear upon that portion of the roof which was in front of our place of refuge, and at last I was obliged to draw a line upon the dried mud and intimate that I should deal in a summary manner with any who overstepped that boundary. Whatever they had to bring must be laid down at this line, and none but Kazem might pass over it. The precision of this arrangement met with the entire satisfaction of the family. But there was one member—a black cat—whom I could not instruct, and through the evening and night this green-eyed monster sought, often with success, to violate the sanctity of our mud-cabin. To secure greater privacy and higher temperature, I had nailed a camels'-hair rug inside the imperfect door, and as a fortification against the cat, had weighted the lower end with heavy stones. As for the wooden door, that, like nine doors out of ten in Persia, presented no hindrance, and with time on his side, the tom-cat was always more successful than I with the rug. Twice in the bitter cold of the night I expelled the enemy and renewed our defences. But the cat was always victorious, and in the morning I found he had been successful in carrying off the greater part of a tongue, which had been placed in a position, as I believed, of absolute security. On the whole we were not sorry to leave Kinara. But forgetting the squalor of the village and the lodging, looking across the five miles of level plain, to the still visible ruins of Persepolis, with their high background of mountains varied in colour as in shape, we were ready to admit that it would be difficult indeed to name a scene of greater natural beauty or of higher antiquarian interest.

Our way to Zergan, the next station, wound through low hills, at nearly a continuous level. About midday, we came to a bridge crossing a river which was swollen and foaming with melted snow. There was a wretched hovel at hand from which half a dozen of Houssein Khan's ragged tofanghees emerged, and hovered round us while we sat in the only patch of shade, to make a luncheon of lamb and eggs. During the morning their chief had possessed himself of two more sheep from flocks which were feeding near our path, and we felt so indignant at the continuance of this system of robbery, carried on under our eyes, and probably in the opinion of the victims, with our connivance, that we resolved to be silent no longer, and desired Kazem to ask Houssein Khan for an explanation of what, we wished him to tell the Khan, appeared to us nothing better than robbery. The captain of the guard sat on a stone close by, with his ivory-hilted sword laid across his knees, a dagger and two pistols in his belt, when Kazem delivered my demand for an explanation of his conduct. I could see he was very much disturbed by the inquiry. He came himself to explain that he had done no wrong in taking the sheep; he declared that they represented a payment on account of loans he had made to the peasants, and that this was the only way he could obtain consideration for his advances. Although Kazem smiled incredulity, as he assisted me in comprehending Houssein Khan's explanation, I was obliged to accept it and to admit that possibly it might be correct, although I do not believe there was a word of truth in his statement. It is, however, unquestionable that in Persia, money lenders are most often soldiers, the only class which feels strong enough to secure payment. This is so general, that a defaulting debtor is looked upon as in a particular degree obnoxious to the military class, who, if they get an opportunity, subject him to severe ill-treatment *pour encourager les autres* in the payment of their borrowings. I have met with people who have seen the dead body of a debtor stripped naked and dragged by the heels with a rope in the midst of a party of soldiers through the bazaars of one of the chief towns in Persia, by way of warning to those who owe money not to fail in discharging their obligations to the usurious military before they pay the debt of nature.

Houssein Khan was in a very black humour when we resumed our journey, towards the end of which, there lay between us and Zergan a vast morass, extending for miles from mountain to mountain. The charvodar and he had a quarrelsome difference of opinion as to which was the best path, and I decided, much to the disgust of the soldier, that the muleteer should select the way for the caravan. He had the greater property at stake. He and his mules were inhabitants, natives in fact, of the village we were approaching, and the result justified my decision.

We met a string of dromedaries coming out of Zergan. Their swarthy riders were seated between the humps of the animals, enduring the swaying motion and passing us with imperturbable gravity. "English reserve" is a common subject of joke, but it is certainly not greater than Oriental reserve. It is more true, perhaps, that the reserve practised on some occasions by Englishmen appears inconsistent with the absence of reserve upon other occasions. But in the deserts of Persia and Arabia, it is common experience to meet but one or two persons in a whole day's journey, and not by any means uncommon to pass these without uttering a word. Sometimes the ejaculation "salāām" is exchanged between one or two of the members of a caravan, but a prolonged greeting is of very rare occurrence.

I was about to say that the situation of the chaparkhanah at Zergan is very remarkable, but I am conscious that in all Persian scenery there is a sameness in certain features, though these have invariably a peculiar beauty of form and colouring. The mountains are never out of sight, and in January there is always snow in the landscape. When the plains and hill sides are visible there are always the browns peculiar to Oriental scenery, and when there is a village, the flat roofs of mud and straight walls of the same colour and material give an unmistakable character. At Zergan, the plain was so narrow that all these features were brought in unusually close contact. At sunset, when the moollah of the village, too poor to have a minaret, was standing on the roof of his mosque and crying, "Allah-ah-ah-ah-u Akbar-ar-ar-ar" (God is great) in the tones to which we had become accustomed at night and morning, I walked for a long time on the roof of the stables (which is, as it were, the terrace of the bala-khanah) enjoying the scene, watching how the silence of the plain seemed to deepen with the lengthening shadows and the rose colour of the distant snow turned first to a pale gilding and then to iron grey, and the bell of a mule coming to rest for the night resounded for miles in the still clear air, given over by the parting sun to the dominion of frost, which immediately sealed all until the morning.

I was awoke by a direful wailing of many voices, and hastily turning out upon the roof, saw a funeral passing from the village to the graveyard upon the plain. In Persia, as in Turkey, great haste is generally made in burial; the bearers hurry along, unwilling to keep the soul from rest in earth. In this case, the body was wrapped or swathed in white linen, and laid on a bier, the mummy-like form of the corpse being entirely exposed. In front, the wailers, professionals probably, trotted at a pace a little faster than would be possible had they walked at their utmost speed; the bearers, of whom a relay followed the body, did their best to keep up, and the succeeding crowd of mourners and sympathisers straggled onwards as they could.

This was the twenty-sixth of January, and we were happy in the thought that we were about to rest in Shiraz after the fatigue of travelling. For eighteen nights, from Ispahan, we had endured the miseries of chapar-khanahs and caravanserais; with the exception of one day's painful rest at Yezdikhast, we had ridden on an average for eight hours every day, and as we rode up and down the snowy hills towards Shiraz, we longed for a sight of the famous city in which we were to be for some time the guests of an Englishman. The snow was deep, and the road almost the worst we had met with. Underneath the soft snow, there were hidden boulders of every shape, upon which our horses and mules stumbled and slipped. In places where the sun had power, the hoofs of the animals were covered with slush at every footstep. We had not gone half way from Zergan to Shiraz, when the sun disappeared behind thick clouds, and the magnificent panorama was closed by a heavy fall of snow. In the mountains, slouching through the snow, we met two rather large parties of armed men, who would possibly have shown themselves to be robbers had we been less strong, and at length in a hollow we dismounted at a ruined caravanserai, and awaited Kazem's preparation of a stew. The good little man was bringing it towards where I sat, almost shivering, upon the framework of a well, near to my wife, who did not leave the shelter of her takht-i-rawan, when his foot slipped and the savoury mess fell into a hopeless quagmire of mud and snow. We had to put up with less comforting provision. But what did that matter; in three hours we should be in Shiraz! We mounted again, and rode up and down over hills of which we could not see the end. Progress became very difficult on account of the snow which every hour fell fast and faster. I saw it was the intention of our guard to creep away and leave us to walk through the storm. Houssein Khan himself set the example. When a projecting rock hid him from my sight, he pressed his horse onward and was soon out of sight. My contempt for the whole troop was too great to permit of entreating the soldiers to remain and trudge slowly through the snow with the baggage mules, and the takht-i-rawan.

Every man of them soon trotted off, and we, attended only by our muleteers and servants, moved slowly along, the whole caravan white with the falling snow, the takht-i-rawan and the baggage fringed with icicles. We had passed the last summit and were descending from the pass of Allahu Akbar in a gorge, the grandeur of which was perhaps enhanced by the severity of the weather, when we met the English doctor, Mr. Odling, who had kindly invited us to stay at his house in Shiraz, attended by a stalwart Persian groom. Both were mounted on splendid horses and well armed. The doctor wore a long coat of English frieze and riding boots; a young man with the strong, quiet manner characteristic of Yorkshiremen, a man of whom at first sight one would say that he was well chosen for the service in which he had engaged. He had some difficulty in reining his fiery horse to our caravan pace. Worse travelling I have never known. Snow and stones and mud beneath, and above a cold blinding drift and fall, which froze where the lingering warmth of the body did not melt it into greater discomfort.

From the high hills by which Shiraz is approached by way of Ispahan, a broad path leads down to the city. In other places it would be called a road, but where wheels are never seen such a word might be misleading. Had the day been clear, we should have enjoyed from these hills one of the finest views in

Persia. Close beside the path as it slopes into Shiraz, is a graveyard with a garden attached, an enclosure in which dark green cypress trees rise high above the walls. In this place rest the remains of the poet Hafiz, and about a mile further to the left in another enclosure of the same character, Sa'di was buried. Upon the right of the road is a garden, also set with cypress trees, with a pavilion or palace at the higher end, a very favourite resort of the Shirazees, who carry their teapots there, and sitting on their heels upon the open floor of the pavilion, enjoy the view over the flat roofs, the blue domes, the minarets, and the green "chenar" or plane trees of the city, bounded by the opposite mountains rising high above Shiraz, and enclosing that which they fondly believe to be "the hub" of the universe. This quotation is the more permissible, because there is some parallelism between the reputation of Boston in the United States and that of Shiraz among the Persians. Shiraz is pre-eminently the literary city of Persia.

But in the snowstorm we had no disposition to turn to right or left, even to do homage at the grave of Hafiz. Straight on we pushed, until, at a council including the doctor and the charvodar, it was decided that the takht-i-rawan, three feet wide, seven feet high, and in length perhaps not more than that of three mules, could not pass through the town, and that it would be necessary to ford the river and enter the walls as near as possible to Mr. Odling's house.

I shall never forget the mud inside the gate of Shiraz. It was about a foot deep and spread from wall to wall. A labyrinth of walls and narrow ways rendered the further progress of the takht-i-rawan impossible. We had at the entry of this famous city to place my wife on a led horse, and to have the takht-i-rawan carried in the hands of men, because with the more extended length of harnessed mules, it could not follow the windings of the miserable streets of Shiraz. That operation of "swopping horses while crossing a stream," which Abraham Lincoln condemned as the height of impolicy, is as nothing compared with the manœuvre we were forced to effect in this sea of mud. At last we arrived at a brick wall in which was the door of Mr. Odling's house. For the kindness and ability with which he conducted, under the double oppression of a snowstorm and of a Shiraz crowd, the difficult arrival of ourselves and our train, I have an unfading recollection of esteem and obligation.

There is no one of the Englishmen resident in Persia, and we became acquainted with all, of whom we retain a higher opinion than of Mr. Odling, partly because no one is more careful to vindicate the superior characteristics of his country, by the contined observance of them in a land where as a rule, right appears to have no significance but that of might. His home in Shiraz is a good Persian house of the usual style; mud-built of course, and with no view from within of the external world, with rooms arranged upon paved terraces around two small quadrangles, in which there is the usual tank and bit of garden, the latter in his case set with orange trees. The walls of the rooms in a house of this sort are finished with fine plaster and whitened; panelled with recesses in which pictures, books, or china may be placed. The fireplace is always the same; a hole in the wall beneath a flue, and the floors of course are more or less covered with carpets, those best productions of Persian industry, with their unrivalled blending of soft colours. When we arrived, and indeed during the few days of our stay in Shiraz, the quadrangles of Mr. Odling's house were heaped high with snow, including a large quantity thrown from the roofs. It is obviously unwise to allow a great weight of snow to melt on the mud roof of a Persian house. Careful housekeepers always remove it quickly, and upon the roof of every Persian house in which there is pretension to good management, a cylinder of stone is always kept to solidify the roof by rolling after wet weather and upon the occasional application of a new layer of wet clay.

Houssein Khan had orders to report our safe

arrival to the Firman Firma (the Decreer of Decrees), and I sent at the same time by a servant a letter of thanks to his Excellency, together with a Vizierial letter from his brother, Mirza Houssein Khan, the Sipar Salar. Early the next morning the inevitable present arrived. This time it was much bigger, more imposing in its arrival, and more useless in fact, than before. Preceded by the Firman Firma's major-domo, whose every stride was marked with a movement of his silver-mounted wand, walked several servants, followed by negroes bearing the present on their heads in huge trays of metal, each a yard in diameter. Three were piled with oranges, and in others there were arranged ten large china plates, full of sweetmeats. Shortly after all this was delivered, a handsome young Persian, the Governor's aide-de-camp, the "nazir" of his Excellency's household, arrived with the following letter from the Firman Firma, which is not only in the French language, but is without the slightest touch of Persian manner:—

"Monsieur,—J'ai eu le plaisir de recevoir la lettre de S. A., et je m'empresse de vous réitérer mes sincères félicitations pour votre arrivé dans cette ville.

"Demain, vendredi à midi, je vous attends avec le plus grand plaisir. En attendant je vous prie de vouloir bien présenter mes respectueux hommages à Madame Arnold. Je m'imagine des fatigues qu'elles a du endurer pendant un voyage en ces froids.

"Je vous prie d'agréer l'assurance de ma parfaite considération.

"YAHIA."

One may live for months in a Persian house without acquiring any knowledge whatever of that which is to be seen outside the door. Upon our arrival in Shiraz I had been so confused by the falling snow and the mingled noise of porters, muleteers, soldiers, and servants, that I had taken no notice of the surroundings. In the bustle of arrival I had not even observed the mud hut in which a dervish lived close by Mr. Odling's door. On coming out, this holy man took care there should be no such omission, lifting his voice with ever-increasing loudness until he attained his object. It is a common circumstance in Persian towns for one of these religious mendicants to plant himself near the gate of any house of unusual importance. Of course the residence of a giaour was not the cause of this particular dervish's presence. A Moslem house joined the residence of the Christian doctor, and one of the city gates lay close at hand. The situation was therefore a good one for a religious beggar; and a dervish, though upon one occasion he will not be sparing of his curses, which are always the only words fit in his mouth for Christians, has, as a rule, no objection whatever to money from the hands of unbelievers. The dervish at the door is regarded by Persians as a nuisance which must not be rudely expelled; much as an English squire or farmer of the olden fashion looks upon the summer birds which build their muddy nests in the angles of his porch, with a lingering belief in his mind that after all there is perhaps something in the old doggrel, which says—

"Martens and swallows are God's best fellows."

For my own part I would far rather hear the twitter of the swallow as a morning call, than the "Allahu akbar" of a self-imposed dervish at my gate. But then there is no accounting for taste; and the dervishes find that a lazy life, with a noisy devotion to religion, insures an easy livelihood.

Twenty steps past the dervish over the frozen slush, we arrived in the smaller "place" or meidan of Shiraz. On one side stands the Governor's palace; the other three sides are occupied with the blank walls of houses and yards. Paving has never been attempted in Shiraz, and the meidan is in hills and holes according as the traffic and the exigencies of the people, in the disposition of rubbish, have made it. There are two or three miserable trees before the Governor's palace, which was apparently at one time fenced from the open space by a wall of mud-bricks, with stone piers. But the stones have long since been cast down; they lie broken on the ground with much débris from the wall. The front of the palace has no architectural pretensions; under a heavy châlet roof there are windows, one storey above the ground floor, but the windows and frames are broken, the mud plaster has fallen off in large patches from the wall, and on every side of this meidan the walls are in the same condition. Over all there is the usual aspect of ruin and poverty, so general throughout Persia.

Under the gateway lounged some of the Firman Firma's servants and soldiers. On seeing us, they led the way to a brick staircase, with steps inconveniently high, to a part of the palace at some distance from the meidan, pulled aside the hangings of Manchester cotton stamped with Oriental pattern, from a doorway, and we were in the presence of his Excellency Yahia Khan, brother of the Prime Minister, and husband of a sister of his Majesty the Shah. Yahia, commonly known as "the Firman Firma," is also Motemid-el-Mulk, and the title of the Princess, his wife, is Izzet-ud-Dowleh. Her Highness was the widow of the murdered Ameer-el-Nizam. The Shah's repentance for the crime of consenting to the death of the Ameer led his Majesty, as we have seen, to betroth his two young daughters to the sons of the Ameer; and the same feeling induced him to bestow the Princess, whom he had made a widow, upon the Motemid-el-Mulk, whom he afterwards styled "Firman Firma."

Yahia Khan is the most accomplished and Europeanised man in Persia. His manners are charming, and there can be but very few Asiatics who have such easy command of the French language. If he were a man of firmness, vigour, of strong and lofty ambition, Yahia Khan might do great things for his country. But one sees at a glance that though superior to his brother in culture, and probably in moral worth, he has not the energy, the boldness, or the power of intrigue of Mirza Houssein Khan. He wore a military undress of European cut—the only Governor who had not received me with all the jewels and ornaments at command. In this and many other points, the superior civilisation of Yahia Khan was evident. His apartment was not unlike a barrack-room in officer's quarters: the walls white and bare, the floor covered with matting, with two carpets laid upon it. Chairs are always scarce in Persia; there were only three in the Firman Firma's room, two for Mr. Odling and myself, beside the arm-chair of the Governor, which he compelled me to accept. The British Agent, a native of rank, the Mirza Hassan Ali Khan, 'a man of very agreeable manners and of much cultivation, arrived as soon as we were seated, and gracefully accepting Yahia Khan's apology for the absence of a fourth chair, took his seat, in probably greater comfort, upon the floor. All the weakness of the Firman Firma's amiable character appeared in his conversation. Of the ills in the condition of Persia, he was in no way ignorant; of amendment he had nothing to say. I did not expect much in that direction from a man who, while drawing a splendid income from the province, was content to leave the front of his house a heap of ruins. It is this supine submission to the process of decay which is the bane of Persia. From highest to lowest everything is administered as if the only object of those in power was to seek their own momentary advantage, as if, in fact, the Persians held the country as yearly tenants, and nothing more. When Sir Lewis Pelly was (in his capacity as Political Resident at Bushire) in official communication with the Government of Shiraz, he showed his true appreciation of the political system of Persia in a report to the Bombay Government:—" A.," he wrote, "gives to his sub-farmers permission to collect the revenue by force; this is done; next year some of the peasants are fled; some of the land is lying waste. The country, in brief, is revenued as if the Government were to end with the expiry of the Governor's lease."

The Firman Firma had but one word of explanation concerning the condition of Persia; the country, he said, was "very, very poor." There had been a few robberies lately in his province, but he believed it was generally quiet (he has since been recalled, owing to his inability to control the turbulent people of Shiraz); he should provide us with an armed escort from Shiraz to Bushire, which he had intended should be ten men and an officer; but as I preferred to have only two sowars, he would give orders that but two, and those the most trustworthy, should accompany our caravan. He provided the customary entertainment, of tobacco, tea, and coffee, and was most polite in desiring to do anything which could conduce to the comfort and pleasure of our stay in Shiraz.

I had one favour to ask—a very small one—but I thought it would be more proper not to put it to him personally; and on leaving I directed the attention of his "nazir," or controller, the same agreeable young man who had brought the Firman Firma's letter soon after our arrival, to the large tent adjoining the palace, in which during the first days of the Mohurrem, then just commenced, there was acted the representation of the closing period of the life of Houssein, the grandson of Mahommed. I was aware that this taziah, or theatre, was visited daily by the Firman Firma and the ladies of his anderoon, as well as by hundreds of the people of Shiraz; and I requested if his Excellency thought my visit would not be displeasing to the people, and therefore a possible embarrassment to himself, that he would kindly make provision for our admittance to witness the performance.

For days this strange "Passion-play" of the last days of Houssein had been going on, and for days it would continue. On the tenth day, the tearful tragedy of his death at Kerbela, with that of seventy of his followers, would be represented. The canvas of the large tent had, I should think, been purchased in England or in India. On three sides the theatre was closed in by the walls of the precinct of the palace. Upon the top of these, and covering the fourth side, the canvas was arranged. The whole of the centre of the tent appeared to be the stage. It seemed that no scenery was introduced, but the events were made life-like by the employment of soldiers, camels, horses, and mules, of which there were generally some standing outside the theatre. These were for the most part splendidly equipped and lent for this sacred occasion by the Governor and great people of Shiraz.

The young nazir called at Mr. Odling's the next evening and, expressing the great regret of his Excellency, said that the Firman Firma thought it better we should not visit the theatre. The moollahs would certainly object, and he feared there might be a disturbance. We therefore failed in this respect in Shiraz as we had failed in Tehran.

The Persians are so strict in excluding Christians from their religious places that we had some doubt if we should be able to enter the cemetery in which is placed the tomb of Hafiz. We rode in single file through the crowded bazaars, and soon gained the broad way by which we had entered Shiraz. Leaving our horses outside the gate, we entered the mud-built gate and walked among the dark cypresses. An open mosque stood at the higher end of the graveyard, which was full of tombs, and at the other end there were charming views through the cypress groves, of the blue sky and the snow-covered mountains which lay on the farther side of the valley in which is placed the city of Shiraz. There were two moollahs near the mosque wearing white turbans and long robes of green. One of these ran towards us, but not with the intention of objecting to our entry. Mr. Odling's dog had unobserved left the grooms and followed us into the cemetery. It was against the presence of the Christian "dog" that the demonstration of the moollahs was made, and though we aided in expelling our dog we thought it an affectation of religious zeal on the part of the guardian priest, inasmuch as all the while there stood near the quiescent moollah a Persian, and, by hypothesis, a Moslem dog, which appeared quite at home and welcome in this pleasant and most picturesque retreat.

Our offending dog having been thrust outside, we were at liberty to look at the grave of Hafiz, which is placed about the middle of the square enclosure. The ground is thickly beset with tombs, mostly flat, like that of Hafiz, but none so exquisitely carved nor, like his, of marble. Hafiz' tomb is covered with a single block of the beautiful marble of Yezd, of which about eighteen inches appear above the ground. The upper surface of this fine slab is nine feet long by two feet nine inches in width. In the centre there is an ode, written by Hafiz himself, of which the following is a translation founded upon that made by Mr. Binning:—

"Proclaim the good tidings of oneness with the, that above this transitory life I may be lifted immortal. A bird of Paradise am I; my heart's desire is to fly to thee, away from the traps and temptations of this world. If thou shouldst deign in thy great mercy to call me thy faithful servant, how joyously would I take leave of the mean concerns and miserable vanities of this transitory existence.

"O Allah! from the bright vapours which surround thy throne, pour out upon me a flood of the graces of thy goodness, before I am borne away like dust before the wind.

"Come hither, O my loved ones, to my tomb, with wine and music, and possibly at the sound of your cheerful voices and the music of your melody, I may rise from slumber, and rise from among the dead.

"Though I am aged and weak, do thou, if it be but for one night, fold me in thine embrace, so that on the morrow I shall arise from thy side re-endowed with the bloom and the vigour of youth.

"Come forth and show thyself, O type of all good; manifest thyself, so that Hafiz may bid adieu to this life and to this lower world."

Raised in low relief, this ode, in the beautiful letters of the Persian alphabet, occupies the centre only of the slab. Round the edges, in a band about four inches deep, appears another ode, which has been rendered into the following words of English:—

"O my soul, be thou the servant of Allah, the king of the universe, and be thyself a king. Seek to abide for ever under the care and protection of Allah.

"The enemies of the true faith may be many; but a thousand of them shall count as naught and they shall be as nothing, even though hosts of such unbelievers should cover the hills.

"To day, O Ali, we live by thy power. By the souls of the holy Imāms be thou a witness on our behalf in the world to come.

"He who bears not true love towards Ali is no better than an infidel, even though he be most devoted in his prayers and the most learned in the mosque.

"Go, kiss the sepulchre of the eighth Imām, the prince of the faith, Réza, and stand expectant on that sacred threshold.

"O, Háfiz! choose thou the service of Allah, the all-powerful, and go forward boldly in the right path."

The tomb is probably not yet two hundred years old. From this interesting place we passed to the "New Garden," which is not far distant, and commands the same charming views of the valley and mountains of Shiraz. There we met with a party of "softas," theological students, who had brought a samovar and charcoal, cups and saucers, sugar and tea from the town. They invited us to join them in a cup of tea, which we all enjoyed upon the ruined floor of an "imaret," a palatial pavilion which had been gay and grand in the days of Shah Abbas.

CHAPTER VII.

Literature of Persia—Hafiz and Sa'di—Contemporary of Dante—
Mr. Bicknell's translation of Hafiz—Consulting Hafiz as an oracle
—Nadir Shah and Hafiz—Hafiz' fragments—"Tetrastichs" of
Hafiz—Sa'di's "Bustan"—Sa'di's "Gulistan"—Extracts from
"Gulistan"—Sa'di's wit and wisdom—Gardens of Shiraz—Slaves
and slave-brokers—English surgeons and Persian patients—Influence of Russia—Mr. Thomson and Mr. Bruce—Indo-Persian
telegraph—Major Champain's reports—A view of the neighbours—
Persian homes—Government of Shiraz—Ecliats in Fars—Attack
on a caravan—A vengeful Government—Cruel execution of robbers—Firman Firma superseded—Taxation in Persia—The Shah
and Shiraz.

THE literature of Persia is not extensive, and that which exists is little known outside the Empire. But in any survey of Persia, however hasty, some notice must be taken of the works of the two great poets, Hafiz and Sa'di, both natives of Shiraz. There is, no doubt, immense difficulty in translating their writings. Hafiz, the later of the two, has been dead nearly five hundred years. Imagine a Persian with a smattering of English (Europeans very rarely acquire a thoroughly competent knowledge of the Persian language), as it is spoken to-day, set to translate Chaucer into Persian! Dante was contemporary with

Hafiz. Fancy the difficulties which the writings of Dante would present to a Persian who had but an imperfect acquaintance with the colloquial Italian of the nineteenth century!

For my own part, I have no confidence that in such translations as have been made, we obtain a thorough understanding of the poet's meaning. But we should not therefore reject them. Mr. Herman Bicknell has made a very praiseworthy attempt to render the poetry of Hafiz into English verse.* This is not the place to express my opinion of his success. I have read the greater part of his work, and I am not sure if the difficulty inseparable from the undertaking is not injuriously and needlessly increased by fitting the translation into rhymes. Mr. Bicknell had undoubtedly a rare acquaintance with the manners and customs, the thoughts and fancies of the East; and it may be justly said that any comparison of the difficulty of translating Hafiz truly into English with that of rendering Chaucer and Dante into Persian, is not strictly fair, because the East is not as the West. The changes which have taken place in Persian and in Persia since the time of Sa'di and of Hafiz would seem as nothing when placed beside those which divide England and Italy of the fourteenth century from those same countries in the nineteenth century.

* "Hafiz of Shiraz: Selections from his Poems." Translated from the Persian by Herman Bicknell. London. T ubner & Co.

There can be no question of the high repute in which Hafiz has been and is still held by his countrymen. He died at Shiraz in 1388. Mr. Bicknell, in the introduction to his work, alludes to a custom of which I have often heard in Persia, and which, I believe, is still practised in Shiraz. He says:—" The admiration for the Odes had increased to so great an extent before the death of Hafiz in the year of the Hijrah 791 (A.D. 1388), that it became customary to consult them to discover future events; and this practice is still continued in the East in various ways. One method, after breathing over the volume, is to utter an invocation such as the following:—

O Hafiz of Shiraz impart
Foreknowledge to my anxious heart!

The book is then opened at hazard, and the first couplet which meets the eye is taken as an answer to the question of him who consults the oracle.

"When Nádir Sháh was engaged in hostile operations against the Afghans it is related that he performed a 'ziyárat,' or pious visit, to the tomb of the poet, and had recourse to the Díván to know whether it would be expedient to continue the war. The couplet lighted on was the following:—

O Hafiz, by thy dulcet song, 'Irák and Fárs are raptured;
Now haste that Baghdad and Tabríz may in their turn be captured!

Such an omen was, of course, hailed as auspicious. Baghdad and Tabríz were accordingly attacked and rescued from the Turks. On account of the supposed heterodoxy of certain passages in the Díván, difficulties were raised as to the interment of Hafiz with the rites of religion. The poetic oracle, however, being consulted, all doubts were set at rest by the following couplet:—

> Wish not to turn thy foot away from Hafiz on his bier
> He shall ascend to Paradise, though steeped in sin while here."

The following is Mr. Bicknell's translation of one of the Odes of Hafiz :—

" Thou whose features clearly-beaming make the moon of Beauty bright,
Thou whose chin contains a well-pit which to Loveliness gives light.

When, O Lord! shall kindly Fortune, sating my ambition, pair
This my heart of tranquil nature and thy wild and ruffled hair?

Pining for thy sight, my spirit trembling on my lip doth wait
Forth to speed it, back to lead it, speak the sentence of its fate.

Pass me with thy skirt uplifted, from the dusty, bloody ground :
Many who have been thy victims, dead upon this path are found.

How this heart is anguish-wasted, let my heart's possessor know :
Friends your souls and mine contemplate, equal by their common woe.

Aught of good accrues to no one witched by thy narcissus eye :
Ne'er let braggarts vaunt their virtue : if thy drunken orbs are nigh.

Soon my Fortune sunk in slumber shall her limbs with vigour brace :
Dashed upon her eyes is water sprinkled by thy shining face.

Gather from thy cheek a posy, speed it by the flying East ;
Sent be perfume to refresh me, from thy garden's dust at least.

Hafiz offers a petition, listen, and 'Amen' reply;
On thy sugar-dropping rubies let me for life's food rely.

Many a year live on and prosper, Sakis of the court of Jam,
E'en though I, to fill my wine cup, never to your circle come.

Eastwind, when to Yazd thou wingest, say thou to its sons from me
May the head of every ingrate, ball-like 'neath your mall-bat be!

What though from your dais distant, near it by my wish I seem;
Homage to your king, I render and I make your praise my theme.

      Shah of shahs, of lofty planet,
      Grant for God what I implore;
      Let me, as the sky above thee,
      Kiss the dust which strews thy floor."

From among the "Fragments" which Mr. Bicknell's volume contains, I have taken this :—

"O Shah, an envoy came from Heaven, of húri aspect fair,
Rizvan-like in his majesty, of Salsabíl-like hair,

Of language sound in sense, and sweet symmetrical, refined,
Both fair and slight, of virgin mien, and unto jest inclined.

I said: 'To this retreat of mine what cause has made thee wing?'
He answered: 'For the Shah I come, that angel-minded king.'

Of me, O Shah, for poor am I, that youth has weary grown:
To gratify his heart's desire, accept him for thine own."

The key to this poem is contained in a note which informs us that the "envoy" is the genius of Hafiz, who, in the last couplet, is soliciting the Imperial patronage. I will make one more extract from the same work, that of the following lines, which are placed with the "Tetrastichs" of Hafiz :—

   "Pure wine beside a brook   'Tis good to have
   Release from sorrow's nook   'Tis good to have
   Life lasts ten days, as doth the rose's time;
   A smiling, beaming look   'Tis good to have."

Without in the least disparaging Mr. Bicknell's work, which I am not competent to criticise fully, I must say he has not led me to abandon the opinion that there is a needless loss of Persian aroma in forcing the interpretation into rhymes.

The full name of Hafiz was "Mahommed Shams-ud-deen Hafiz." Probably the first of these three names was all that he possessed in his childhood. Shams-ud-deen, which means "Sun of the Faith," and Hafiz, which implies "One who knows the Koran," are appellations of honour, which were probably conferred upon him in the zenith of his fame.

A greater than Hafiz, in the opinion of many of the most learned Persians, is that older poet, the Sheik Sa'di, also of Shiraz. In view of Shiraz, yet farther in the mountains, we found the reputed tomb of Sa'di. Sa'di is supposed to have been born in 1194, A.D.

In the preface to his translation of Sa'di's "Gulistan" (Rose Garden), Mr. Eastwick says:—"It appears that his (Sa'di's) father's name was Abdu'llāh, and that he was descended from Ali, the son-in-law of Mahommed; but that, nevertheless, his father held no higher office than some petty situation under the Dīwān. From Bustan, ii. 2, it appears that he lost his father when but a child; while from the sixth story of the sixth chapter of the Gulistan, we learn that his mother survived to a later period. He was educated at the Nizāmieh College at Baghdād, where he held an idrār or fellowship (Bustan, vii. 14), and was instructed in science by the learned Abū-'lfarj-bin-Janzi (Gulistan, ii. 20), and in theology by Abdu'l Kādir Gilāni, with whom he made his first pilgrimage to Makkah. This pilgrimage he repeated no less than fourteen times.

"Sa'di was twice married. Of his first nuptials, at Aleppo, we have a most amusing account in the thirty-first story of the second chapter of the Gulistan."

The following is Mr. Eastwick's translation of this marriage story:—

"Having become weary of the society of my friends at Damascus, I set out for the wilderness at Jerusalem, and associated with the brutes, until I was made prisoner by the Franks, who set me to work along with Jews at digging in the fosse of Tripolis, till one of the principal men of Aleppo, between whom and myself a former intimacy had subsisted, passed that way and recognised me, and said, 'What state is this? and how are you living?' I replied—

STANZA.

From men to mountain and to wild I fled,
Myself to heavenly converse to betake;
Conjecture now my state, that in a shed
Of savages, I must my dwelling make.

COUPLET.

Better to live in chains with those we love,
Than with the strange 'mid flow'rets gay to move.

"He took compassion on my state, and with ten dinārs redeemed me from the bondage of the Franks.

He had a daughter, whom he united to me in the marriage knot, with a fortune of a hundred dinārs. As time went on, the girl turned out of a bad temper, quarrelsome and unruly. She began to give loose to her tongue and to disturb my happiness, as they have said—

DISTICHS.

In a good man's house an evil wife
Is his hell above in this present life.
From a vixen wife protect us well,
Save us, O God! from the pains of hell.

"At length she gave vent to reproaches, and said, 'Art thou not he whom my father purchased from the Franks' prison for ten dinārs?' I replied, 'Yes; he redeemed me with ten dinārs, and sold me into thy hands for a hundred.'

DISTICHS.

I've heard that once a man of high degree
From a wolf's teeth and claws a lamb set free;
That night its throat he severed with a knife,
When thus complained the lamb's departing life:
'Thou from the wolf didst save me then, but now,
Too plainly I perceive the wolf art thou.'"

It is well, in reading the translations of Sa'di, to remember the Eastern saying, that "Each word of Sa'di has seventy-two meanings."

In the "Gulistan" (Mr. Gladwin's translation), Sa'di speaks of a man. "stringing himself upon the cord of our acquaintance," and adopting his metaphor, I will endeavour to string this illustrious Persian more thoroughly upon the cord of our acquaintance, by a few additional quotations from the "Gulistan."

He was evidently anxious above all things to obtain the favour of the King for himself and his work, though there is no reason to doubt that the following loyal effusion contains the expression of his genuine convictions:—"A king," he writes, "is the shadow of God, and a shadow should be the image of its substance; the disposition of the subject is not capable of good unless it be restrained by the sword of the sovereign; any peaceable demeanour which is observed in the world originates in the justice of princes; but that sovereign's judgment can never be just whose rule is founded in wickedness." This last sentence being, as Sa'di evidently supposed, of a most venturesome character, he adds, that it "met Abaca-an's fullest concurrence;" and then with regard to the work in hand, the "Gulistan" itself, he writes, "it will be really complete when it shall have met a favourable reception at Court, and obtained the indulgent perusal of that Prince, the asylum of the world, shadow of omnipotence, ray of gracious providence, treasury of the age, refuge of the faith, fortified from above, victorious over his foes, arm of triumphant fortune, luminary of resplendent piety, most illustrious of mankind, glory of orthodoxy, Sa'ad, the son of the mighty Atabak, all-powerful Emperor, ruler over the necks of the people, lord-paramount of Arabia and Persia, monarch of the sea and land, successor of the throne of Solomon, Mozuffar-u'd-deen," &c.

In a less servile mood, Sa'di avows, "I swear it were equal to the torments of hell to enter into paradise through the intervention of a neighbour;" and in a higher tone he says, " Be undefiled, O brother, in thine integrity; washermen beat none but dirty clothes against a stone."

The ways of kings and of their followers have not it seems, changed in Persia during seven hundred years. Sa'di lays it down as proverbial, that "from the plunder of five eggs, made with the sanction of the king, his troops will stick a thousand fowls on their spits." But subjects must not complain of kings, for "to maintain an opinion contrary to the judgment of the king, were to steep our hands in our own blood; verily, were the king to say, ' this day is night,' it would behove us to reply; 'Lo, there are the moon and the seven stars!'"

"Draw the foot of contentment within the mantle of safety" is an expression of rare wisdom, one which may well have made any one of Sa'di's readers " drop his head on the bosom of reflection."

" Do not sprinkle his sore with the salt of harsh words," and " Withdraw the hand of reproach from the skirt of my fatality" (or destiny) are among the sayings of this work.

Sudden death, in the flowing Persian of Sa'di, is rendered:—"All at once the foot of his existence stumbled at the grave of being, and the sigh of separation burst from the dwelling of his family."

Sa'di could say pretty things of a lady as of a king. An Irish peasant once said to an English peer:— "May every hair of your head be a mould candle to light yer to glory!" But Sa'di was even more extravagant:—"Wert thou," he wrote, "to seat thyself upon the pupil of mine eye, I would court thee to remain, for thou art lovely."

The following sentences must conclude my extracts from this very remarkable work:—

"While the body of a fat man is getting lean, a lean man must fall victim of hardship."

"If in place of a loaf of bread, the orb of the sun had been in his [a stingy merchant's] wallet, nobody would have seen daylight in this world until the day of judgment."

"Whenever thy hand can reach it, pluck out thy foe's heart; for such an opportunity washes anger from thy brain."

"Whoever sees gold lowers his head, even though, like the scales of Justice, he has iron-bound shoulders."

"Were they to take the ass of Jesus to Mecca, on its return from that pilgrimage it would still be an ass."

"The money of the miser comes out of the earth when he himself enters into it."

The works of these great writers will not pass away; they are safely enshrined in letters which are frequently reproduced. We should be glad if we had the same confidence that the remains of the tombs, and halls, and palaces, of Cyrus, of Darius, and of Xerxes, which adorn the road from Ispahan to Shiraz, were equally assured against neglect and injury.

Shiraz is famous for its "gardens," which, however, are not gardens in the English acceptation of the word, but rather shrubberies, groves of orange and cypress trees, delicious in their chequered sunlight and shade, in the views from between the trees; containing lovely vistas of grove ending only at the far off mountains; enclosures, melancholy with ruined marble tanks and imarets (as the pavilions are called) falling slowly to decay.

Inside a Persian city, there is nothing picturesque except in association with the many-coloured dresses of the people. In the larger meidan or open space of Shiraz, I saw one man kill an ox and another a sheep, and begin to dress them in the place where they fell, which seemed a "note" of great barbarism, as if it were no matter at all where the slaughtering of butchers' meat was carried on. Slaves are very numerous in Shiraz, and there are persons who act as brokers for the sale of this "property," not by public auction, but by transfer from one family to another. In this way the children of the slaves of one household are sold into another. A young boy was pointed out to us who had been lately purchased for thirty-five tomans. The English doctors in Persia, and also the French doctor who attends the Shah, are in great request among the higher class of natives, especially in cases where surgical skill is required. But the European doctors never undertake a very serious case without a bond, sealed by the patient and his nearest relatives. By this document it is arranged that half the sum to be paid for the operation is to be delivered beforehand, and the other half if the sick man recovers. It is always further agreed that under no circumstances is the doctor to be held liable for the results of his operation, which, as is natural in the very grave cases to which alone their attention is summoned, are not rarely followed by death. The operation most commonly undertaken in this way is lithotomy, and I have heard it said of the French surgeon who resides in Tehran, that he has been successful in a greater number of cases than even Sir Henry Thompson himself.

"Morning calls" form a recognised part of Persian etiquette, and among those who honoured us with this sort of attention during our stay in Shiraz, was the priest of the small Armenian community, a man most pitifully poor and apparently without hope of improving his miserable condition. If he could send a sufficient present to his bishop, then he might get nominated as priest to some position in India or Java, where he would obtain a good income. But he sighed hopelessly at the impossibility of acquiring the amount of silver which was requisite to move his spiritual father. The ritual of the Armenian Church is very severe, and the priests are enjoined before administering the sacrament of bread and wine, to spend half the previous day in the "hamām" or bath, and then to fast all night without sleep. Such Christians in a place like Shiraz lead a fearful life; under every disadvantage that bigotry, injustice, and the absence of any possible publication of their wrongs, or official representative of a foreign Power to whom they may appeal, can bring upon them. If a case of flagrant oppression and cruelty occurred as far north as Tabriz or Tehran, it is probable that if his attention were called to it, the Russian Minister or Consul would interfere, and there is no doubt that the Russian Legation at Tehran can command the action of the Shah's Government.

I have not observed an equal readiness to move on the part of the English Minister even in those affairs in which his influence would be greatest. When Mr. Bruce had telegraphed a message informing Mr. Thomson of the dangerous invitation to murder, which the Zil-i-Sultan had rashly and thoughtlessly uttered in Ispahan, Mr. Thomson neglected the common obligation of courtesy, and of proper consideration for the dangerous circumstances of the missionary. He sent no acknowledgment whatever of the receipt of this urgent message. Mr. Bruce thought it his duty in a matter of such great consequence to support this message with a full statement of his case, and to send by special messenger to the British Minister in Tehran, an elaborate report of the past and present circumstances of his school. I was favoured with an opportunity of reading this paper, a copy of which was I believe addressed at the same time to the Church Missionary Society in London, and I was much impressed with the tone of fairness, moderation, and respect in which it was composed. There could be no doubt that the school had done and was doing a great and good work, affording a valuable education to the impoverished Christians of the districts of Ispahan, and thus enabling them to improve their condition by emigration to British India. It was plain to any one that the missionary was isolated and in great need of the friendly and personal support of the Minister. When, in these circumstances, he had sent at his own cost a messenger upon an eight days' journey across the snows of Kuhrud to Tehran, I should not have thought it possible that Mr. Thomson, or any one in his position, on receiving this statement would have sent the messenger back upon his long journey without a word of acknowledgment. On hearing of the return of his servant, the missionary hurried from his room to meet the messenger. There was a congregation of people to witness the man's return after a twenty days' absence, and all heard Mr. Bruce's anxious and impulsive question: "You have a letter from Thomson Sahib?" "Nothing, Sahib," was the reply; "I was told there was no answer." I shall never forget the blank disappointment of the missionary. He knew how grievously this reply and his chagrin, obvious to all the bystanders, would augment the dangers and difficulties of his position. We were not at all surprised to hear the next morning that in the bazaars of Ispahan and Djulfa, the common talk was that "Thomson Sahib" cared nothing for what the Ispahanees might do to Mr. Bruce, and it was said that when "Thomson Sahib" got the missionary's letter he tore it in pieces and threw the bits at the messenger. This and much more of the same purport Mr. Bruce heard from his neighbours in Djulfa. I feel sure Mr. Thomson was not inactive in making representations to the Persian Government, but he was wrong in leaving Mr. Bruce without a word of support in a position of very unusual difficulty.

For the measures which followed, and for the reopening of the school, I hardly think Mr. Thomson can claim credit. Immediately upon hearing of the

Prince's decree, I wrote from my bed, in which I was suffering from fever, to several friends possessing much influence at home, begging them to move in the matter, and I think it more than probable that Mr. Thomson was impelled by consequent instructions from England in any measures he took to obtain a reversal of the Zil-i-Sultan's arbitrary decree.

If any one were to ask me, What is there to be seen in Shiraz? I should answer, Nothing of interest beside that which I have mentioned. No great building, no historic ruin claims attention. One of the best houses in the place is the office of the Indo-Persian Telegraph. It is entered from the larger meidan. Inside, in the spacious courtyard or garden, there were usually some piles of telegraph stores, iron poles, and earthenware insulators. The inspectors report that about Shiraz, a large number of these earthenware appliances are destroyed by bullets. Proficiency in placing a bullet in the head of an enemy or in that of an antelope, is an object of desire, and what mark is so good, or when hit so telling, as the white insulators suspended on telegraph poles, over all the lonely plains and the desolate hills from north to south of Persia? Besides, there is in these a prize, an iron hook, which falls to the ground like a bird when the mark is well hit, and is valued more highly than a dead snipe or a partridge.

In the report for 1875-76 by Major Champain, the

Government Director of the entire service of the Indo-Persian Telegraph, the following occurs under the head of "Interruptions:"—"The total interruptions were fewer than in any previous year, and amounted in the aggregate to only fifty-nine hours fifteen minutes. One break in May, 1875, which lasted thirty-one and a half hours, was caused in a rather curious way. The line crossed a village not very far from Bushire, and this village having been attacked and burnt to the ground by robbers, the wires were severed by heat, and could not be immediately restored. The remaining twenty-seven hours of interruption were caused by excessive cold on the high ground in the interior of the country.

"Wilful damage has, I am happy to say, somewhat decreased within the past year, although the south of Persia is probably in a more lawless condition than ever, and robberies and outrages of the worst kind continue. In fact, the road from Bushire to Ispahan, and some parts between Ispahan and the capital, are so infested with robber tribes that travelling is out of the question except for strong and well armed parties. The marauders, however, display no special hostility to the Telegraph, and rarely touch it except between Bushire and Kazeroon. In that district, every man and boy carries a gun, and the temptation to try the effect of their bullets on the iron poles seems to be irresistible."

In Major Champain's report for 1874-5 he quotes a statement on this subject made to himself by the local director, Major Smith, who reported:—" The line between Shiraz and Bushire has suffered greatly from wilful damage of the most purely wanton nature. In that part of Persia every man is armed, and it would appear that in default of more tempting objects, the people amuse themselves by trying their guns on the cast-iron sockets of the telegraph poles. Many insulators have also been destroyed in the same part of the country for the sake of their iron hooks. An effectual remedy for these unfortunate propensities of the natives is provided by the 12th Article of the Telegraph Convention of the 2nd December, 1872, to which the Persian Government have hitherto refused to give any effect on the frivolous pretext, as I understand, that the Article refers only to the wire and not to the mere adjuncts of posts and insulators. There is no doubt that if the provisions of the Article were duly enforced, the wilful damage would entirely cease. As it is the new iron poles are shot down faster than we can put them up. The bills for the repair of wilful damage already amount to upwards of 7000 tomans, of which not a penny has yet been paid."

At the Telegraph office in Shiraz, the garden of fifty yards square has three broad pavements leading from the meidan to the house, one in the centre, the others at the side walls. Between these there are plane trees, and at the end there is a low terrace of brick, upon which is the ground-floor of the house. In this, the large room to the left is the Persian office, while in that to the right, the Indian and European business is conducted. From the roof of this house, which is of unusual height, trouble has been made. It commands a view of the interior quadrangle of several Persian houses, and many complaints were consequently made when it was first occupied by giaours. It is understood that the Persian neighbours have now grown used to the possibility of this observation, and that some are not even displeased when it occurs. When we ascended in order to obtain one of the most comprehensive views over Shiraz, I observed that our appearance excited considerable interest, and certainly no displeasure. And if one can withdraw one's eyes from the eternal beauty of the mountains and streams round about Shiraz, from the general aspect of the flat mud-roofs, above which rise the white stems of plane trees, the dark green spires of the cypresses, with here and there a brown minaret, or a dome covered with a glazing of greenish blue; if in sight of all this one does feel interested in the details of Persian housekeeping, these are well exposed to view. The ladies may be seen lolling upon the floor of their apartments, the anderoön, the front of the rooms all open to the welcome warmth of the wintry sun. There is nothing on their horizon but the narrow walls of home, and it is not surprising if the apparition of persons in strange garb upon a neighbouring height is to them the most exciting event of the day. Their slaves cross and recross the quadrangle from room to room in the performance of household duties. The ̍ ̶ ͏k-eyed children roll and play in the same open The father, who is patriarch, master, ruler of ҄ rarely appears. He is hunting, or in the bazaar, or smoking, or sleeping, or at the palace or the mosque. One cannot be surprised that as the despotic ruler of his domestic realm, in which there can be no interference from without, he hates the vantage ground of this roof from which people of a monogamous race presume now and then to look in upon his polygamous household.

The district of Shiraz, which is, I believe, identical with the ancient province of Fars, has, and probably deserves, a bad name for disorder. Crimes of robbery and violence are much more frequent in this than in the northern part of Persia. To some extent the crime of Fars may be attributed to the mountainous nature of the country, which affords shelter from observation, and probable security in case of pursuit, for bands of robbers; but it is also owing to the fact, that there is a large nomad population, wandering tribes of Eeliats and others, which, according to the season, pass from north to south, or from south to north, in this province, and live a gipsy life, with the assistance of flocks and herds, and, if they are not belied, of much robbery. From Ispahan to Shiraz, there are few plains lower than five thousand feet above the sea-level. At four days' march south of Shiraz, on the road to Bushire, the path rises to above seven thousand feet. Soon afterwards it falls to near the sea-level, and the climate changes in a march of thirty miles from the rigour of winter to the genial warmth of verdant spring. To these lower lands, the thousands of Eeliats and the other nomads of Persia, wend their way in autumn, blocking the mountain passes with their cattle; and back again they come to the high lands when the summer sun has clothed the hills with green, and burnt up the vegetation of the lowlands upon which they have passed the winter. The unsettled habits of these people are supposed to conduce to a lawless life. Certain it is, that by some people or other the province is kept in perpetual terror; anywhere in Fars the talk of the road is of robbers and of robbery. The traveller who passes safely through the realm of the Governor of Shiraz is universally held to be fit subject for congratulation. Travellers gather together for mutual protection; and Europeans complain, when they are victims, that the English Government does not exact retribution and indemnity with sufficient vigour and determination. Perhaps if this charge is well founded it may find some excuse in the unwillingness of the agents of any civilised power to rouse the Persian Government to such indiscriminate and wholesale vengeance as it is ever ready, upon the motion of the Minister of a European Power, to wreak upon its miserable subjects. Shortly before we travelled through this ill-reputed province, the eldest son of Lord Napier of Magdala passed through Shiraz, on his way from India to Tehran, charged with a special mission of observation in the Persian capital. He was accompanied for some distance by Dr. Waters, who was attached to the Residency at Bushire, and from whose narrative of the incidents of their journey I gather the particulars of the attack upon their caravan. Fortunately for themselves, these gentlemen were not with their baggage when it was stopped and rifled by a band of about fifty robbers, who killed one of the mounted guards with a bullet, and with an iron-headed mace—the common walking-stick of the Persian peasantry in Fars—smashed the jaw of an Armenian, who for the better security of money upon his person, had joined the caravan of the Englishman.

Major Napier was of course in no way responsible for the manner in which the Persian Government pursued and punished the men who were guilty, or were assumed to be guilty, of this crime. I have been told that the prisoners were taken somewhat at hazard, the main evidence being that they were near the spot;

but there is no doubt that three-and-twenty men had their throats cut by the public executioners in Shiraz on account of this robbery and murder; nor that this is a humane punishment compared with that by which the Firman Firma's predecessor, the Hissam-us-Sultan, endeavoured to repress crimes of this sort in the province of Fars. He tried throat-cutting, and left the bleeding bodies exposed to the view of all comers in the meidan of Shiraz. He tried crucifixion, nailing the wretches by the hands and feet to the walls of the town, and leaving them under a guard of soldiers to die of exhaustion and starvation. Finally, he tried burial alive in pits or cylinders of brickwork, of depth such as to allow the criminal's head to appear above the top. Pinioned and naked, the robbers were placed in these short open columns of brickwork, and a white plaster, not unlike plaster of Paris, was then poured, neck deep, over their bodies, around which it set into the hardness of stone. I questioned several persons living far apart as to the particulars of this horrible punishment, and their substantial agreement left no doubt on my mind that it had been inflicted, or that the miserable men who were subject to this most cruel death, were in their dying hours barbarously ill-treated in their exposed and defenceless heads by the rabble and the soldiery of Shiraz. On finding the Firman Firma too weak for the place, the Shah's Government have lately endeavoured to persuade the Hissam-us-Sultan to return to Shiraz. But he has successfully pleaded age and increasing infirmity, and another has been appointed.

Such ruthless punishment, always uncertain in its vengeance, has never been successful in exterminating crime. The sins of the Executive of Shiraz are visited upon the people, and upon all who travel among them. The Government of Shiraz, in degree worse probably than that of any other province of Persia, is a system of oppression, made with all the power and authority and force of the State, for private advantage. The taxes are farmed, and, as a rule, the amount demanded is limited only by ability of payment; soldiers are taught robbery by being officially engaged in making demands for money, which they know to be unjust, from the all-enduring peasants; the Customs are farmed, and collected by the armed servants of the contractor, who is subject to no surveillance, and who renders no accounts. Those are exempt from direct taxation, who, possessing the means to render them independent of exertion, are the most able to pay. Direct taxation in Persia is levied solely upon those engaged in production, and the merchant or tradesman pays only in respect of his store in the bazaar. In the summer of 1875, the dismayed population of Shiraz heard that their Sovereign, the Shah, intended to make a royal progress to the south of his dominions. An order was published, that no corn was to leave the province, because all might be required for the use of the Shah and his retinue. The great people of Shiraz, who, of course, could evade this or any other edict, took advantage of the circumstances, and made money. The poor suffered most cruelly. Some say the Shah was bought off; that in consideration of receiving so many thousand tomans, his Majesty agreed not to quit Tehran; and this which sounds so scandalous, is never spoken of by Persians as a very extraordinary or even uncommon way of dealing with the intentions of the Sovereign, his visits being always regarded as involving extortion and loss, owing to the rapacity of his followers; and as an evil which, like capital punishment in Persia, may by gift of gold be averted.

CHAPTER VIII.

The road to Bushire—Yahia Khan's portrait—To Cinerada—Last view of Shiraz—Difficult travelling—Khan-i-Zonoon—A caravan in trouble—A cold caravanserai—Murder of Sergeant Collins—Death of Sergeant MacLeod—Advantage of an escort—Dashtiarjan—"Eaten a bullet"—Plain of Dashtiarjan—Ghooloo-Kojeh pass—A lion in the path—Mr. Blanford's "Interview"—Up a tree—A wounded horse—Kaleh Mushír—Mount Perizan—Kotul Perizan—A solitary rock—View of Mian-Kotul.

OPINION was unanimous that it was impossible to march with a takht-i-rawan from Shiraz to Bushire. For three days it was agreed that a conveyance of that length might proceed, but farther than three days' march the paths in the mountains were too narrow and dangerous to admit of this mode of travelling. We therefore left the takht-i-rawan in Shiraz, and my wife had to face the prospect of riding for twelve days through a country certainly not less dangerous than any other, and reported by those who have traversed the Himalayas and the Rocky Mountains to be the most difficult road in the world. When we were packing up, another incident occurred, displaying the habitual cruelty of the Persian muleteers to their animals. One of the string of mules which was brought to Mr. Odling's door for the conveyance of our baggage, had terrible sores upon its legs and back, caused by badly-fitting harness; and it was proposed to load this suffering animal for the long journey to Bushire. We refused to have it in our caravan, and the muleteer, to whom the notion of the animal's pain seemed as strange as it would be to others to learn that a flint suffered from the presence of quartz in its side, departed to exchange the injured mule for one in a sounder condition.

On the first day we had only two farsakhs to ride to the caravanserai at Cinerada. Early in the morning before we set out, the Firman Firma sent by his agreeable nazir a large photographic portrait of himself, "pour souvenir de Shiraz." The nazir also brought with him two sowars, who had been specially selected as our escort to Bushire. Their horses were very much better than ours to look at. Somebody suggested to Mr. Odling, who rode out of Shiraz with us, that we looked rather like prisoners of war compelled to ride our sorry nags into captivity. But in a few days, when we came to the rolling stones of the mountains, our "yaboos" covered their shabby appearance with glory.

Shiraz is not a large place; it does not occupy more than half the ground upon which Ispahan stands, and we were soon upon the plain, on a westerly course to Cinerada. The snow had melted away in many places, but there was sufficient to give a very wintry appearance to the scene, and the weather was cold enough to make my Persian coat of sheep's wool and leather, a very agreeable companion. Shiraz stands at the junction of three wide valleys. One slopes from the north, the way from Ispahan; another to the west, in the centre of which lies the path towards Bushire; the largest valley falls away towards the north-east.

We took leave of Mr. Odling about four miles from Shiraz at the gate of one of the gardens in the neighbourhood of the city, and stayed a few minutes for a last look at Shiraz. Persian towns seen from that distance leave no vivid impression, and this is as true of Ispahan and Tehran as of Shiraz. If they were grandly built, if they contained monuments of real value and of permanent interest, these would probably look unimportant in the wide plains and beneath the mountains of Persia. But their buildings are so insignificant, so impermanent, such rubbishing masses of mud-brick, with no beauty of form or ornament, that even large cities have no appearance of dignity, and are indeed overlooked in the contemplation of the grander features of the landscape.

My wife was mounted on a stout grey pony, which had very decided ideas of its own as to the proper mode of going to Bushire. By no persuasion could it be induced for more than a moment to alter its pace from a steady, plodding walk, and my chestnut was very much of the same opinion. The snow became more wide-spread, and the wintry afternoon darkened as our path wound through the valley. We could see far before us up the snowy steep, and were beginning to think it possible we had misunderstood the distance to Cinerada, when suddenly, behind a spur of rock, we came upon the caravanserai.

We had no more troublesome march in the whole journey than that from Cinerada to Khan-i-Zonoon. Several caravans had gone before us since the last great fall of snow, and the mules, treading always in the same track, had worn the snow in high ridges, higher than those of a deeply ploughed field. When the sun shone out the bottoms of these furrows became filled with water, which froze in the night, and sometimes the ice between the ridges would bear the weight of our horses, and sometimes not. When it bore, the animals often slipped; when it was thin their feet crashed through with a jerk distressing to the horse and to the rider. There was but one track, and the whole caravan passed up the mountain in Indian file. Soon after noon, we had ascended about two thousand feet from Cinerada to a height of nearly seven thousand feet above the sea level. But we found it impossible to keep the caravan together. Kazem had fallen at least half a dozen times in the deep snow, and his black mule, his saddle-bags, and himself bore many traces of these tumbles. The baggage mules had similar disasters, and after four hours' toilsome ride we had lost sight of servants and baggage, a circumstance which the sight of one or two ugly-looking parties of armed men who had met us in the narrow track, rendered more disquieting. There was no place in which we could dismount, and nothing to eat if we had done so, for Kazem, our storekeeper, was far behind—we knew not where; and we were in a wilderness of drifted snow, crossing ridge after ridge, always hoping that each would be the last, and always disappointed.

Our two soldiers, Abd-ullah and Hassan, had kept up with us. I sent the latter back to bring up and protect the baggage, and with Abd-ullah and my wife's gholam we resolved to push on and, hungry as we were, to get to the caravanserai as quickly as we could. On the way we met a large caravan bringing merchandise from Bushire, some of the loads upon the mules extending six feet from side to side. This involved our plunging out of the track into the deep snow and occasional sad knocks of the knees and shins against the passing packages. Far behind we could see Hassan, with his carbine erect upon his knee, standing on the summit of the mountain waiting for the stragglers, whom we assumed from his contented attitude were in sight from the point on which he stood. Presently the caravanserai of Khan-i-Zonoon was seen like a speck upon the far-extending desert. A rill began to trickle down the mountain, which widened to a stream, and lower became a river, of which the surface, frozen from side to side, remained unaffected by the midday sun. Upon the narrow plain, at the end of which lay the caravanserai, there was a scrubby forest, through which we passed upon a slippery and dangerous path. Some donkeys loaded with bags of wheat were being driven by two miserable-looking Persians through the wood, and of the number more than half had fallen, and lay helpless on our path beneath their heavy loads. In a hollow, the sides of which were a mass of ice, there was one of the loads with no animal beneath it; the donkey, in its struggles after falling, had probably succeeded in extricating itself from sacks and saddle-bags. Abdullah and our muleteer were in advance of us, and we saw them seize the saddle-bags as a prize, and turn out from them a quantity of bread, which they began to stuff into their pockets. We had been nearly eight hours on the road with nothing to eat, and they seemed to regard this as a godsend, taking no thought that this bread was probably the only food of the donkey-drivers during the same journey, in a much colder time of day. We rode up to them and forced them to put back the bread which, although the caravanserai was now close at hand, they did most unwillingly. It seemed to us that this readiness to rob on the part of two men, really superior to the lowest class of Persians, was very indicative of the predatory instincts of this uncivilised and ill-governed people. We made a fire in one of the smoke-dried brick arches of the caravanserai, and as there was nothing with which to construct a seat, had to stand about or sit upon the earthen floor for two hours until the baggage-mules arrived. Then a covering was nailed over the door-hole, matting and carpets laid down, our iron bedsteads set up, one on either side of the chimney-hole, in which some logs were burning cheerfully, a cloth spread upon our camp-table, and we sat upon our folding stools until Kazem appeared with a hot stew of rice and meat, and a bottle of very good Shiraz wine. Our fire had been burning for hours when we took to our beds at ten o'clock, and placed a cup of milk in the recess close by the chimney. The fire continued burning till nearly midnight, and at half-past five in the morning the frost was so intense that although the ashes in the fireplace were still red, the milk was frozen in a solid block, and some soapy water which I had left in a large brass handbasin on going to bed was in the same condition. Yet we were in 29° of latitude, and very little more than six thousand feet above the sea-level.

Our ride to Dashtiarjan was hardly less difficult, on account of the ridgy snow, than that of the previous day. We found it impossible to do more than two miles an hour. The road was in such a bad state we could not walk, and in the early hours of the ride we were blue with cold. The path was unlevel, and would have seemed varied and picturesque if it had not been for the unchanging glaring white of the deep snow. In a basin between two hills, a pole standing erect by the side of the path, marked the place of the most recent murder of an Englishman by Persian robbers. We had already heard the particulars of this fatal attack. The victim, Sergeant Collins, of the Royal Engineers, engaged in the Telegraph Service, was riding with his wife and servants from Shiraz to the next station, which is at Dashtiarjan. He was challenged, surrounded, and fired at from the woods; he returned the fire, and killed one man. But he was soon afterwards shot down, a bullet entering the back of his head; his body was mutilated, and his wife carried off to the mountains, where she remained for some days in captivity. I believe the murderers were never found, and that no one suffered punishment for the crime. Another sergeant died not long ago in a similar way; but the circumstances of his death were homicidal rather than murderous. The attack upon his comrade preyed upon his mind, already disordered by illness and drink, until he fancied that every man he met with on the road was a robber; and in this delirious humour shot an unoffending Armenian. Then he entirely lost self-command, and flourishing his revolver, rode about vowing he would shoot the first Persian robber he met with.

It was, at a caravanserai in which we had passed a night that this mad assassin made his next attempt, regardless of the fact that there were several men with guns in the caravanserai, which, as almost everybody in Persia carries firearms, is usually the case. The wretched sergeant was flourishing about, threatening everybody he saw with his pistol. It was then that some of the bystanders having placed a wall between him and themselves, shot him down, really in self-defence; and thus the second Englishman died the death of a mad dog.

In travelling in Persia, it is undoubtedly safer not to be too "ready with the pistol." For our own parts, we felt no very confident assurance that we should get safely through the country. All the English we met with in Persia told us it was highly probable we should be robbed, and that it was quite certain our escort would not be very energetic in defence. In these circumstances we had deliberately framed our plans of action, or rather of inaction. We had a letter of credit from merchants trading in Persia, upon which we could obtain money in Ispahan, Shiraz, and Bushire; so that the silver we carried was only sufficient for the expenses of the road between any two of those places. We knew that the resistance of robbery by incautious firing involves the maximum of danger, and were quite prepared to say "Inshallah" to any band against which successful resistance would be impossible, and submit to be robbed. We believed that nothing less than a band of forty or fifty determined robbers would venture to stop a caravan belonging to Europeans, and without the least desiring or expecting that one, two, or half a score of soldiers could or would drive off such a force, we always preferred to have an escort, because they never failed to communicate to the people we met with, and by this means to all the neighbourhood, that we were specially under the protection of the governor of the province; and because attack is not improbably prevented by the fear of subsequent recognition by the soldiers of an escort.

The view from the hills over the plain of Dashtiarjan was very remarkable. A plain looks small in Persia when like that of Dashtiarjan it is about four miles broad and twelve miles long. Near the higher and northern end, lay the buildings of the Telegraph Office, and not far distant the mud hovels of the village. About the centre, a large brownish patch, three miles long, in the unblemished white of the all-surrounding snow, indicated a deep morass, which is perhaps the cause of the ill reputation of this plain for the deadliest fever. Dashtiarjan is well known too as a hunting ground for lions; and upon the edges of this morass there are said to be a great number of wild hogs. At the foot of the hills, an armed guard of the Telegraph Service met us. They had been sent out by the clerk and inspector, Mr. Anderson, who stood on the steps of his bungalow to receive us. His house looked like an island in a Polar sea, and the face of this intelligent young Scotchman, who lived alone in this wild place, beamed with the pleasantest welcome.

"I've been expecting you for two months, and longing for you for a fortnight!" were almost his first words.

Mr. Anderson gave us a large empty room; and partly from his larder and partly from our own stores a good dinner was provided, of the cooking of which Kazem took charge. Whether this habit is universal, or affects only travelling servants, I cannot say; but we always found that no servant, even in his master's house, regarded the cooking place, or indeed any function, as particularly and exclusively his own. When we were guests in a strange house, even for one night, our servants seemed to fall into the work as if they were quite accustomed to it. At Dashtiarjan, Kazem appeared as cook and butler, as hopeful about his dishes, his soup and his stews, as he did when we had no one else to look to upon the road.

Mr. Anderson often had to trust to his rifle for supplying his dinner, and to judge from the noise made at night, wild beasts of all sorts seemed to be suffering hunger in the snow. A Persian who came in, using an idiom I had not heard before, said that one of these beasts had "eaten a bullet," which Mr. Anderson explained is the common mode of saying that any person or animal has been shot. The loneliness of such a life as that of this young man is greater, and in some respects more trying, than I think the Indian Government should call upon any one to endure. For months he has no opportunity of hearing his own language spoken. In winter, the road may be closed at any time for weeks by snow. He lives surrounded by wild beasts, with the semi-savage population of Dashtiarjan for his only neighbours. Mr. Anderson seemed to be fighting bravely and resolutely, with the aid of a small library of good books, against the difficulties of his situation; but we thought that the real trials of such an existence are not sufficiently estimated by his superiors, who would do well so to arrange their stations, that not less than two European officers should inhabit the same place.

Mr. Anderson and one of his tofanghees rode out with us in the morning along the plain of Dashtiarjan, when the drifts of snow were in some places ten or fifteen feet deep. The work of finding and following the shallowest depths made our path very circuitous. We skirted the morass, and in about two hours arrived at the foot of the Ghooloo-Kojeh pass, a hill covered with scrubby trees, the trunks of which were deep in snow. From among the trees, and from the over-towering height, we heard the shouts of muleteers urging their caravans through the snow. Mr. Anderson left us when we began the ascent. He had no opportunity for the use of his rifle, though there were footmarks of wild beasts in every direction. No one seemed to fear or to anticipate the presence of a lion, though the district we were passing through is a famous haunt, and it does now and then happen that a villager of Dashtiarjan falls the prey of a hunted or hungry lion.

It was exactly at this point that Mr. Blanford, F.R.S., the distinguished naturalist attached to the Persian Boundary Commission, met with a lioness, in March, 1867. His own account of the adventure is very spirited and interesting:*—"It was not till sunset that I entered the oak forest south of Dashtiarjan, with five miles of steep mountain road before me. Contrary to my usual habit, I carried no gun, being unarmed with the exception of a Colt's revolver of the smallest size. I was mounted, I may say, on a bay Arab, fifteen hands high. I had crossed a tiny rivulet, said to be a favourite drinking place of lions, and where indeed I had often seen their foot-prints, and had just begun the ascent of the hill by a path covered with loose boulders, when a tawny shape moved noiselessly out of the trees some thirty yards

---

* "Eastern Persia," vol. ii. p. 31.

in front. Whether my horse stopped or I pulled him up I do not know, but there we stood; the lioness, for it was evidently a lady, gazing at us, motionless, but for a gentle waving of the tail, and the horse and I looking straight at her. I mentally execrated my folly at not having brought a gun, for a fairer shot it was impossible to imagine. After the lapse of a few seconds, thinking it time to end the interview, I cracked my hunting-whip and gave a loud shout, to intimate to her ladyship that she had better clear out, never dreaming for a moment that lion or tiger would have the courage to attack a man on horseback.

"To my astonishment, instead of sneaking back into the forest as I expected, she deliberately charged us down hill, and sprang at the horse's throat. Whether from miscalculation of the distance through the unevenness of the ground, or from my jerking the horse's head up with the curb, I cannot say, but she missed her spring and came down under my right stirrup. With a good-sized pistol I could have broken her spine as she stood bewildered for a moment, but to fire a bullet hardly bigger than a pea, with only a few grains of powder behind it, into the loose skin of a lioness, would have been folly; so I stuck in the spurs, with the intention of making tracks as fast as the nature of the ground would allow. But the poor horse was paralysed with fear; not an inch would he budge, till the lioness, recovering from her surprise, made a swift half circle and attacked us from behind; not leaping on the horse's back with all fore legs, as is so often represented in pictures of Persian sporting, but rearing on her hind legs and embracing the horse's stern with her forepaws, while trying to lay hold of his flesh with her teeth. As may be supposed, I lost no time in jumping off, with no other damage than a tear in my strong cord breeches, and a slight scratch in the thighs. Directly the horse felt himself relieved of my weight, he reared and plunged violently, sending me head over heels among the stones in one direction, and the lioness in the other. Expecting the brute to be on me at once, I pulled out my miserable little pistol, and picking myself up as soon as possible, looked about me. There stood the lioness, not five yards off, sublimely indifferent to me and my proceedings, waving her tail and gazing intently at the horse, which had trotted twenty yards down the road. She made a few swift steps after him, when I fired a couple of shots over her head, hoping to drive her off. The only effect was to start the horse off again, when the lioness again charged him from behind, and clinging to his quarters both disappeared among the trees.

"So far 1 had had no time to feel much fear, but, as soon as the source of danger was no longer visible, my nerves began to get somewhat shaky. Perhaps I ought to be ashamed to say that I did not lose much time in ensconcing myself in the branches of a convenient oak, some twenty feet from the ground. A few minutes at that secure altitude sufficed to restore my nerve somewhat, and I reflected that there were the regulation three courses open to me, to stay where I was, to go forward, or to go back. The first involved spending a March night on the top of a tree, the bottom of which was seven thousand feet above the sea, and I hate cold. The second presented the not more agreeable prospect of a five-mile walk over a villanous road through the forest, with the chance of meeting more lions without a horse to take off their attention; moreover, my holster and saddle-bags contained valuables, and even if the steed was killed, I might recover these by prompt action. I therefore made up my mind to follow the horse and his enemy, and as the shades of night were fast gathering round me, lost no time about it. Half a mile down the road I found my unfortunate steed, bleeding fast from a wound in his quarter, and still in such a state of terror that he declined to let me approach him.

"There was nothing to be done but to drive him out of the forest into the plain, which was not many hundred yards off, and to walk on to the nearest village for assistance.. This was the little walled hamlet of

Kaleh Mushír, a mile or so off, which I reached without mishap, save an alarm from a herd of pigs, which charged past me towards the lake as if a lion was after them.

"A single family tenanted Kaleh Mushír during the winter. From them I got a little acorn-bread and dates. No bribe would induce the man to come out with me that night with torches to find the horse; but I found him the next morning at daybreak, after a night made sleepless by the most vigorous fleas I have ever met. The poor brute was grazing quietly in the plain, and allowed himself to be caught without difficulty. Although his quarters and flanks were scored in every direction with claw marks, only one wound had penetrated the flesh, and this to a depth of two inches, making as clean an incision as if cut with a razor. This I sewed up, and in a week the horse was as well as ever, though he bore the scars of his adventure for the rest of his life. It is perhaps worthy of remark, that the distance apart of the scratches made by the two outer claws of each stroke with the paws, was between fourteen and fifteen inches."

When we met the caravans, whose noises we had heard upon the hill where Mr. Blanford had this encounter, the difficulty of passing presented itself as serious. Our soldiers, after the manner of their kind, began to bully the poor muleteers, and to force the donkeys into the deep snow. The shouting was tremendous, and the mules and donkeys vied with each other in obstinacy, some of them resolving that, at all costs, their loads should graze my shins. Three or four times on the pass we had a battle of this sort, in which at last the inconvenience was arranged pretty equally, each caravan taking turn with the other in plunging through the deep snow. When we got clear of the jungle, we could look back over all the plain of Dashtiarjan, but the path ascended yet far higher to the top of Mount Perizan (the Old Woman), and when at last, after much toil, we gained that elevation, the sowars and gholams threw up their arms and screamed with delight. I had no need to ask the cause of their rejoicing. In a moment, a strange transformation had taken place in the prospect. For weeks, our eyes had found no repose from the glare of the snow; for weeks we had seen none but a snow-covered landscape. Here, in a moment, the scene was shifted as if by magic. From the top of the Perizan Mountain, we looked upon valleys, brown upon the sides and green upon the level plain. We had nearly done with frost, but we had the worst part of the road before us.

There is no portion of the way through Persia more picturesque than the half-dozen miles from the Perizan to the caravanserai at Mian-kotul. This word "kotul" is only met with between Shiraz and

Bushire. Between those two places, there are three "kotuls"—of which the first is the Kotul Perizan. The word is one of terror to the traveller, for it appears to signify a road the most difficult and dangerous which it is possible to conceive—a path upon a mountain's side, sometimes upon the edge of a precipice, at others upon a descent so rapid as to render riding impossible. But always upon the kotuls the path is beset with stones, so numberless and awkward that horse and man pause at almost every footstep to consider where the next advance may be most safely made.

If one rides down a kotul, as we did at Perizan, a feeling of recklessness soon sets in. When at any step a fracture of the skull is not at all unlikely, one ceases after the first half hour to think much of the danger. We passed corners where mule and merchandise are sometimes lost by a fall from the precipice into the stony valley beneath. But the beauty of the scene culminated at a point where a single peak of rock rises seven hundred feet from the centre of the valley and stands, grey and jagged, with large birds flying about its summit. We might have thought it inaccessible but for the evidence of conquest upon the topmost rock, where a Telegraph post was fixed supporting wires which at great height spanned the valley on each side of this precipitous elevation.

Another remarkable view, which in words can be

but poorly painted, is that which meets the eye after passing this eyrie of the Indo-Persian Telegraph. We were slowly descending a deep wide valley from the hollow of which we were still raised three or four thousand feet. On the farther side, ran a chain of mountains, their summits appearing to cross the horizon in almost a level line. Like a great ridge or furrow these mountains crossed our road from north to south, and about half way down, in the slow descent we were making through the scrubby jungle which clothes the western side of Perizan, upon a projecting platform of rock, lay the caravanserai of Mian-kotul (the Middle of the kotul). We were so high above it that we could see nothing but, as it were, the ground plan of the building; the mules, moving like specks from side to side of the yard, the roof of the surrounding stables, like a line; the whole caravanserai but a spot in the immensity of the prospect.

CHAPTER IX.

Mian-kotul Caravanserai—Tofanghees on guard—Feuds between villagers—Kotul Dochter—Travelling on the Kotul—The Mushir-el-Mulk—Lake Famoor—Encampment of Eeliats—Ruins of ancient Persia—Plain of Kazeroon—Songs of Persian soldiers—Kazeroon—Anniversary of Houssein's death—"Ah! Houssein"—Fanatical exercises—Orange gardens—The Sheik of Kazeroon—Plain of Kazeroon—Attack on Major Napier's caravan—Village of Kumaridj—Plain of Khan-i-Takhte—Hospitality in Persia—Kotul Maloo—A difficult path—Dalki river—Arabs in Persia—Palm-leaf huts—A loopholed bedroom—Petroleum at Daliki—Barasjoon—Rifle practice - Indian officers in Persia—Functions of Political Resident Sowars from Bushire—Caravanserai at Ahmedy—Arrival of Captain Fraser—The Mashillah—A wet day's ride—Bushire.

THE caravanserai at Mian-kotul was no better and no worse than others. A black arch ten feet by eight, with no windows, opening by a doorway in which a carpet was the only screen, upon a stone platform raised about three feet above a yard full of mules and asses, some of them knee deep in the dirt of the place, is not a very charming residence. For the last time, the night was cold and frosty; the next day we were to descend more than five thousand feet into a land of palm trees and orange groves, where the raggedness of the people would look less wretched and pitiful, and where poverty would lose much of its misery. Kazem was delighted at his own accomplishment when, under my direction, he turned out a dish of eggs and bacon, but looking at the slices of the forbidden meat (which had been exported from the United Kingdom by a merchant of Shiraz), he laughed and said, "No Irān man eat." His bright eyes beamed with pleasure at the coming change of climate, though he grew more and more apprehensive as to the safety of the road. " Very bad robbers," he said, in an interval of cookery, pointing forward on our road to Bushire. Like a prudent man, he had turned the heap of silver which represented his wages and allowances into paper at Shiraz. Mr. Odling had kindly taken the silver and telegraphed the amount to Kazem's credit in Tehran, so that of this money he could not be robbed. The transaction had given much ease to Kazem's mind.

Outside the caravanserai of Mian-kotul, the way to Bushire descends through a grove of trees to a small plain, also covered with stunted oaks and some growth of underwood.

We had advanced about a quarter of a mile into this wood when there suddenly appeared seven wild-looking men, each armed with a gun and a long knife. They might be robbers or friends; I really could not tell which as we approached them. That they were waiting for us was quite clear. Without a word, they surrounded the caravan, and presently, without appearing curious as to their quality, I gathered from Kazem that they were men living in the neighbourhood who proposed to accompany us through part of our way to Kazeroon as an extra guard for our greater security. Several of them went on before dispersed like sharpshooters in the wood. Sometimes they fired at birds, but I think none fell to their aim. After walking about four miles to the centre of a small plain below the Kotul, they gathered round me and made "salaam," at the same time asking for money.

It struck me that there could not be very great difference between declared robbery, and a request which was so much like a demand, made by seven armed men, two of whom had their hands upon my saddle. However they were satisfied with a small present, and before dismissing them, I asked why they wished to leave us in a part of the plain where, if their presence was at all useful, it was certainly most desirable. They told me they could not go any farther because they were "at war" with the men of the next village. That led to another explanation in which Kazem and the charvodar joined. From this it appeared that in the parts of Persia south of Shiraz, there are, as a rule, feuds existing between village and village, arising in the first place from some dispute, agricultural or matrimonial, between two men, and having a fatal result. The friends of the murdered man have then to undertake the sacred duty of revenge. Any one of them will at sight, shoot or stab in cold blood any one of the relations of the murderer, or perhaps more correctly, the man-slayer. This homicidal disposition ultimately spreads to the villagers on each side, and the feud thus becomes a war between village and village.

In the south of Persia, we never saw a man or a boy unarmed. The donkey-drivers carried long guns slung at their backs; the peasants who were scratching the earth in patches with wooden ploughs, were armed in the same way, and most of them carried in addition a long sword-knife in their girdle. Every man, in fact, was a tofanghee, and one of the traveller's difficulties is to get rid of those men who spring up at the sight of a caravan from the bushes or stones, and are ready to be paid guards, or to remain in something very like the attitude of robbers if no money is forthcoming. If we had not had our two sowars, we should possibly have had trouble with these tofanghees of Mian-kotul.

At the end of the plain, a concealed outlet over a low elevation led us to the summit of the Kotul Dochter (the Daughter-kotul). Four tofanghees joined us at this point, and when we were obliged to dismount, owing to the difficulties of the road, we found them useful in getting our horses down the Kotul. If they had really been robbers, instead of men with perhaps a tendency in that direction, they could have chosen no more satisfactory place for attack. No horse can make more than two miles an hour over a kotul. One might more easily try to trot or gallop over the lava of Vesuvius than upon the stones of a kotul; and of all the kotuls, the "Dochter" is by far the steepest and most difficult. No one attempts to ride upon the Kotul Dochter. It is a way, partly natural, partly built, and partly hewn, in the side of a precipitous rock about two thousand feet high.

Half an hour's labour by the small strength of our caravan would have closed it altogether. With stones alone a dozen strong men could defend the almost perpendicular zigzag against a host. Such "gates" are a security to a country; but what a high road for the commerce of Persia! When one thinks that every piece of Manchester goods passing to the markets of Shiraz and Ispahan has to be carried upon a mule, stumbling and slipping, toiling up these rude stairs by a path so difficult that camels are not employed, it is easy to see the advantage of Russia, who sends her manufactures by way of Tabriz and Resht. The Mushir, the Vizier of the Firmah Firma, who has made himself rich by the subordinate government of the province of Fars has, let it be said to his credit, done much by the erection of retaining walls to render the Kotul Dochter less dangerous. Many were the loads of goods, and many the mules which were dashed to pieces before the improvement of this ladder of stone by the Mushir.

But the Mushir-el-Mulk, as this functionary was called, has, I hear, since we left Persia, met the fate of all energetic rulers in that country. For alleged offences, perhaps for the high crime of getting rich and failing to share his profits with the Shah and the Imperial Government, the Mushir-el-Mulk has, I am told upon high official authority, been summoned to Tehran, where he has received "the sticks," has been compelled to make a large disbursement, and has been formally deprived of the profitable position he held as Grand Farmer-general of the Province of Shiraz.

Until we saw the Kotul Dochter, we had not fully realised why it was not possible for a takht-i-rawan to pass that way. In the corkscrew windings of the Kotul Dochter there was at times scarcely room for the body of a mule, and though we followed closely, one almost upon the heels of the other, yet the leading horse of our caravan was sometimes a couple of hundred feet below the rear-guard. When we turned our eyes from the rock we were descending by a sort of irregular stone ladder, two thousand feet long, we looked over a fertile plain—a tender green where there were patches of young wheat; set here and there with groves of palms, which seemed to be the only trees; and to the left lay the shallow tranquil waters of Lake Famoor. It was the 5th of February, and the rose bushes beside the stony path upon the spur of the mountain which led from the foot of the Kotul Dochter to the plain, were gay with blossoms. These seemed to welcome our arrival from the snow, which for nearly fifty days had been always under our eyes. A river runs from the lake through the plain, and beside it on the greensward, the pasturage of which belonged to any man, was an encampment of the much-dreaded Eeliats, their low tents of goats'-hair cloth stretched on sticks, in which only a year old baby could stand upright—reminding us of the very similar abodes of Bedoueen Arabs in Northern Africa.

At the point where the path to Kazeroon is at last level, and quite clear of the mountains, there are some interesting ruins of Ancient Persia. By these we dismounted, and enjoyed our luncheon in a genial climate. The ruins are those of a tomb or a temple, and their interest centres in a large bas-relief, carved upon the smoothed face of the overhanging rock. A monarch, heavily bewigged with false hair, in the fashion of Ancient Persia, and as marvellously bearded, is seated with a lion before him, his chair of state encircled by attendants. In front of this work there are the ruins of an enclosure, in which we lingered until it was necessary to get on over the plain to the town of Kazeroon.

We had passed in three hours from winter to

summer. My Cabul sheepskin coat was no longer endurable; the way was level and grassy. Birds fluttered in the air, the graceful foliage of the palm trees waved about us, the swarthy, Arab-like Eeliats who had migrated from the plains of Ispahan and Shiraz on the coming of winter were here tending their flocks, every one of them with a gun at his back and a knife in his belt, and in the far distance, where the palm trees were congregated in dense groves, lay Kazeroon, in which there is an Office of the Indo-Persian Telegraph kept by an Armenian, who we knew was prepared to receive us. Hassan and Abd-ullah, our sowars, were singing, as their own way, taking turns in the monotonous dirge, which is the only singing voice of the Mahommedan nations, when suddenly Abd-ullah shouted in Persian the word for "antelope." In the twinkling of an eye, to say a moment would seem an exaggeration, their horses were at a gallop, and they were chasing furiously over a patch of wheat. Away they galloped, so far as to be almost out of sight. First Hassan fired without slackening speed; then Abd-ullah shot; but there were no results, and presently they returned and resumed their doleful song, which was a somewhat stupid rhyme about the charms of an imaginary lady, repeated again and again without the slightest apparent consciousness, interest, or weariness. Sometimes the songs of Persians, delivered all in the same tone, are in language highly indecorous. Among the Turks as well as the Persians, it is observed with surprise by Europeans, that even in the superior classes, talk is habitually indecent, and that this immoral flow is not arrested by the presence of women and boys. The Vizier of the Zil-i-Sultan, who called upon me in Ispahan, a man of great position and of an ability rare in Persia, invited me to an entertainment at his house which I was too ill to attend. Mr. Bruce, the missionary, went, and told me on his return how he had been shocked at the filthiness of the general conversation carried on, especially by the host and father, in presence of his youthful sons—two boys whom I had seen riding in Ispahan, attended after the manner of people of their class by a dozen mounted servants.

It may be that Kazeroon appears more beautiful on approaching it from the snowy mountains than in coming from the greater heat of Bushire. To us, it seemed the very ideal of an Oriental town. There were orange gardens with the golden fruit upon the dark green leaves; there was scarcely a house which was not shaded by a palm tree. The inhabitants live for the most part on dates. There were mosques with domes of mud and minarets of sun-baked bricks. The poverty of the people, the squalor of their huts (many of them made of mats hung on poles), all this was as evident as on the higher and colder regions. But nobody shivered or looked pinched and hungry. Two pounds' weight of dates makes a good meal, and can be bought for about the value of a halfpenny in English money. We were delighted with the promise of rest as we rode into Kazeroon, and by no means sorry when the charvodar rode up with Kazem, and salaaming, begged as a favour that we would not travel the next day, as it was the day of Houssein's death, and they wished to keep the solemn festival in Kazeroon.

A tofanghee from the Telegraph Office had met us about a league from the town, and now ran forward to announce our arrival to his master, who received us very kindly, placed a large empty room at our disposal, and having done this, set himself to telegraph the news of our arrival to north and south. We were out betimes in the morning to see the doings of the people of Kazeroon in honour of the lamented Houssein. From the courtyard of the principal mosque we heard the continuous cry, "Ah! Houssein!" "Ah! Hous-sein!" arising, and standing in the doorway, saw the whole place was full of men, the surrounding roofs crowded with women and children. In the centre, about fifty men had formed themselves into a ring holding each other's hands. In this formation, they expanded and contracted the circle, advancing and retreating with the cry "Ah! Houssein!" uttered in the tone of profoundest grief. This was kept up with mechanical regularity for about an hour. Then when every man's brain was reeling with the exercise and with watching it, at a word from their leader, the men sat down and each one beat his bare breast with his open palm, and then clapped his hand upon his thigh with the common cry. This too, was done with the same precision. We left them at this work, and soon after it was understood that the two parties, one holding that day to be the proper anniversary and the other preferring the morrow, were disposed to fight over the difference. There was some tumult, and the Governor ordered that there was not to be the usual procession in the streets, of which the leading feature is the slashing of their faces and persons with knives, and the consequent staining of their white garments with blood, by the most devoted mourners for Houssein. The Telegraph clerk and I went into the streets to see how this order was obeyed, and had got into a narrow place when we heard from a hundred voices the cry "Ah! Hous-sein!" coming towards us. We hurried to an outlet, and reached an open space just in time to avoid a rushing crowd of men, each one of whom leapt into the air as he shouted at every step "Ah! Hous-sein!" and at the same time beat his inflamed breast with his hand. Men in the condition of those forming this crowd were virtually insane with frantic exertion and the continuous exercise of the same movement. Had we met them in the narrow way, we should very likely have been knocked over and trodden to death. I felt that looking on as we were, a single word of hatred for the infidel would have been sufficient for the sacrifice of our lives. This production of irresponsible fanaticism by shouts and oft-repeated movement, by exercises such as these and such as those of dancing and howling dervishes, is as much a part of the recognised machinery of the Mahommedan Church as the celibacy of the clergy and the domestic fulcrum obtained in the confessional-box, are of the Roman Catholic Church.

From this scene of noisy and dangerous fanaticism, it was pleasant, when we were joined by my wife, to pass into the largest of the orange gardens, a grove of magnificent trees, most of them more than two hundred years old and all loaded with fruit. The central path through this orange garden is a sight to be remembered. From the ruins of the tank in the centre, the surrounding orange trees, the largest we have ever seen, presented a delicious appearance. Possibly there would not have been so much fruit remaining on the branches had the oranges not been of the sour variety. We have not met with sweet oranges anywhere in Persia as a product of the country. They are imported from Bagdad and other places. I can hardly suppose that the deficiency of Persia in this respect is due to want of the proper climate or soil for ripening sweet oranges. No part of the world would seem better adapted for the growth of oranges than the region about Kazeroon. At Bushire it may be too hot; at Shiraz, the winter may be too severe. But Kazeroon, though it is two thousand seven hundred feet above the sea, has the climate of Seville ; the palms prove that the cold is not severe, and the cornfields that there is abundant moisture and genial sunshine. On returning from the orange garden, we met a small crowd, in front of which walked an old man with beard dyed red. His dress was rich ; he had a huge ring of silver upon his hand and a heavy pair of spectacles upon his nose. He was the religious Sheik of Kazeroon—the Sheik-ul-Islam he would have been called in a capital ; the ecclesiastical mayor and judge of the place, and the crowd was composed of his numerous attendants. The Telegraph clerk presented me to the old man, who shook hands and welcomed us to Kazeroon with grave politeness.

The weather was showery, and there were signs that the half of the population which did not assent to the celebration of the previous day was preparing to realise its own idea of the anniversary of Houssein's death when we rode out of Kazeroon. I think Kazem favoured the day of our departure, and the charvodar that after our arrival, as the proper date of this ceremony. However, no objection was made to our progress, though we passed through the plain of

Kazeroon, of which only a few patches are cultivated, under a heavy shower of rain. There were abundant evidences of natural fertility in the soil, which seemed to need nothing but industry to be highly productive. At the end of the plain, the path mounted towards a small caravanserai, adjoining which was a hut built of palm leaves. We had this swept out and sat on the floor to eat a luncheon of eggs and dates, and then, still in the rain, rode up and down among the hill-tops, though some of the most favourite haunts of robbers, until we looked down upon another plain, that of Kamaridj, in the middle of which stood the white dome of some Mahommedan tomb, and at the farther end, the village in which we were to pass the night. This was the place where the Hon. Major Napier's caravan was attacked and robbed—as pretty a plain as any in Persia. As we looked down upon it from the hills, there were two herds of long-haired goats, the only life upon the plain. The ground was sloppy with the rain; and the palm trees, under which Kamaridj lay, were visible for two hours before we reached the village. That which in grander spheres would be called a reign of terror, prevails always in Kamaridj and the villages of southern Fars. They are at all times liable to that which in higher latitudes would be dignified with the names of siege and sack. Their efforts to win prosperity are blighted by the musket of the tax-gatherer and the pistol of the robber. In good and bad years alike, for every one of their palm trees and their bullocks, the peasants must pay a heavy charge to the costly system of misrule dignified with the name of Government, of which the Shah is the head; and in bad years as in good, the robber urges his claim to maintenance at the expense of the only hardworking class in Persia. For such depredation the site of Kamaridj is most convenient, nestled under hills in which there is concealment for a troop from the eyes of an army.

Kamaridj was all alive with excitement at the sight of our caravan approaching over the plain. Two men, armed of course, ran out about a mile to meet us; and when we entered, not a few of the roofs were occupied with women. We found a fairly good room in Kamaridj; and on the morning of February 8th rode over the hills in a climate which seemed perfection, through a country full of the budding luxuriance of a southern spring, to the plain of Khan-i-Takhte, in which there were continuous groves of palm trees extending for miles an unbroken shade. Our soldiers and muleteers sang—not so sweetly as the birds—and the conductors of the two or three caravans we passed in the day's ride were smiling and talkative. Near a great patch of palm trees stood the Telegraph Office, which was to be our stopping place for the night. It was, we knew, uninhabited, the clerk having recently suffered an attack of apoplexy, in consequence of which he had been removed by Mr. Odling to Shiraz. A tofanghee was in charge of the place. There was something very sad on entering the rooms to see the clock stopped, the instruments all dead and dusty, and the necessaries of a European's daily life lying about in disorder—evidences of the suddenness of the attack by which the greater part of the life of this man had been taken from him.

The simplicity of hospitality in such a country is fully experienced in a case of this sort. In the presence of the master of the house it is very much the same; the reception of visitors is devoid of nine-tenths of the difficulty with which it is encompassed at home. One finds an empty room; the carpets and furniture are taken from the mules' backs, the property of the traveller. For all the trouble they are at, he pays the servants of the house; his own servants prepare and cook his food, and in the morning he leaves not a trace of his sojourn.

We were still eighteen hundred feet above the sea. We were now to descend by the Kotul Maloo to Daliki, where we should be but two hundred feet above the line at which our ride was to end—the level of the Persian Gulf at Bushire. From the plain of Khan-i-Takhte we looked back on that high, serrated ridge of mountains, the other side of which we had seen from the caravanserai of Mian-kotul. Indeed, the plain appeared to be locked on all sides by mountains, but we rode on towards the southern end, where the path suddenly disclosed a steep descent upon the side of an almost perpendicular cliff. There has been no building at the Kotul Maloo. Somehow or other in the course of years the hoofs of mules and the feet of men have worn a track from one huge stone to another, and a zigzag has been formed, which descends at gradients of about one in three, but so unequally, that every step is more or less of a climb. Looked at from the bottom one would hardly suppose the piled-up rocks of the Kotul Maloo to be accessible. It is prudent to make some noise in the passage, so that if a caravan is ascending the mules may be made to stand aside in the few places where it is possible for one loaded animal to pass another with a similar burden. At the foot of the Kotul Maloo the ravine widens, and there is a splendid view in the valley beneath of a river, the waters of which were rushing when we saw them, and green with the nauseous salts which they contain. To the side of this river we gradually descended into a valley, through which it passed in a broad stream towards a bridge, which is certainly the finest in Persia—another work of the Mushir who then governed Fars in the name of the Firman Firma. Near this bridge, the stream, which is known as the Daliki River, turned abruptly round high rocks, through a southern outlet by which we also passed, after sitting awhile near the bridge, in a thick growth of beautiful ferns, to eat our luncheon.

It would have been utterly impossible for an unguided stranger to have followed without error the path by which we accomplished the remainder of that day's journey. It lay, unmarked because of the hardness of the rocks, through a labyrinth of hills. Sometimes we forded the river, at others passed for a mile upon boulders which seemed to bear no trace of a track. Then we left the stream, and, crossing a hill, entered upon an entirely new scene. No part of the way from Shiraz was more curious and fatiguing. At last our tired horses climbed a rounded hill, which was the final elevation. From this we had a prospect over a sandy plain of apparently illimitable extent. We could not see the Gulf, but, in fact, had our sight been sufficient, and the Persian belief in the flatness of the earth established, we might have seen ships riding at anchor off the town of Bushire. Near the foot of this last hill lay the village of Daliki—a wild place, more Arab than Persian—the inhabitants living in huts made of mats or of palm leaves. The general plan of Daliki, like that of all the villages upon the plains around the Persian Gulf, is very simple. A mud bank about a foot high encloses the area of each hut, and upon this is made a framework of palm branches, covered or thatched with the broad fronds or leaves of the same tree, or with mats plaited with strips from the palm leaves. Daliki is environed with palm trees. The people of Daliki have terrible blood feuds with neighbouring villages, and suffer greatly from occasional raids by bands of robbers from the mountains. Major Champain, R.E., the Director of the Indo-Persian Telegraph, informs me that in passing Daliki a month after we stayed in that village he saw two dead bodies lying exposed, those of men slain by robbers who were still in sight, hastening with their booty into the fastnesses of those hills by which we approached the village. There are two huts in Daliki which have a bala-khanah. Of one of these we took possession. But the roofing over the mud stairs was so very low that we were obliged to hoist up some things with a cord, and to throw up the smaller articles to one of the large holes intended for windows. The room was nine feet by twelve, and had loopholes on all sides, twenty-four in number. The night was not cold; we could afford to laugh and call this liberal provision of draughts, "airy." At times in the night there came through some of the numerous holes in our room a smell which reminded me of Russian Baku, the Asiatic Petrolia on the Caspian—an odour of naphtha, from the natural springs which lay neglected and running to waste a little to the southward of the village.

By a slight détour we visited these springs in the morning on our way to Barasjoon, the next station.

There seems to be no doubt about the quality or quantity of the petroleum. All the streams around us were coloured and covered with the outflow. But no one attempts to make use of it. There may be underground a practically inexhaustible supply, and doubtless Englishmen would be found ready to sink wells and to engage in exportation if it were safe to deal with the Persian Government. The wells would not be more than fifteen or sixteen miles from the waters of the Persian Gulf at Sheef, and the price of coal in India is certainly high enough to encourage enterprise of this sort.

The smell of petroleum was still on the plain when we were joined by a number of ruffianly-looking men, who after walking with us for a mile, to my great relief departed in the direction of the mountains. The ground between Daliki and Barasjoon is unlevel, but not hilly. Cultivated patches, all unfenced, are few and far apart. In these, wheat was waving five inches high around bushes which the cultivators had not taken the trouble to remove. The sun shone very hotly on the 10th of February, as we approached Barasjoon, which consists of a Telegraph station, a caravanserai, and a village. Throughout the evening there was a continual noise of firing. The one amusement of the men of these villages seems to be rifle-shooting. They are always striving to improve themselves as marksmen, and as nothing else. Their agriculture is careless; their homes are miserable; their food, for the most part, dates; they are subject to the most cruel tyranny. The Governor collects his taxes from them at the head of an irresistible force; their one delight is to be ready against their neighbours with their rifles. The head-man or sub-governor of Barasjoon, enthusiastic like the rest in this direction, was, we were told, taking shots one evening not long ago from the roof of his house, and was unable to resist the tempting mark offered by a harmless shepherd upon whom he inflicted a wound from which the man died in two days. A resident at Barasjoon told me the story was quite true; that the head-man killed the shepherd only because he was seized with a cruel desire, at sight of the man, to have a living mark for his shot, and that no punishment whatever had followed this wanton murder.

On the morning following our arrival at Barasjoon, we received a most welcome reinforcement. We were really delighted to see the red uniforms and British accoutrements of two Bombay sowars, who had been sent to meet us with a letter of invitation and welcome, by Colonel Ross, the Political Resident at Bushire. Perhaps this is as good a place as any in which to allude to the connexion, amounting to something like co-ordinate authority, which has at one time existed in greater degree than at present, but which is still maintained on the part of the Foreign Office and the

Government of British India, in Persia. At one time I believe the Legation in Tehran was a Mission from the Indian Government, despatched by and maintained solely at the cost of that Government. At present the Indian Government makes, I understand, a contribution to the cost of the Legation in Tehran and maintains at Bushire a Political Resident, who is protector of the commerce of the Gulf, and mediator-general (backed by a force of gunboats) between the tribes upon the Arabian and Persian shores, the object being to secure safe and unrestricted intercourse between the towns of the Gulf, and free communication from India and Great Britain with the inlet to the Tigris and Euphrates at Bussorah and up to Bagdad.

The Political Resident at Bushire is not subordinate to the Minister in Tehran, and they are, I should suppose, sufficiently far removed to render their occasional intercourse free from embarrassment. The lines which separate their authority are probably not defined. In Shiraz, Mirza Hassan Ali Khan, the British agent, told me that in applying for leave of absence, he obtained permission both from Mr. Thomson and from Colonel Ross, though the latter has no connexion with the Foreign Office, and is an Indian officer on special service, under the orders of the Bombay Government, reporting only to that Government.

The sowars he had kindly sent to meet us and to

conduct us to the Residency, were Sikhs, fine men on good horses, wearing scarlet turbans and long tunics of the same British colour, high jack boots, and armed with short carbine and cavalry sword. I noticed they could not make themselves understood by our Persian sowars or servants. They had spent the night at Ahmedy, and after some hours' rest, their horses were fresh enough to return with us to that caravanserai. It was a tedious ride upon almost a dead level of damp sand, with small groves of palm trees each a few miles apart. In the last hour when we were in sight of the caravanserai of Ahmedy, rain fell very heavily, which made us arrive in great discomfort. But the caravanserai was strong and new; it was possible to have a fire; there was not more than one open hole in our room, and when the sky cleared, we spread our wet clothes upon poles on the roof, and enjoyed the look out from that place of vantage. The scene was one of life near the Tropics with an Arctic back ground. There were behind us the brown hills over Daliki, and above these, the high snowy ranges we had passed through from Shiraz. All around in the immediate neighbourhood of the caravanserai was a level of brown sand which met the shallow waters of the Gulf at an almost invisible distance. A stream beset with palm trees ran near, and towards this our string of mules was being led out to water after the removal of their loads. In this sea of sand the rectangular walls of the caravanserai were the only interruption. It may strike the reader as it did myself that the panorama, though remarkable and thoroughly Oriental, was one which could be painted with little liability to error, even from these few and imperfect words of description.

Over the sand from the direction of Bushire there came galloping a group of white horses. The new arrival was Captain Fraser, Assistant Political Resident at Bushire, who was out on a sporting expedition, attended by two sowars, comrades of those who had joined our caravan, and two servants. From his arch in the caravanserai he sent his card to our arch; and shortly afterwards I paid him a visit. He had come out on a shooting expedition, and when I left him, we received a present than which nothing could have seemed more delightful and acceptable. One of his soldiers brought us, with Captain Fraser's compliments, a small loaf of exquisitely white bread, in a cloth of equal purity. We had been living upon a supply of Persian bread brought from Shiraz, now eleven days old. We had not seen white bread since we left Russia, five months ago; and this loaf, good as any in England, had for us, in its setting of snowy linen, a charm which it is not possible to describe. When Captain Fraser joined us afterwards upon the roof, we were rejoicing in his thoughtful gift.

Between Ahmedy and Bushire there is an expanse

of wet sand extending for about twenty miles, to the possession of which the sea on both sides makes pretensions. It connects the dry land about Bushire with the main land of Persia. Sometimes the "Mashillah," as it is called, is dry, and even dusty, but after rain it is sloppy, sometimes worse even than when we crossed it. We rode over the Mashillah under a downpour of almost continuous rain. At every step our horses sunk over the hoofs, and the muleteers were obliged to walk barefoot, lest they should lose their shoes in the wet sand. We were enveloped in mist, we could see nothing but the wet quagmire over which we were struggling. The clothes of our soldiers, Indian and Persian, were wet through, and the men looked as sulky and miserable as Asiatics always do in rainy weather. For half the way we were splashing through water, and the rest was swampy. The gholams, who had charge of the baggage, failed utterly to keep up with us, and I was obliged to send two soldiers to look after them, and to bring the mules forward. They were not very willing to go back through the rain, and an hour passed before they reappeared with the baggage, but without the gholams, whom they left to plod on at their own pace.

At two miles from Bushire the ground became harder; there was a small bank, on which we found a caravanserai. We made a fire and had luncheon there in great discomfort; but it was advisable to wait for some time in order to get the caravan together, for our march into Bushire. To reach the town we had to cross a level stretch of sand, a fine field for a gallop with better and less tired horses.

We can hardly express the joy with which we saw the Union Jack flying on a high mast planted before the sea-front of the Residency. Colonel Ross's numerous guard of Bombay Native Infantry turned out to present arms on our arrival; and in the wide courtyard of his house, the Resident himself gave us a kindly welcome. Our ride through Persia was ended.

CHAPTER X.

Bushire—The Residency—Arab towers and wooden "guns"—Government in Persian Gulf—The Arabian shore—Arabs and Arabs—The Sultan's power in Arabia—Oman and the Ibadhis—Pilgrims to Mecca—Destiny of rotten steam-ships—Pilgrims' coffins—Six hundred Arabs drowned—Persian land revenue—Collecting customs' duties—Trade and population—Commerce of Bushire—Cultivation of opium—Opium and cereals—Export of opium—British expedition in 1857—Occupation of Persia—Persian army in 1857—Interests of England—The Indo-Persian telegraph—Persia ripe for conquest—Persia and India.

AFTER the chapar-khanahs and caravanserais of the road, how Elysian seemed the apartments and the comforts of the Residency! We gladly parted company with all our travelling baggage, and Kazem's eyes glistened with delight as we made him a present of bedsteads and bedding, fur coats and jackets, saddles and bridles, pots and pans, chairs and tables. We had a week to enjoy the hospitality of Colonel and Mrs. Ross before the next boat of the British Indian Company would sail for Kurrachee and Bombay.

The Residency is a large pile of buildings, with a great deal of court below and a great deal of staircase and verandah above. On one of the flat roofs is a structure which is common to all the superior houses of Bushire, a room built like a cage, with poles and laths, in which the hot nights of summer are passed. The town lays behind the Resident's house. In front, about fifty yards from the gate, there is a sea-side terrace, a quarter-deck as it were, belonging to the Residency, but open to all comers; and below this the waters of the Gulf ripple or beat upon the sand. At each end of this walk is the ruin of an Arab tower, a relic of the days of barbarism and piracy. In Arab fashion, timbers have been built into the rough masonry, and upon the outer side of the shell of these towers the weather-worn blocks of wood project, about three feet apart. I am precise about these timbers because, by a curious chance, I had happened in Shiraz to meet with an old copy of a London newspaper, containing a letter from a travelling correspondent in the Persian Gulf. He was writing of Bushire, and assuming close acquaintance with a place which he had evidently seen only from three miles' distance —in fact, from the deck of a steamer, while passing down from Bussorah. He particularly drew attention to the "armament" of these Arab towers, which, he said, were encircled with an array of "guns." This is not the first time, perhaps, that wooden poles have been taken for cannon. But the fact is that Bushire is entirely without any remarkable defences. The Resident's gunboat, a part of that unknown force, the Anglo-Indian Navy, is generally in the offing, and the military duties of the Persian Governor of Bushire are as a rule confined to oppression of the inland subjects of the Shah. Looking out from the front of the Residency, the Gulf narrows to the right in the direction of Bussorah, and on the left, where the sandbank (at the end of which is Bushire) rises rather higher than elsewhere, is the ground on which the British troops encamped in 1857. If the opposite shore were in range of sight we might see to the south, Bahrein, the emporium of the Pearl Fishery. The annual value of the pearls found in the Persian Gulf exceeds 400,000*l*. a year. The oyster-shells have a considerable value, for these are as large as a cheeseplate, and the inside is the best of that lustrous substance known as " mother-of-pearl."

Upon that—the Turkish-Arabian side of the Gulf—slaveholding tribes are allowed by the Governments of the Empress of India and of the Sultan, to engage in a moderate amount of fighting among themselves. On great occasions, the Resident at Bushire and his subordinate, the Resident at Muscat, interfere; and it is understood that the Indian Government permits no fighting on the water. On land, a system of chieftainship prevails, and he who is strongest wins Bahrein. The Sultan of Turkey is nominally the sovereign ruler of this wild shore, and suzerain of the chief at Bahrein, and also of the petty Sultan of Muscat. But the Turkish Sultan's authority is never seen and rarely heard of. Sir Lewis Pelly, who was the predecessor of Colonel Ross as Resident at Bushire, in remarkable, if somewhat unofficial language, reported to the Government of Bombay concerning these tribes:—"The Arabs acknowledge the Turks as we do the Thirty-nine Articles—which all accept and none remember." I am inclined to think that even this is an exaggeration of the Turkish authority. I do not believe it is accepted by these lawless tribes, who seem to have but one rule of life, which is this: that a man's slaves are his own and that the African is an amphibious creature, who, with the cruel alternative of a wire whip applied to his back, must live as long as possible under the waters of the Persian Gulf in search of pearls for the benefit of Arab masters. The reign of anarchy at Bahrein cannot be more strikingly displayed than in the official report of the Bushire Resident that "Bahrein once hoisted in succession Turkish, Persian, and English flags." It is even added, "she has been known, when attacked, to hoist them all at once."

Further to the south, still upon the Arabian shore, we come to Muscat and Oman, and all that is known of these regions goes farther to show that the Sultan's writ does not run in the East of Arabia. Colonel Ross, who was for some time Resident at Muscat, found the tribes divided under the general names of Hinawi and Ghafiri. But it appears that this division is not ancient. At the beginning of the eighteenth century, in civil wars of unusual magnitude, one set of tribes ranged under Khalf the Hinawi and another under Mahommed the Ghafiri, whose contentions established divisions which have since endured. In the native chronicles of these tribes, their historians, or writers, have divided all the tribes of Arabs into three classes—1. *El Arab el Arabeh*—*i.e.*, pure Arabs, those whom they believe to have been created with a natural disposition for speaking Arabic; 2. *El Arab el Mota' arribeh*, those who have achieved the position of Arabs by acquiring command of the Arabic language; and 3. *El Arab el Mosta' ribeh*, the naturalised Arabs.

Of these three classes the teachers of to-day hold the first to have been lost, or become extinct. But their devotion to the God of Mahommed, and to the great Meccan as the foremost and chiefest of the prophets and interpreters of God, endures, though it has become sectarian. For instance, the Ibadhis, a very numerous religious body on this coast, reject both the Turkish and the Persian doctrine, as to the devolution of Mahommed's powers and functions. With the Turk it is a necessary article of faith to believe that the Sultan administers the Koran, as the rightful representative of the Prophet. He has no confidence in civil law, which differs from the code of Mahommed. The Sultan is the inheritor of

Mahommed's authority, though not of his prophetic powers; yet probably millions would accept as the inspired word of God any pretended revelation he might make by way of addition to the Koran. These are not times favourable for promulgating supernatural revelations; but if a man gifted with as much original genius and power and capacity for leadership as Mahommed possessed, were to arise in Turkey, he might add Suras to the Koran at his pleasure. But his revelations, unless enforced by the sword, would have no authority among tribes like the Ibadhis of Arabia, nor with the Persians. The latter have a belief, somewhat like that of Christians, that their Imām, or head of their religion, will some day reappear in likeness of the form he had on earth. But the Ibadhis have another belief: they have a visible successor of Mahommed, a true Imām, whom they select. They are much given to pilgrimages, which, living as they do in the Holy Land of Mahommedans, are for them comparatively easy.

In his "Annals of Oman" Colonel Ross says:— "Amongst the Ibadhis, a man must have amassed sufficient for expenses, and one year's ordinary expenditure in addition, before he makes the pilgrimage to Mecca." The observances of pilgrims from this shore are not very different from those of other sections of Mahommedans. In the Mina Valley they throw the three stones, typical of Abraham's

conflict with Satan, when the Evil One sought to tempt the father of the faithful. They are taught to regard as essential the following five points of ritual :—
1. The spirit or intention in which the pilgrimage is undertaken and carried out. 2. The duty and excellence of prayer on Mount Arafat. 3. Shaving in Mina Valley. 4. The proper making of the circuit of the House of God. 5. Running seven times from Safa to Merwa. It is obligatory that after putting on the *ihram*, or garment of pilgrimage (which Mr. Bicknell, who made the pilgrimage, says consists of only "two towels"), the pilgrim must hunt no game, and take no life; he may not even hunt to death the vermin upon his body; and if in a fit of natural irritation a death of this sort should occur, he is liable, upon confession, to the payment of expiatory offerings.

The modern pilgrim, whether he is bound for Mecca or for Paray-le-Monial, does not select the most troublesome mode of travel, and even native-born Arabs prefer a British steamship to the perils and hardships of crossing the sandy, foodless, waterless desert, which lies between the shores of the Persian Gulf and the holy places of Mecca. At sea, it i true, they endure a maximum of the perils of naviga tion; but they are ignorant of the comparative safet with which Europeans are conveyed in well-appointe ships, and they may think that the annual sacr fice of life enhances the grandeur and importance and the glory of pilgrimage. Since the invention of steam navigation, the shores of Asia have been strewn with the bodies of Mahommedan pilgrims. Mr. Plimsoll once told me that the shipbreaker's trade is virtually extinct; that old ships are not broken up. He has found that our coasting trade is to a great extent carried in rotten ships; and I myself, while bathing, have seen one of these touch the sand, and fall to pieces in twenty minutes; so that, by the time I had dressed after my bath, there was not a trace upon the sea of a brig of three hundred tons burden, which had stranded in ten feet of water. This, no doubt, is the general destiny of old sailing ships of the smaller class. They are broken up by storms, and sometimes the crew are saved, and sometimes all hands are lost.

But it was not until I travelled in Asia that I became fully aware of what is done with rotten steamships; they are, in fact, the pilgrims' coffins. From Japan to the Red Sea, the superannuated and dangerous steam-vessels—useless in a supervised trade, in which it is not permitted to drown passengers and crew by glaring neglect in regard to the seaworthiness of the ship—are engaged in what is known as the native carrying and coasting trade. While we were at Bushire news arrived of the complete loss (with the exception of two survivors of the crew) of a steamship on the well-known rocks outside the port of Jiddah, the landing-place for Mecca, in the Red Sea. Six hundred pilgrims were drowned, and a fortnight afterwards we met the survivors as fellow-passengers in our voyage to Bombay. They were natives of India, and from them we learned that the ship, a very old one, had been bought by a native merchant in Bombay from an English firm, and chartered for the conveyance of pilgrims from the Persian Gulf to Jiddah. The men said she went to pieces the moment she touched the rocks, like a rotten shell. Though they were close to shore, there was no time to get a boat out, nor to make any effort to save the crowd of passengers. The thing—homicide is perhaps the fittest name for it—occurs frequently; and the difference between the drowning of Europeans and the drowning of Asiatics is graduated in the English newspapers just as it is in the shipowner's mind. The destruction of six hundred Arabs is recorded in London in a single line of small print. If the original owner of the vessel had sent it to sea with half the number of his countrymen on board, with the same consequences, the largest prints with an array of headings, would have signalised the natural result of his neglect. The parade of virtuous airs by shipowners, who sell old vessels of this sort with the knowledge that they are to be engaged in the carrying trade of Asia, while, for reasons which are obvious, they provide vessels for service at home which comply with reasonable demands for the assurance of safety, remind me of the old lady, widow of a Southern planter and owner of many slaves, who, professing a languid horror of slavery, said to an Abolitionist visitor: "I cannot bear it; it goes against my conscience to keep slaves. *I* mean to *sell mine!*"

If an Arab of Bahrein or Muscat should produce a bag containing the smallest "seed pearls," and offer, in consideration of a hundred rupees, that a handful may be taken, my advice to any one receiving such a proposal would be "don't." There are no men in the world, not even the jewellers upon the Ponte Vecchio at Florence, who know the value of pearls better than these Oriental merchants. But they are not much seen at Bushire, which is engaged with the import of British manufactures and the export of Persian produce; the former consisting chiefly of cotton-piece goods, and the latter of raw cotton, wool, corn, opium, almonds, and raisins. The world, I think, cannot furnish another example of a trade carried on under circumstances as deplorable as those which indisputably exist at Bushire. There is no security for the safe conduct of commerce. The Political Resident has lately reported that "the district of Bushire, in common with all Southern Persia, has been infested with bands of robbers, whom the local authorities have proved wholly unable to repress." But this is only a part of the insecurity which extends to all the relations of Government. Take another remark by Colonel Ross:—"The Government collects the land revenue, paying a fixed sum to the central Government," which means, that no inhabitant of the region is secure in his gains against the rapacity of the local government. That government is free to extort all that it can get, upon condition of making a certain annual payment at Tehran. The consequence is, that the entire province is kept in perpetual disorder by the demands of armed men, who plunder under the pretence of taxation, and who, by the peasantry, are scarcely preferred to robbers. Then, with regard to Customs. In describing a dinner party in Ispahan, I have mentioned the Khan, to whom Colonel Ross alludes in his report to the Bombay Government, in which he states that "the Bushire Customs were let to a person of Ispahan, in 1873, for 32,000 Tomans, or Rs. 1.28.000." A less civil but more correct mode of expressing the circumstances would be to say, that a man with the reputation of an ex-brigand has amassed a fortune by purchasing from the Shah for the above-mentioned sum the power of extorting all that he can in any manner get, by way of Customs, in or about the port or district of Bushire.

Imagine such a system of Customs carried out by such " a person" under the following circumstances, for which the Political Resident may be quoted as the highest authority:—"The farmer of Customs employs his own servants to manage, Government officials not interfering. The transactions are kept secret, no returns being required by the Government." Colonel Ross, in language which I have already quoted, adds, "The system is felt to be inconvenient to traders." He is too able a man not to have experienced some difficulty in restraining his pen to such moderation in regard to a "system" which is indeed infamous—the repression of trade by the licence of robbery.

To all this must be added the uncertain burden of export duties, which, in the article of raw cotton, "are so large as to prevent trade," and the difficulties of a road, nowhere good, which culminate in such places as the Kotul Maloo and the Kotul Dochter.

The trade, and I believe the population of Persia also, are declining. In transmitting to the Government of India the Trade Reports for the Persian Gulf and Muscat for the year 1874–75, Colonel Ross states, that " there has been a very marked falling off in trade, as regards the Persian coast, during the year under report. At the port of Bushire, the decrease is shown both in imports and exports, and amounts to an aggregate of over eighteen lakhs of rupees. The decrease would have been still greater but for the removal of the prohibition on the export of grain and increased exportation of opium." The following shows the total value of the exports and imports from and into the port of Bushire for the years 1873 and 1874 :—

	1873.	1874.
Imports—Total value	Rs. 39.85.820	Rs. 34.72.720
„ Specie	6.17.405	1.25.000
	46.02.925	35.97.700

There is thus a decrease in the total value of imports, including specie, of more than ten lakhs of rupees. The exports are :—

	1873.	1874.
Exports—Total value	Rs. 28.67.333	Rs. 26.45.775
„ Specie	10.53.396	4.46.000
	39.20.729	30.91.775

The decrease in one year of the exports is thus shown to be considerably more than eight lakhs of rupees. In this one year the demand of Persia for cotton goods of English manufacture declined in value to the extent of three lakhs of rupees, while the value of her export of raw cotton declined only to the extent of one lakh.

The two chief items in the port statistics of Bushire are the import of cotton goods and the export of opium. With regard to the former, although there has been the signal decline above referred to, it was the opinion of those most competent to judge that at the close of 1875, the market was overstocked, and that a further depression of trade was to be expected.

With reference to opium, of which in 1874 there was exported from Bushire a quantity valued at more than fourteen and a half lakhs of rupees (about two lakhs more than the value of the export in the preceding year), an interesting report by Mr. Lucas, one of Colonel Ross's assistants at Bushire, has been presented to the Government of India, from which it appears that opium is cultivated principally in Yezd and Ispahan, and partly in the districts of Khorassan, Kerman, Fars and Shuster. The opium grown in Yezd is considered to be of superior quality to that produced in Ispahan and elsewhere; owing to the climate and soil being better adapted for the production of the drug. But in the district of Yezd there cannot be any considerable increase in the area devoted to the growth of poppies, owing to the utter insufficiency of the water supply. In the province of Ispahan, water is more easily attainable, and there an increase in the production of opium would seem possible. Mr. Lucas appears to have made the discovery that the terrible famine which afflicted Persia in 1870-71 was due in no small degree to the withdrawal of land from the production of cereals, owing to the temptation which the far greater profits of opium held out to the cultivators. He says that, a few years ago, the profits of the opium trade having attracted the attention of Persians, almost all available or suitable ground in Yezd, Ispahan, and elsewhere was utilised for the cultivation of opium, to the exclusion of all cereals and other produce. It was then supposed by some that the cultivation of opium would be indefinitely extended in Persia. But the attempt of the natives to enrich themselves by cultivation and growth of a profitable article of trade, and their neglect to provide the necessaries of life, combined with drought and other circumstances, resulted in the famine. The costly experience thus gained has made the Persians more prudent, and although the cultivation has improved, and the yield from the same area has been greater, the export in 1874 was less by 600 cases than in 1869-70.

The crop is harvested in May and June, manufactured and exported in the winter. Of the 2002 cases exported in 1874, nearly three-fourths were shipped for Hong-Kong, and the remaining 583 cases for London. In order to avoid the duty levied at British Indian ports, the opium intended for China is carried from the Persian Gulf to Suez, where it is transhipped into vessels of the Peninsular and Oriental Company. The Persian opium is, however, said to be not much liked in China, owing to its having a peculiar flavour, caused by the mixture of a large quantity of oil during the process of preparation, and also because it is not always free from adulterating matter. It is in greater favour with the wholesale druggists of London, inasmuch as it contains, on an average, a larger quantity of morphia, than the opium produced in India.

Bushire (which is sometimes spelt Abushebr and Bushahr) is a collection of mud hovels, no better and no worse than other towns in Persia. The population is a mixture of Persians, Arabs, Indians, and Armenians. The rupee is current coin at Bushire. I have no doubt that the British Expedition in 1857 did much to familiarise the people of the Gulf with the coinage of India. But of that war in which Outram and Havelock were engaged, no traces are visible at Bushire. That it was ended by a satisfactory submission on the part of Persia, and that those gallant leaders were thus released from one of the most ineffective wars our country has ever waged, in time to give their aid and that of their forces in suppressing the Sepoy mutiny, was most fortunate.

If another difficulty should arise, Indian officers will know more about Persia than they did in 1857. They will understand that before any one of the great cities of Persia can be reached, there are for an army terrible obstacles to be surmounted in the mountainous paths, and in the extreme severity of the winter. Nothing that our expedition accomplished was calculated to strike the Persians with terror. The people of Tehran, of Ispahan, and of Shiraz, know little, and care little, for the towns of Mahommerah and Bushire, to which, together with the island of

Karrack, our occupation was limited. The force tried the road to Shiraz, but found it inaccessible, and in the small advances that were made the sufferings of the troops from cold were very severe. We may some day be forced to occupy the province of Fars, but that is a policy which England does well by all the means in her power to avoid. It implies the abandonment of all that is most valuable in Persia to Russia, whether Russia annexes North Persia or not. Even now the manufactures of Russia compete with us, and successfully, as far south as Shiraz. A prolonged hostile occupation of Bushire and the coast by the British, would make Ispahan wholly Russian; and the rich provinces upon the Caspian, including Tabriz, the most populous town in Persia, would be virtually, or in fact, part of the Russian Empire.

The occupation of Persia is for the Tsar a very much more easy matter than for the Empress of India. The year 1857 was well chosen for us to be at war with Persia, the year after the Treaty of Paris had been forced upon the young Tsar, who loves and longed for peace. Even then we might not have continued it with impunity; and such an occasion is not likely to recur. The Shah's power exists by favour of England and Russia, but the authority of England in Persia is probably inferior to that of Russia, because Russia is absolute in the Caspian; and thus, with a secure base of operations by land and water, can overrun Persia by passing her armies through the Caucasus, or down the Caspian, without fear of molestation. Though we met with no physical trace of the war of 1857, we heard an incident which is very characteristic of the Persian army. After the loss by the Persians of Mahommerah in that war, the officers of the Khelij regiment, which was thought to have behaved badly, were punished by having rings passed through their noses in the Shah's camp, near Tehran; to these rings cords were attached, and the unhappy men, harnessed in this fashion, were then driven in disgrace through the lines. It was said that Prince Khunler, who was in command, especially deserved punishment, but that as he was able to pay a douceur of fifteen thousand tomans, he received, instead of disgrace, a sword and dress of honour.

The true interests of England in Persia are easily appreciated. It is our interest to promote reform in the Shah's Government, and to improve his army, in order to secure better government in Persia, which is impossible without a sufficient and well-trained military force. The Persian army would be a respectable force, if it were well drilled, and led by men of competent education, sufficiently well paid to be removed from the paltry temptations which are now enough to lead Persian officers from the line of duty. As a rule, they are scandalously ignorant, greedy of bribes, vicious, and cruelly oppressive. Our interest in Persia is synonymous with that of the Persians. The present condition of Persia, fast becoming worse, invites foreign occupation. It is our interest that Persia should stand; prospering, improving, and independent; and to this end there is needed great intelligence and activity, together with the most complete knowlege of the policy of England, of India, and of Russia, which it is possible to obtain, in the person of the Minister accredited by the English Government to the Shah. This indispensable provision has not been duly regarded by the Foreign Office, and until it has been made the first and most necessary step towards the promotion of British interests in Persia will not have been accomplished.

England has, however, planted in the Indo-European Telegraph an "institution" in Persia, which, though it adds nothing to her strength in the country, and does not in any degree fortify her position as against Russia, is a monument of her power, and an emblem of her civilisation. The Persian system of government must, indeed, be execrable, when we find that it has not benefited by this great addition to the power and resources of a wise administration. Nothing but the inherent badness of that Government could have led to this failure. The decline of Persia has not in any perceptible degree been arrested by this annihilation of space in the service of the Government, in a country where space is a chief obstacle to good government. I have often thought, when following these wires across salt deserts, where there was no sign of life, and in the mountains, where the iron cords were sometimes strained almost to breaking by the weight of frozen snow, that under the rule of the Marquis of Salisbury, the government of an Empire, compared with which that of Persia is insignificant, was passing there; and thus I have been led to reflect what a blessing it might prove to that most miserable land if conquest were to secure peace and order, and give to Persia, with those most precious gifts, the scientific discoveries of Europe.

CHAPTER XI.

The Province of Fars—Memorandum by Colonel Ross—Boundaries of Fars—Government of Fars—Six first-class Governments—The districts of Bushire—Kárágash River—Eeliats—Nomad tribes of Fars—Numbers of the tribes—Eel-Khanee and Eel-Begee—Chief routes in Fars—Taxation and revenue—A revenue survey.

ENGLAND is more interested in the Province of Fars than in any other part of Persia; and in a memorandum by Colonel Ross lately communicated to the Government of Bombay, I have found so much valuable information upon the affairs of that province, which includes an area of not less than sixty thousand square miles, that I propose in this chapter to give the facts almost in the words of the Political Resident. Fars includes the whole of Southern Persia Proper, Lar being considered one of its subordinate governments. On the Persian Gulf, Fars includes the seaboard belonging to Persia, from 50° East longitude to 58° East longitude, from Bunder Dilam to the boundary beyond Cape Jashk. The northern limit of Fars, identical with the jurisdiction of the Shiraz Government, I have mentioned in an earlier chapter, in describing our brief stay at the caravanserai of Ahminabad, which is certainly the most northerly house in Fars, between the thirty-first and thirty-second parallels of North latitude.

On the west, Fars is bounded by Khuzistan and Luristan; on the north-east, the district of Aberkah lies between Fars and Yezd, belonging to neither at present, and from the north-east comes to a point at no great distance north of Bunder Abbas; the frontier of Fars is identical with that of the Persian province of Kirman. The districts of Bunder Abbas lie in the strip between the Gulf and Kirman and Bashkard, and are included in Fars in a political rather than a geographical sense.

The marked contrast of climate which I have shown as existing between that of the uplands from Ahminabad to Daliki as compared with the region which we crossed in riding from Daliki to Bushire, has given rise to a division of Fars into the "Garmsir," or hot districts, and the "Sardsir," or cool districts; the former being the lowlands and the latter the highlands.

Colonel Ross states that a great part of the province of Fars is still, as regards Europeans, *terra incognita*; and he adds, that even the courses of the most important streams are matter of conjecture. Very much has been added to our knowledge of "Eastern Persia" by the work of Major St. John, R.E., in connexion with the Boundary Commission, recently published by authority of the Indian Government.

The Governor-General of Fars, who is also Governor of Shiraz, and whose seat of government is in that city, reigns in the name of the Shah over this extensive and important province. He is assisted by the Mushir, to whom I alluded as the builder of the excellent bridge over the Daliki river, at the foot of the Kotul Maloo, and the improver of the Kotul Dochter. The Mushir (whose full title is "Mushir-el-Mulk") is the person most feared in the province; but this does not appear to exempt him from the ordinary vexations of Persia, for a caravan conveying goods on his private account from Bushire was not long since pillaged near the Kotul Dochter.

For administrative and fiscal purposes, there are in Fars six subordinate Governments of the first class, under sub-governors, who are responsible for the revenues and management of their districts. Of these we have met with one in the person of Mirza Réza Khan, Governor of Abadeh, whose letter to myself has been printed in an earlier chapter. Besides the divisions of the first class, there are considerable districts not administered by these six Governments. The outlying districts are usually managed by a "head man," directly responsible to the Government in Shiraz.

The six subordinate divisions of Fars are—1.

Bebehan; 2. Bushire; 3. Lar and Salia; 4. Bunder Abbas; 5. Darale; 6. Abadeh and Iklid, each of which is subdivided.

The district of Bebehan is ruled by the Ihtisham-el-Dowleh, Sultan Awiss Mirza, son of Ferhad Mirza Motemid-el-Dowleh. The revenues of this Government are, in part, obtained from chiefs of Eeliat tribes. The Political Resident states that Bebehan is little known to Europeans, and he thinks the routes to Shiraz and Kazeroon require further surveying.

His Highness the Sipah Salar (Commander-in-Chief), who is really Sadr Azem (Prime Minister) gave us a Vizierial letter to Houssein Kuli Khan entitled Saad-ul-Mulk, the Governor of Bushire. But his Excellency was out tax-gathering with a considerable force, and consequently we had not the honour of meeting with him. Formerly Bushire and the adjacent district were administered by a Governor directly responsible to the Imperial Government in Tehran. The present Governor is the subordinate of the Governor of Shiraz.

The Bushire districts are dependent almost entirely upon the rainfall for the watering of their crops. The rivers of Khisht and Daliki, skirting the district of Dashtistan, unite and flow into the Rabillah Creek, some miles north of the town of Bushire. The lower part of Dashtee (a sub-district of Bushire) is traversed by a river which flows into the creek called Khor

Ziaret. It is supposed that this is the stream which further up the country is known as the Karagash (the ancient Silakus), which Colonel Ross says is believed to rise near Shahpur, and to flow round to the eastward of Firozabad. He continues :—" The Khor Ziaret can be entered by vessels of not exceeding six feet draught, and is navigable for such craft for some miles. I recently proceeded up the creek for about twelve miles, and the information elicited from the inhabitants of the district tended to confirm the conjecture that here is the embouchure of the Karagash river. It would be an interesting and useful undertaking to march up this river as far as possible."

We visited Lingah, in the Lar districts, on our way down the Persian Gulf. These districts, says Colonel Ross, "are little known to Europeans, and the geographical position of the town of Lar but vaguely known." We also landed in the districts of Bunder Abbas, to which we have made a reference in the notes of our passage from Bushire. In the Government of Darah, which we nowhere traversed, there are some interesting ruins, and Colonel Ross states that "iron mines exist in this part of Persia." In the sixth district, the Government of Abadeh and Iklid, we stayed in our ride between Ispahan and Shiraz, both at the chief town and at Zurmak, in the same district.

A very interesting portion of Colonel Ross's

memorandum is that which relates to "The Eeliat o
Nomad Tribes of Fars," races to which I have alread
made more than one allusion. He says:—

"Some of the Eeliat tribes found in Bebehan hav
already been mentioned, and it was stated that the
are Looree tribes. In other parts of Fars, the Eel
are 'Toorks' and 'Arabs.' These pastoral peopl
roam with their flocks from one pasturage to anothe
according to the seasons. In the winter they fre
quent the comparatively lowlands, and when the in
creasing power of the sun commences to scorch th
grass, they move off to the cooler uplands. The winte
encampments are termed 'kishlak,' and the coc
summer quarters 'zelak.' Each tribe usually fre
quents the same tract year after year. In the earl
part of summer, the Eeliats are on the move witl
their flocks, and robberies are then frequent. It i
necessarily difficult to form any estimate of th
number of those tribes, but they form an importan
part of the population of Fars, and contribute som
12,000*l*. to 15,000*l*. of revenue yearly.

"The Eeliat population has greatly diminished o
late years, as during the last famine many perished
with a large proportion of their cattle and flocks
others have of late abandoned the nomadic life an
become members of the settled population, and thi
has been particularly the case with the once note
'Feelee' tribe.

"Of all the Eeliats of Fars, the Kashkaee are most numerous, and although the number has greatly diminished since the famine they muster about eight thousand houses. This tribe have been great breeders of horses, but at present comparatively few are reared amongst them. The families (*teerah*) of Kashkaee are Ader-Ban, Chardeh, Chireek, and Lashnee.

"The Arab Eels have about three thousand houses (or rather tents), and roam from their *kishlaks* in Salia to the summer pastures, or *zelak*, in Bowânât. They claim descent from the Benu Sharban tribe of Arabia.

"The Basseree tribe, numbering about one thousand houses, are found in Mervdasht, Sirhadd-i-charhar-dongah, and Servistan.

"The Baharloo tribe, of about one thousand tents, inhabit Darab; others are the Arayâloo, the 'Napar' and 'Abu'lwardee,' the 'Tewalallee' and 'Amlah Shâhee,' the 'Mammasennee,' of about one thousand houses inhabit Shoolistân.

"The following tribes are nearly extinct as nomads, having mostly settled in towns:—'Feelee,' 'Bujat,' 'Berkushadee.'

"The Eeliats are for the most part governed immediately by chiefs of their own, who are appointed by the Government of Persia, and held responsible for collection of revenue and the conduct of the tribes.

"The Kashkaee tribes have at their head an Eel Khanee and Eel-Begee. The former is the highe title, and the nominal Eel-Khanee now, is the Sooltar Mahomed Khân; but as matters are, this personage' office is practically in abeyance, and is administere by a Persian officer, Nowzer Mirza.

"The present Eel-Begee is Dârâh Khân, brother c Sohrâh Khân, who was put to death by the Persia Government at Shiraz. The residence of the Eel Khanee of Kashkaee has till lately been Firozâbâd where the late Eel-Khanee, Mahommed Khoolee Khân, commenced to build a pretty villa somewha in European style."

It will also be interesting to quote what th Political Resident has to say in the current year, a to the routes in the province of Fars :—

"The chief caravan road traversing Fars is tha which leads from Bushire to Shiraz by Kâzeroon, anc from Shiraz northwards towards Ispahan.

"Another route from Bushire to Shiraz passe through Firozabad. This road is somewhat longer but from the gradients being greater, is considered more capable of being made practicable for wheeled conveyances or artillery. At present this road is not used as regards the seaport traffic.

* * * * *

"The roads to the summer haunts of the Eeliats in the north-west of Fars, where the great mountain,

Koh-i-Dana, or Koh-i-Pádána, rises to a height (according to Major St. John) of about seventeen or eighteen thousand feet, have, it is thought, never been explored by British travellers, though these districts are interesting enough to repay the toil of a journey through them.

"More accurate topographical information regarding the various districts of Fars (as of other provinces), and the roads traversing them, would be of great advantage to the Persian Government. In fact, the acquirement of such knowledge would evidently be one of the first steps, and an indispensable condition, to any real reform of the fiscal system and administration of the country generally. There are at the present extensive tracts and districts the extent, capacity, and even position of which are but vaguely known at the seat of Government.

"Information regarding the resources of many districts is necessarily derived by the Government of the country from interested persons.

"In some cases, it is said that in one case, out of 10,000*l.* actually realised from a district, about 2000*l.* goes to the Government, and the remainder into the private purse of the official who farms the place. The Persian Government very frequently puts the leases up for sale to the highest bidder; and this system, though a partial safeguard against such extreme cases, has many unsatisfactory results. Be it remarked

that it matters nothing to the peasantry what th
assessment may be, as in any case they are taxed t
the utmost. But the question is one immediatel
affecting the resources of the Government, and ir
directly the whole well-being of the State.

"It would be difficult to suggest a measure ca
culated to have a more beneficial result to Persia tha
a well and honestly conducted revenue survey. Thei
is reason to believe that the more enlightened of th
Persian Ministers are alive to these consideration;
and disposed to adopt this measure; but so many ar
interested in perpetuating existing ignorance, tha
the scheme would have many powerful opposers.]
adopted, however, not only would result a knowledg
of and increase of her resources to Persia, but justl
and properly fixed assessments would tend to chec
the system of dishonesty and fraud, which, com
mencing at the sources, as at present, taints the whol
stream of official life in Persia."

CHAPTER XII.

British India Steam Navigation Company—Crew of the *Euphrates*—Pilgrims in difficulty—Streets of Bushire—German Archæological Expedition—Sermons in bricks—Leaving Bushire—Slavery in Persian Gulf—Fugitive Slave Circulars—The Parsee engineer's evidence—Ships searched for slaves—Pearl fisheries of Bahrein—Anglo-Turkish ideas—Lingah in Laristan—Bunder-Abbas—Landing at Cape Jahsk—"Pegs" and pale clerks—A master mariner's grievance—The end of Persia—Coast of Beloochistan—Shooting sleeping turtles—Harbour of Kurrachee—Kurrachee boat wallahs—The orthodox Scinde hat—Faults of Indian society—English ladies in India—Intercourse with natives—Unmannerly Englishmen—Exceptional behaviour.

A CHEERY, bright-eyed, broad-shouldered man, some way on the younger side of thirty, who could laugh louder than any, and beat most of us at a game upon the Residency billiard table, was Captain George Stevenson, of the British India Company's Steamship *Euphrates*, which on her arrival from Bussorah had cast anchor about three miles from Bushire. A vessel drawing seventeen feet of water cannot with safety get much nearer. Captain Stevenson's gig had been pulled ashore by six Indian sailors—the crew of the *Euphrates* did not include a single European—neatly dressed in blue, and with blue caps surrounded with

a scarlet turban. Another steamer had been lyin
for two days before the Residency under rather pecu
liar circumstances. She was loaded with pilgrim
who had received tickets for Bussorah; but the shi
was chartered only to Bushire, and the captain pro
fessed to be ignorant that the pilgrims had shippe
for the more distant port. The Political Resider
was informed that the pilgrims would not allow th
captain to come on shore in order to explain his diff
culty; they held him, in terror for his life, a hostag
and surety for the performance of the contract which
had been made with them; and for my own part
was delighted to see Colonel Ross firmly on the sid
of the pilgrims. He sent off the Assistant-Secretar
to communicate to the captain his opinion, which
was that he [the captain] would do well to fulfi
the engagement declared upon the tickets, and carr
the pilgrims on to Bussorah. It was, I think, owing
to the praiseworthy firmness of the Political Residen
that the British flag did not become in the eyes o
these two hundred Persians a deception and a snare
and that they were not landed, many of them with
out food or money, upon a shore of which they knew
nothing, and where they had no means of communi
cation with their homes. Worse indeed might have
happened; and in a fight between the pilgrims and
the British officers of the vessel, the justly exas
perated Moslems would probably have succeeded in

making the ship their own at a terrible cost of life. We were all very glad to see the vessel steaming quietly towards Bussorah.

After rain, the narrow streets of Bushire are in many places, sometimes from wall to wall, covered with green pools of stagnant filth, through which one may pass dry-shod on bricks or blocks, which have long been used as stepping-stones across these shallow cesspools. These filthy places might be filled up by a hundred men in one day's labour; but throughout Persia there is no regard whatever for sanitary considerations. He will not fail to prefer the work of nature to that of man, who, after gazing over the blue waters of the Gulf, plunges into the labyrinth of mud walls and noisome passages, through the squalid bazaar, among the mud hovels of Bushire to the other side of the narrow peninsula on which the town stands. But when the horrors of this middle passage are overpassed, the view is even more beautiful than that from the front of the Residency, including the sweep of the sandy Mashillah, and the snowy highlands of Persia.

About four miles from Bushire, a scientific expedition, directed by Dr. Andreas, an Armenian, and carried on at the cost of the Berlin Government, has been for some time engaged in excavating a mound which evidently enclosed the ruins of an ancient temple. That the mound contained matter of interest appeared probable to some officers of the Indian Navy, who examined it at the time of the British Military Expedition in 1856-7. Architecturally, Dr. Andreas's discoveries do not appear to have been very significant. From the ruins he has unearthed, it seems that the building over which the mound had formed was used as a "Fire Temple;" but the material of the walls included bricks which can be made to speak—bricks having one of the sides covered with cuneiform inscriptions. These bricks evidently formed part of some older work, from which they have been carried and then built into this structure near Bushire. I have seen several of these bricks; they are rather longer than the common brick, and very hard; the cuneiform letters are raised on one side and have endured twenty-five hundred years' wear and tear with surprising steadfastness. We had the pleasure of meeting Dr. Andreas and his colleague at the Residency before we embarked for Bombay. But in quitting Bushire, we were not to leave Persia. We had nearly six hundred miles to travel down the Gulf before passing the boundary which separates Persia from Beloochistan at the little promontory of Gwadur.

There is nothing in Nature more delicious than the spring sunshine of southern latitudes; than the exhilarating air of such a morning as that on which Captain Stevenson took us off to the *Euphrates* in his gig, pulled by six Suratees of his crew. The first of those ill-advised Slave Circulars, which the Government issued and withdrew from the storm of anger they evoked, had just reached us, and formed the subject of much talk. It was well known that the supposed difficulties of naval commanders in the Persian Gulf had been the cause of this movement. It was believed in the Gulf that Sir Lewis Pelly was, more than any one else, responsible as the adviser of the Government in this unfortunate business. He had been Political Resident at Bushire, and had found, as all resident officers in such places must discover, that the real difficulty in the matter rests with officers on shore rather than with naval commanders. At Bushire, a considerable portion of the population is held in slavery; it is considered by those well acquainted with the facts, that the proportion of slaves increases in descending the Gulf. But I could find no one who wished for more definite instructions. The agent for the British India Company's line of steamers trading from Bagdad and Bussorah, through the whole length and breadth of the Gulf to Kurrachee and Bombay, told me he had in seven years had but one case brought to his knowledge. One of his captains informed him, on this occasion, that he had two fugitive slaves on board his ship, and asked what was to be done with them. This occurred six years ago, and the agent wrote to the then Political Resident, referring the matter to him. He acted as Political Residents are generally disposed to act; that is, with a leaning towards the slave-owner's claim for the restoration of his "property." He did not write a reply: British officers do not like to commit themselves to slavery in black and white; he sent a verbal message to the agent to the effect that he might give up the slaves if he pleased. But the agent found the captain not at all disposed to take this view of his duty. Sailors are generally opposed to the notion of surrendering slaves to the ignominy of their former life, and to the cruelty which they well know the attempt to escape will bring upon them by way of punishment. He declared that he should take the fugitives to Bombay; and so he did.

We had to row three miles from the shore at Bushire to where the *Euphrates* lay at anchor, and to pass the Resident's gunboat, which is supposed to be specially concerned with the suppression of the slave traffic, and the maintenance of general peace upon the waters of the Gulf. The chief engineer, a Parsee, joined us as a fellow-passenger. He had been four years on this particular service, and could speak English. He said that, during those years, ten or a dozen slaves had come on board the gunboat. Sometimes they had swam off from the shore at night, some had "come on board with the coals," others had been found hiding in the ship. In no case, he said, was there on the part of the captain, or officers, or crew, any desire to send them ashore. If a slave swam off at night, the men on watch were always ready to give the poor wretch a hand on to the deck; and if a fugitive slave was discovered when the vessel was at sea, it was just the same—everybody was ready to pass him on to Bombay, or to some place where he would be free and safe. But it generally happened, said the Parsee engineer, that the owner on shore discovered his loss, and at once suspected the British ship. If the owner came off by himself, and even if he were permitted to look through the vessel, the probability was, said the engineer, that he would not find his missing slave. The slave-owners, however, are generally wiser than this, and succeed in clothing their claims with the authority of the Queen of the United Kingdom and the Empress of India. Wherever it is possible, they resort to the Political Resident, acquaint him with their loss and their suspicions, and obtain from him a letter to the commander of the vessel, requesting that, if the fugitive slave is on board, he may be given up. In most cases, the Political Resident being the superior officer, this of course amounts to an order; and the engineer said this was the plan so generally adopted that it might be said that it was only when the slaves came from "foreign ground," which he explained to mean any part of the coast upon which there was neither Resident, nor Agent, nor Consul, that they were taken on, or passed on, to Bombay. The fact appears to be, that owing to the leaning of the Resident British Officers to the ideas and interests of the slave-owners among whom they dwell, there is a very small chance of escape for a fugitive slave where the British Crown is represented, and a very good chance wherever the British flag is flying at sea, out of sight and out of reach of any British authority on shore. I met with a captain of one of the British Indian Company's vessels, who had twice allowed his ship to be searched by slave-owners upon a requisition from the Political Resident at Muscat. A first-class engineer in the same employ, a Scotchman, who had served in the Gulf for three years, told me that he had seen but one fugitive slave on board his ship. He found this man hidden in the screw-tunnel (the casing in which the rod connecting the screw with the engines is placed), and allowed him to work his passage as a coal trimmer to Bombay.

Of the large number of slaves upon the shores of the Gulf, both on the Persian and the Arabian side, it is certain that but very few attempt escape. All the severe and dangerous work of the pearl fisheries is sustained by slaves, the result of these fisheries being, as I have said, estimated as worth 400,000*l.* a year. There is abundant evidence that the pearl divers prefer to risk the perils of the water, which swarms with sharks, rather than be flogged on shore; and I am surprised, hearing of the lashings with wire whips, and of other tortures to which they are subject, it so rarely happens that one or two swim off to any ship displaying the British flag.

That the difficulty, such as it is, culminates in the Persian Gulf, must be admitted. The numerous sovereign tribes which hold and rule the shores of the Gulf, are restrained from hostilities and piracy by the influence of the Resident Officers of the British Indian Government, who believe that the maintenance of their authority would be much more difficult if they appeared to acquiesce in that which is regarded as the confiscation, for the advantage of the British, of Arab, or Persian " property." Most people find it easier to adopt a local opinion than to maintain the ideas of the higher society in which they have lived. I met lately with an account of "harem life in Turkey," written by an Englishwoman, who had lived as governess for six years in the house of a great Pasha upon the Bosphorus. She appeared to see no degradation of her sex in the ceremonious "dinner party," in which the Pasha sat surrounded with his three wives and their children, together with the children of his slave-wives. These last performed the offices of the table, and though not thought worthy to sit with their own children, were privileged to wait upon them. As to the Pasha's property in his slaves, she appeared to think it quite right that the eunuchs should look closely after them, because it must be remembered that, in any attempt to get away, they were not only leaving a kind master, but were "thieving themselves," a feat which seemed in her eyes to be an act of most atrocious wickedness. With regard to the Fugitive Slave question, which is for the present relegated to its former condition by the substitution of a colourless and indefinite circular, the result of my inquiries in the Persian Gulf was, that I could find no one who desired more precise instructions; and it appeared from the evidence I could obtain, that a fugitive slave is rarely met with, and that when seen his chances of escape are excellent, provided the British Crown is not represented on the land from whence he has taken flight.

After staying a few hours before Lingah, in the province of Laristan, we steamed on to Bunder Abbas (landing-place of Shah Abbas), the principal place of entry—for it is not a port—in the Persian province of Kirman. We had been two days at sea, and were glad to land upon the shelly beach at Bunder Abbas. But the people, black and yellow, pressed upon us in their eagerness to see an Englishwoman, and our progress in the squalid town and bazaar was slower than we desired. Many of the women bore upon their faces by way of covering, a half-mask of stiffened cotton upon a bamboo frame, finished with a metal ornament upon the nose, and supported upon the face by a string passing over the head. The town looked like a sore upon the beauteous landscape. To have wandered on the shore strewn with pink shells, or inland among the palm trees, in sight of the mountains, would have been delightful. But the people of Bunder Abbas would allow us neither pleasure. Where we walked they followed, laughing, screaming, "larking"—as English street-boys would say. If we stopped to pick up a shell, twenty hands were indiscriminately filled with shells, and the contents pressed upon us.

This is the "Gumberoon" of "Lalla Rookh," and over the waters of the Gulf we could see the pale coasts of the Island of Ormus, the commencement, now neglected, of our Indian Empire. Probably the most ancient traces of European occupation are to be found in this island, which was once the emporium of Portuguese, and subsequently of British, commerce. Sailing up the coasts of India, this was the first detached land—the first spot in which those who were secure of the sea, but not of the land, could establish themselves with safety. Ormus is now the home of a mixed but very scanty population, engaged for the most part in fishery—catching sharks for the sake of trading in their fins and bones, and edible fish for sale along the coast. We had lovely weather in the Straits of

Ormus, and anchored in smooth water under Cape Jahsk, where we soon obtained a number of beautiful shells. On the flat and feverish land of Jahsk there is a large station of the Indo-Persian Telegraph, inhabited by half a dozen young Englishmen, who are attracted by a salary which to a youth appears high, into a most unwholesome place, with little chance of promotion. The pale-faced lads whom we saw there assured us that in summer Jahsk was the hottest place in the world; and this is not far from its general reputation. We were touched by the sight of their faces; not bronzed with sunny health, as are those of many Anglo-Indians, but paler than those of Lombard Street clerks, who so very rarely see the sun. Most of the clerks at Jahsk were resolved to "give it up" at the end of their three years' engagement; but I suspect that when that time comes, and they have to face the alternative of recommencing life in England or India, they will settle into that state of acquiescence or chronic discontent, which, in those who survive, is so often the sequel to the first impressions of life in low latitudes.

Near the sand and rocks upon which we landed there was a village of bamboo huts, inhabited by the servants of the Telegraph staff, and about half a mile distant were the large, low buildings of the Office, which included a billiard room and comfortable quarters for the clerks. It was at Jahsk that I first heard of "pegging" as a familiar habit. Every one of the pale clerks whom I met with was full of kindness and hospitality, of which, however, his first notion seemed to be that I was in want of a "peg," upon which the pegholder of the Anglo-Indian, the brandy bottle, was produced. To see the thermometer at 90° in the shade, and a pale youth—towards whom as a fellow-countryman in that far distant island one feels an indescribable tenderness—looking for support to a bottle of brandy is a pitiful sight; and it is one which, even in the flying glimpses we had of Anglo-Indian life, appeared far too common.

A fresh wind was blowing as we rounded Cape Jahsk, and steamed out from the coast on to the broad bosom of the Indian Ocean. After dark, Captain Stevenson set out a grievance which certainly deserves, and I understand has since received, the attention of Government. He is one of a highly respectable class of British subjects who have obtained certificates as navigating officers from an Indian Board of Examiners. Possessed of a certificate as master from the Board in Bombay, he, and those in a similar position, are empowered to take charge of any vessel trading from or into any Indian port. If the Directors of the British Indian Company ask him to take charge of a homeward-bound ship, he can do so and navigate her into the port of London or Liverpool, or to any port in or belonging to the

United Kingdom. But there the validity of this certificate ends; and the commander who is thought by uninsured owners, trustworthy and competent for the navigation of their vessel into a British port, cannot bring the same vessel out of port, unless he has been examined and obtained a certificate in the United Kingdom. If he has this certificate, his Indian diploma is worthless, because the British certificate is valid everywhere, and the Indian certificate is not. Captain Stevenson had been placed in this position; he had been offered the command of a large steamship chartered for London; but he was obliged to decline the flattering proposal, because he would have to leave the port of London as a passenger only, in the vessel which he was held competent to command on the homeward-bound voyage.

There seems in these circumstances to be a grievance demanding a remedy, which is surely simple and easy. Either the Indian Boards are incompetent, or their certificates should be held valid throughout the dominions of the Queen-Empress. So far as I can learn from inquiry, I am led to believe that the Indian examiners at the chief ports of the three Governments are highly competent, and that nothing but advantage would result from giving force to their certificates in the United Kingdom. Navigation demands education as well as experience, and charts are brought to such perfection that perhaps the more important work of the master of a ship is performed in his cabin. No well-trained captain finds difficulty along a surveyed and lighted coast which he sees for the first time; and if it be said that the man examined in London or Liverpool is likely to be better acquainted with the coasts of the British Isles than one who seeks a certificate in Calcutta or Bombay, it is easy to reply that the candidate in London has perhaps the less valuable knowledge, for he is likely to find his danger upon the unlighted shores of Eastern Africa and Southern Asia, the rocks of which are probably known to the candidate in Bombay. I advised the preparation of a petition to Parliament, which I hope will now be needless.

Next day we approached the coast of Beloochistan, and rounding the high land of Cape Gwadur, anchored before the town, where the shore is strewn with the bones of sharks, which are caught and killed for the value of their fins. The eastern boundary of Persia, as settled by Sir Frederick Goldsmid, and agreed to by the Shah, touches the sea at this point. The coast near the shore is generally flat and uncultivated—a sandy desert. We were there in the last days of February, and at that season there are, near the villages, a few patches of green, insignificant oases in the arid expanse. Beyond Gwadur we met with several large turtles asleep on the surface of the ocean; but though rifles were plentiful, and bullets whizzed about, we were not successful in securing the material for soup. Two bullets flew off from a turtle's back as though his shell had been the plates of an ironclad. Twenty-four hours later, the projecting point of high land which marks the westernmost boundary of British India, came in sight, and then a lower headland, over which we could see the topmasts of vessels in Kurrachee harbour.

What a change is marked in passing from the wretched shores of Persia, with no harbour in north or south, to the moorings at Kurrachee, surrounded by the most valuable results of the intelligent labour of Europe! The beacon in the white, English-looking lighthouse; the steam-dredges at work; the huge iron vessels, long and narrow, built for the Suez Canal, and locally known as "ditchers," are pouring out cargoes of railway iron for the Indus Railway; one steamship is coiling from the shore miles of telegraph cable, for the repair of a disaster; another is steaming behind us with the mails from England. Order, activity, utility, nowhere seen by us for months past, appear here to be natural and constant. We are hardly at anchor before the *Euphrates* is boarded by a dozen boat-wallahs, merchants or pedlars, loaded with bundles of shawls from Cashmere, inlaid boxes and needlework of Scinde, caps and trinkets of Kurrachee. They are proof against taunts and trouble. They will expose a hundred articles on the deck without promise of sale, and submit to the exposure of their petty knaveries with unruffled manner. New arrivals probably give a higher price for these goods than that for which the same articles could be purchased in Regent Street. It is easy to find a good carriage at the landing-stage, which is three or four miles from the town and cantonment of Kurrachee. We drove in the first place to the Travellers' Bungalow, intending to stay two nights on shore, but were repelled by the dirt of the place, by the sight of the nasty bedding, the grimy look of the heavy wooden furniture, and the general uncleanliness of the rooms.

The roads about Kurrachee are of unsurpassable excellence, wide (perhaps too wide for a tropical country, where the shade of the roadside is desired by all) and smooth, as well made as any in or out of London. This appears remarkable within a day's journey from the miserable tracks of Beloochistan. One can never be more disposed to admit the material benefits which the English rule has conferred upon India than in passing quickly, as we did, from the countries of the Persian Gulf. From the landing-place to the cantonment of Kurrachee, the ground is low and flat; from the waters of the harbour the roof of the Frere Hall, four or five miles distant, can be seen high above the surrounding houses. When we visited the Hall there were sixteen natives doing the work of two Europeans, in waxing and polishing the floor preparatory to a ball, which was to take place in the evening. The narrow streets of the native town are full of interest. The costumes are mostly white; it is in their head-dress that the people of India are most fantastic, and perhaps they are nowhere more so than in Scinde. The orthodox Scinde hat, which is like an Englishman's hat inverted, the wide straight brim being at the top, the head fitting into the brimless cylinder, is one of the most curious; but scarlet is the prevailing colour in turbans.

The peculiar faults of Indian society had never occurred to me before I landed at Kurrachee. The weariness of a society in which the aims and hopes of all have one goal, in which all bear the same stamp of officialism, in which that very valuable element in society, the leisure class, which asks for nothing, and which has such a refining influence upon the views and sentiments of the employed classes, is conspicuously absent. I can fancy that in the Australian Colonies there is already the nucleus of an established class, which is not engaged in money-making, nor in pushing its way to offices of the State, and which does not consider a return to England, loaded with accumulations of years of exile, to be the grandest hope of life. But it is quite certain that there is no such class in India. There is an intelligent, active, moving class, all, it may be said, of one rank and sort in their origin from the great middle class of English people, existing in an unnatural manner, and dominated by two prepossessions, the hope of promotion on the line to which all belong, and the hope of return to the British Islands, from which all have set out.

Even in such a hasty passing glance as we had at Indian life, it is easy to see that these men are part of the very flower of our nation, some of the best men of their time. But no men can be impervious to the influences which surround their every-day existence for the best part of their lives, and in Indian society there is not sufficient diversity to render it agreeable. It is the same with the women as with the men, but in their case, the faults of Indian society, due to its circumstances, are more marked and even more perceptible. Robbed by the climate of their children, over-charged to the lips with the gabble of the station or cantonment, with a nice knowledge of the relative advantages of civil and military, covenanted and uncovenanted, service, their feminine hopes, and delights, and triumphs, are all upon the same line: success in the ball-room, promotion for their masculine friends, the opening of a "Europe box," and a house in Kensington as the full and final reward of life.

Practically, there is no admixture of the ruling with the subject population. The Government of

India is in the main just and liberal; occasionally in its zeal, it attempts an impossible combination of despotic and constitutional forms. The younger officers are sometimes guilty of gross rudeness to natives of the higher classes, and of harsh treatment to the lower class natives in their service. This injurious and detestable conduct is, as a rule, abandoned in the moment when an officer rises high enough, or becomes by accident so conspicuous as to be subject to public opinion at home. The great value of the influence of English opinion upon the Goverument of India is exhibited in the fact that the most responsible officials are invariably the most benign, considerate, and just in their dealings with the natives of India. Of the natives, many are now put high in place and authority, many are reputed friends of Englishmen. Yet if, as I believe, the few cases which have come under my observation are typical, this "friendship" is not friendship; it is nothing more than intercourse, regulated and sweetened by polite forms, of which none are greater masters than the high-class natives of India.

But if the intercourse of Indians with English must be that of a subject with a governing race, contumelious treatment of natives by Englishmen should be avoided, and, when possible, should be punished. During our stay at Kurrachee, I heard the particulars of a case which exhibited a gross instance of this misconduct. The Prince of Wales was then in India, and a native Prince had chartered two British steamships for the conveyance of himself and suite to Bombay. Into the smaller vessel, his Highness was accompanied by his ministers and personal attendants, the larger was destined for his escort, amounting to about two hundred armed men. When these last went on board, the English captain demanded the surrender of their arms, and he did this, as I was informed, in no very gracious manner. The men had not expected to be disarmed, and thought it implied degradation. To have explained fully and kindly to them that it was the necessary rule of the service, and applied to British as well as native troops, would have been easy and satisfactory. But the English captain not only offended the whole of the force by his manner in demanding their arms, he inflicted an unnecessary wound upon the commanding officer, a first-class passenger, in asking also for his sword. This was an outrage to which an English officer would not have been liable, and I was told by an eye-witness of the scene how pained he was to observe the emotion of the native officer in complying with this insulting demand. From all that one hears of the conduct of Englishmen in India, I most readily and gladly admit that behaviour of this sort is exceptional.

CHAPTER XIII.

Bombay—The *Serapis* in harbour—Suburbs of Bombay—Parsee dead—Towers of Silence—Hindoo cremation ground—Cotton manufacture in India—Report of Indian commission—Neglect of Indian Government—A Bombay cotton factory—Hours of factory labour—Seven weeks' work—Natives of India—Expenditure of Indian Government—The great absentee landlord—Grievance of cultivators—Their enemies, the money-lenders—English and native equity—The Suez Canal—Landing at Ismailia—English at the Pyramids—Alexandria—" Cleopatra's Needle"—Proposed removal to England—Condition of the Obelisk—Recent excavation—Captain Methven's plan—Removal in an iron vessel—Cost of removal—Egypt and the Khedive—Preparing for Mr. Cave—Sham civilization—The horse trampling ceremony—English *en voyage*—Egypt and Persia—Customs' officers at Alexandria—Egypt and Turkey.

THE white *Serapis* and her ironclad companions were lying at rest in the glistening waters of Bombay harbour when we entered upon that magnificent anchorage. Most people know the unimpressive aspect of the town from the harbour, with the salient angle of the Apollo Bunder, or wharf, for a centrepiece. But those who have never been in Bombay, who know that really handsome city only by pictures and photographs, will hardly believe how bad are the hotels, or how beautiful, on a March morning at sunrise, are the suburbs of Bombay. As to vehicles, there is novelty in the harnessed bullocks, ambling through the streets; but the newest fashion of carriage, the tram-car, interested me more than all. A tram-car might be registered as one of the trade marks of democracy. The tramway will do great things in breaking down the barriers of caste among the natives and of lordly prejudice on the part of Englishmen. To see the open benches of the Bombay tram-cars loaded with white-robed Parsees, with Hindoos, with Mussulmans, with one or two lightly clad Europeans; to see this equal representation of castes and classes in a carriage to which all are free to mount, with no distinction whatever, is a lesson in the ways of civilization. And there is no better plan of seeing the busy life and teeming population of the Hindoo quarter of Bombay than to ride through it upon the tramway. But to see the suburbs of Bombay in their vernal beauty, drive in early morning to the Towers of Silence, where the dead of the Parsee community are exposed to the vultures. The road winds and undulates between gardens, in which plants such as in the temperate zone are regarded as the choicest and most splendid exotics, wave their grand foliage, and extend a most grateful shade, in the fullest luxuriance of tropical splendour. There are villas belonging to the wealthy Parsees of Bombay, as elegant in architecture, and as rich in their adornment, as any in the outskirts of London or Liverpool. Riding in this direction has another advantage. By a slight divergence one may obtain practical experience for the guidance of choice in the disposition of the dead. With no great distance between them there are the Towers of Silence, the Hindoo cremation ground, and the European graveyard. In the Parsee towers there is no exposure or exhibition of the dead, except to the vultures which pounce upon the body. I asked a Parsee whether he did not shudder at the thought of such treatment of his own body after death. "Better than worms," he replied, pointing to the graveyard.

But to unaccustomed eyes the sight of these winged destroyers sitting expectant upon the topmost stone of the high towers is most repulsive. When a corpse is brought in, the friends and mourners deliver the body to the guardians of the tower, by whom it is placed on a grating near the top, but entirely concealed from view. The remains of these bodies lie upon the grating until the whitened bones fall to the foot of the tower. One may almost tell by the action of the vultures when a body is being placed. There is a great flapping of wings, and a rising of the birds into view from their horrid feast, when the attendants of the tower mount to place the newly dead. While this is being done, the top of the tower is thickly surrounded with the foul birds,* perched close together; and those who are a mile distant may know when the arrangement is ended, and the dead body left alone, by watching how the vultures flutter down and out of sight, to fasten on the corpse.

Europeans are not admitted to the walled enclosure in which the Hindoos of Bombay burn their dead. This cremation ground is about a hundred yards long and thirty wide, bounded on one side by a high road. On the other side, the soil of the adjoining graveyard rises so high that, standing there, one can observe the processes of cremation. By the side of the wall next the road, there is a long shed, in which the family and friends of the deceased range themselves. At one time, I saw three bodies burning upon as many pyres. The attendants appeared to be very skilful in selecting and building up the firewood, with four strong timbers at the corners, of sufficient substance to hold the burning wood of the pyre together until the body is consumed and these sustaining posts are charred, and fall upon it in ashes. On the ground, in front of the mourners' shed, they build the pyres; the body is laid in a shroud upon wood and covered with sufficient to insure complete destruction. The fires blaze away in the fierce sunlight, the attendants occasionally stepping forward to pull the logs together with a long staff, which each one carries in his hands; and in about two hours from the first cry of the mourners, when the body is first enveloped in flame, the pyre has crumbled into a deep bed of fiery ashes, which are scattered by the wind. I did not find that the operation was offensive; but then I was upon the windward side.

One of the most prominent and notable facts in Bombay is the increase and the character of the cotton manufacture. Familiar with that industry during my four years' residence in Lancashire as Assistant Commissioner in the time of the Cotton Famine, I determined to look closely into the mode of conducting the manufacture without Factory Laws in Bombay; and, with that view, obtained permission to inspect one of the largest and best of the factories. I saw quite enough in one hour to convict the Government of India of culpable delay in regard to to a subject which seems to me to call for immediate action.

A Commission was appointed in 1875 to inquire into the application of the Factory Laws, as enforced in England, to India; and this Commission reported in July of that year,—the majority being hostile to any legislation. Yet the factory to which I am about to refer, is, both in regard to the hours of infant labour and to construction, better than the average of those that must have come under the Commissioners' notice. If gentlemen do not think that circumstances such as these betray neglect on the part of the Executive Government, it is not likely they will be converted by the Under Secretary's promise of "further inquiries in Bromah and Surat." Judging from the conduct of these Commissioners, and the tenour of this reply by Lord George Hamilton to a question put to him by Mr. Anderson in the House of Commons in February of the current year, the Indian Government appears to be playing into the hands of the party interested in opposing legislation, by adopting costly methods of delay and circumlocution.

The establishment I visited had about forty thousand spindles, and, together with the loom shed, employed about eight hundred people, including men, women, and children. The building was in no important respect dissimilar from the Lancashire factories, and the machinery, of Lancashire make, was of the best quality and construction. The hands were leaving the mill for their meagre midday rest of half an hour (the only rest they have in the whole of the working day), just as I was entering the counting-house. I had a very good opportunity for observing their physique. The path by which they passed me was so narrow, that with my sun umbrella I could have touched any one of them. Never have I seen such a wretched crowd of working people—the men pale and haggard, the women and children drooping and grey with cotton dust. The men had been working continuously from a quarter-past six A.M. to one P.M., the time of my arrival; the women and children from seven A.M. The hours of work are—for men, from a quarter-past six A.M. to a quarter-past six P.M.; for women and children, from seven A.M. to five P.M. They have only one half-hour for rest and food; and as I sat waiting for their return, the thirty minutes seemed very short.

At the door by my side, when they re-entered the mill, stood the superintendent, with a stick in his hand, "just," as he said, "to give a tap to them as comes late, for you must be master of 'em." The time was half-past one; and the little children, some of them not more than seven years old—exhausted with the previous six hours of continuous labour—were again at work in the terrible atmosphere of a Bombay factory for another three and a half hours. But this cruelty, involving of course the utter abandonment of education—a cruelty from which the British child is protected by law—is not the worst to which these Hindoo children are subjected. During a period of seven weeks this factory had been closed only for three days. There is no observance of any regular day of rest; and for forty-six out of the forty-nine days preceding my visit, these children had toiled from seven A.M. to five P.M. at their unhealthy and exhausting labour.

It is hardly necessary to state that on every floor of the mill the hands were exposed to many and great dangers from unprotected bands and wheels, and from insufficiently fenced shafting; these are the invariable features of factory labour without any official regulations. On the whole, I cannot conceive a case more clear and simple; the Hindoo children are surely entitled to the same protection which the law has so long afforded to "young persons" in the United Kingdom.

With regard to the natives of India generally, I had of course, in a short stay at Kurrachee and Bombay, no opportunity of looking widely or deeply into their condition. But it appears that there is a strong disposition in the minds of leading men in the Government of India towards fair treatment, and even liberality, in official dealings with natives. There are, however, two grievances, both widespread, and both of the highest importance, which are heard of in every part of India, and which appear to baffle the wisest and most conscientious legislators.

"True," says the native subject of the Empress of India, "you have given us good government. You are mercilessly punctual and exacting in your demands, and the unfailing regularity and uniformity of these charges are, some say, almost perhaps as painful as would be the varying leniency and rapacity of native rulers. But under your rule, that which we have we possess in safety; where we lose, is in the fact that the expenditure of Government and of the governing body is not made in India, but in England." The complaint is indeed very much the same as that which comes with great force from Ireland. The Crown of Great Britain, like a great absentee landlord, collects a vast rent roll in India, which is expended in the savings of civil and military servants transmitted and retained in England; in their clothing, and in the many articles of food and luxury which are purchased in England. Even the trappings of State pageantry bear the mark of London. "In all this," say the natives, "we lose greatly; if we had native rulers, they would not be so invariably just, nor would peace and order be so secure; they perhaps would lavish money in fighting, and squander other sums in semi-barbaric display. But all their outlay would be with us, and among ourselves." It cannot be denied that there is very much which is, to say the least, plausible, in this line of argument.

For the other grievance the means of remedy or alleviation are less difficult. This relates to the land, and to the poverty of the cultivators. They borrow small sums at high rates of interest; they are ignorant; they are sometimes unfortunate; their simple agriculture is peculiarly at the mercy of the seasons. Principal and interest are added and re-added; the money-lenders are perhaps dishonest, and obtain acknowledgment of a document the real nature of the contents of which is unknown to the poor ignorant peasant. At last, the debt, or alleged debt, with its quickly mounting interest, has become big enough to bear comparison with the value of the unhappy rayah's interest in the land, upon which the toil of his whole life has been bestowed. Then he is hurried by the money-lender before the English magistrate; the debt, or alleged debt, is proved. By what process this proof is accomplished the peasant is often profoundly ignorant. No account is taken of the circumstances; the inexorable logic of written evidence—the verdict of the British rule—is all against him; judgment is given, and in the end his little property is sold to the money-lender, who has from first to last made a very successful transaction. Meanwhile the peasant, with a heart full of bitterness, has gone to ruin, bearing with him in his destitution a miserable sense that he has been jostled out of his homestead with the sanction of an English judge.

The Englishman urges that under native rule things would be much the same. Men must pay their debts. "No," says the native, "it would not be so under native rule. Native justice is wilder, less terribly regular, less legal, but probably more equitable. The rayah, under native rule, would have a better chance against the money-lender." And in this conclusion the native objector is no doubt to some extent justified. Here then is one of the most difficult of legislative problems for the consideration of Indian legislators. Would it be judicious —we cannot deny that it is possible—to give tenure which should be free from responsibility for debt—to give the cultivator something which the money-lender could not claim? Every man would like to be, if even to some extent only, invulnerable, so that in whichever direction "the shafts and arrows of outrageous fortune" might fly, these could not wound him irreparably. Everyone would like to have security against being stripped naked by creditors, and turned helpless and shivering upon the desert of utter and extreme poverty. Would not the end be, that the borrowing would continue with heightened rates of interest, and the rayah, under this coveted protection, would fall into poverty more extended and miserable than even he has yet known?

That which struck me most in passing through the Suez Canal is the seeming insignificance of the work. In some places, the water surface is not more than ninety feet wide; and standing upon the deck of a ship of three thousand tons burden one must look almost perpendicularly over the vessel's side to see the water of the Canal. We stuck fast for an hour in such a place, the head of our ship pressing upon one side, the stern upon the other of the narrow channel. This of course involved a similar delay for the vessels which followed us. On gaining the inland waters of the wide expanse which is still called "the Bitter

Lakes," ships are allowed to travel at full speed; and great efforts are made in order to obtain precedence in the succeeding narrows.

We landed at Ismailia, and proceeded by railway to Cairo, a town which resembles Algiers in that it is French in one part and thoroughly Mussulman in another. A more or less accurate notion of the bright bazaars of Cairo is a common possession; and how the English go to the Pyramids, trotting through the dust upon sprightly donkeys, is well known.

At Alexandria I fulfilled a promise in writing the following letter to Lord Henry Lennox, then First Commissioner of Works, concerning the removal of "Cleopatra's Needle," a work which he had been urged to undertake:—

"Hôtel Abbat, Alexandria, April 1, 1876.

"DEAR LORD HENRY LENNOX,—A long time has elapsed since our conversation in July last with reference to the removal of the obelisk commonly known as 'Cleopatra's Needle,' as proposed by General Sir James Alexander to the Metropolitan Board of Works. Detained in Persia by an attack of fever, and by unlooked-for difficulties in travelling, I have arrived in Egypt later by more than three months than I intended when I left England.

"The taking away of the ancient monuments from a

country which they were originally designed to adorn is a policy against which there is much to be said. It is almost pitiful to contemplate upon the now carefully protected Acropolis of Athens, a Caryatide rudely carved in wood doing duty with her four lovely sisters of marble in bearing the entablature of the Erectheum, while the original is in London, instructing the art world, perhaps no better than would a plaster cast, in the beauty and grace of Greek sculpture. But these considerations do not apply, with any considerable force, to the prostrate obelisk now lying upon the shore of the new port of Alexandria. It forms no part of any structure; it is not protected nor in anyway cared for by the Egyptians; and within fifty yards of the ground in which the 'English' column is lying, there is another, apparently of the same age and size, carved with hieroglyphics of similar character. It appears to me, therefore, that the English people could, if they please, appropriate this gift free from any fear or feeling that in doing so they would be 'spoiling the Egyptians.'

"The desirability of removing the obelisk resolves itself into two questions—the cost, and the value and interest of the monument as compared with the necessary expenditure. There can be no doubt as to the feasibility of removal. An opinion has certainly prevailed in England that the obelisk is so much defaced and broken as to have lost all interest. But

I will venture to say that this opinion has not been formed by any one who has seen the whole of three sides which have been exposed by the excavations recently made by Sir James Alexander. The opinion was formed when but very little more than the upper side of the base was visible, a valueless part which appears never to have been sculptured, and to have been intended for burial in the foundation when the obelisk was in position. The column, as at present exposed, is at once seen to be a monument of great value and interest, one which, not only for its antiquity, but also from its quality as a monolith, would be specially notable in London, which, unlike most of the capital cities of Europe, possesses no adornment of this character. The English people cannot see in their own country a carved stone even approaching the dimensions of this colossal obelisk of red granite. As to the condition of the monument, I have examined three of the four sides, and there is no part of any one of the hieroglyphics the carving of which is not distinctly traceable. The edges of the carving are somewhat worn, and the angles of the obelisk rounded; but the interest of the monument is in no place substantially impaired, nor is there discernible any important fracture of the stone. The dimensions of the obelisk are: Total length from extremity of base to apex, sixty-six feet; seven feet square at base, and four and a half feet square at base of apex. The weight is probably about two hundred and fifty tons.

"In considering the method and cost of removal to England, I have had the great advantage of the assistance on the ground of Captain Methven, the senior captain and commodore of the fleet of steamships belonging to the Peninsular and Oriental Company. The base of the obelisk is less than twenty yards from the waters of the Mediterranean; and within about a hundred yards there is a depth of two and a half fathoms of water. It has been suggested to float the obelisk by attaching to it a sufficient quantity of timber. But this is a very crude proposal, apart from the fact that no sufficient quantity of timber is obtainable in this almost treeless country. Undoubtedly it would be possible to remove and to ship the obelisk by constructing a railway on piles for such a distance as would admit of the approach of a vessel capable of carrying it securely to England. In this case, the obelisk would be suspended in slings from running-gear, and moved out to sea until it hung over its destined position in the vessel. But the shore is not the most suitable for this plan, which, moreover, would involve a very large expenditure.

"The position of the obelisk is favourable for the adoption of a third method, which appears both to Captain Methven and to myself to be the most easy, safe, and practicable; and, at the same time, the least costly of any that have been suggested. The ground in which the obelisk now lies seems sufficiently firm (with proper supports at the sides of the necessary excavation) to sustain girders from which the column could be slung without any change in its position. To insure a proper distribution of the weight, it would be desirable that these girders should rest on iron plates, and that they should be of greater substance in the centre, where the weight of the obelisk would be borne. Captain Methven is confidently of opinion that the obelisk could be safely conveyed to England in an iron vessel not exceeding four hundred tons of builders' measurement, one hundred and twenty feet in length, and drawing, when loaded, not more than six feet of water. This decked iron vessel, or barge, would be constructed in England and sent in pieces to Alexandria, where it would be put together in the space to be excavated beneath the suspended obelisk, the channel necessary to get to deep water being at the same time formed by a steam dredge, or, if the shore is rocky, by blasting—a method which has been very successfully adopted on a much larger scale than would be requisite here by the Peninsular and Oriental Company at Bombay. When the vessel was ready to receive the obelisk, the intervening wall of earth between the base of the stone and the sea would be thrown down, and the incoming water would raise the vessel to its burden. The iron barge could then be towed into the harbour, when it would be decked and have so much freeboard added as appeared desirable. Captain Methven feels quite sure that by any competent steamship of her Majesty's Navy the vessel could be towed to England without danger of damage to the towing ship, or risk of losing the obelisk, regard being had to the season and to the state of the barometer on quitting this port and that of Gibraltar. Finally, I would say that Captain Methven seems to be of opinion that all this could be accomplished at a cost of about five thousand pounds.

"Yours faithfully,
"ARTHUR ARNOLD.
"The Rt. Hon. Lord H. G. Lennox, M.P."

In Egypt, we see Mahommedanism through a veneer of Parisian civilisation. The Khedive, a Mussulman in *gants de Paris*, is in fact the *entrepreneur* of the country, concerning which his Highness deals with the financiers of Europe. His personality as a ruler never appears to rise out of the business of entertaining, concessionising, and loan-mongering, in which, to the outside world, his Highness seems always to be engaged. Mr. Cave had just left Egypt when we arrived in the country, and during our railway journey between the two capitals, Cairo and

Alexandria, an incident occurred, which I give for what it is worth; but which seemed to me to be very truly illustrative of the Government of Egypt. Certainly it displayed what Egyptians think practicable and probable in the way of Government by Ministers of the Khedive. A well-known banker of Alexandria, a European, was travelling in the same carriage with us, and, on the way, we had some conversation. At an unimportant station he was greeted by two men of the country, cultivators or corn-dealers of a superior class, Mahommedans, who at once engaged with him in earnest talk. On resuming the journey, I asked my fellow-traveller what had been the subject of discussion, so full, judging from the manner of those engaged, of interest and amusement.

"Oh!" he replied, "they were talking to me about Mr. Cave's report. They say that in anticipation of Mr. Cave's inquiry, the Khedive ordered the collection of a year and a half's taxes in one sum, and in advance, and that the amount was then set down as one year's payment, in order to deceive the British financier. And the worst of it is," he added, "the wretched fellaheen expect that the tax-gatherers will come round all the same, and treat the payment which was said to be for a year and a half as an extraordinary affair, a sort of backshish for the Khedive."

In passing through Egypt, I looked with all the care I could command to find traces of that intelligent government, which has been so often attributed in England, to the Khedive. I compared what I observed with all that I have seen in Turkey and Persia, and though in this comparison there was a marked difference, with much advantage on the side of Egypt, I saw everywhere, in native hideousness in the rural districts, and in the towns, beneath the sham civilisation of modern Egypt, the horrid features of slavery and its twin, polygamy, with the universal degradation which follows in the train of these institutions of Mahommedanism. The people of Egypt are far less civilised, less intelligent, incomparably more ignorant and cruel, than the most wretched of the Christian subjects of the Porte; and Egypt differs notably from European Turkey, in the fact that the overwhelming majority of the people are Mussulmans. There are many in England who, in the devotion of their lives and language to horses, seem as much disposed to serve as to rule the four-footed animal; and that a horse can show itself superior to men is officially demonstrated at least once a year in Cairo, when the mounted Sheik-ul-Islam rides over the prostrate bodies of fanatics, or, as some say, of hirelings. The unwilling quadruped shoved forward by the hands of modern Egyptians, its brute nature revolting from a cruelty to men, while they, the bipeds, affect to regard the animal as the instrument of a miracle, is a spectacle, the human degradation of which is perhaps deepened by the presence of cultivated Europeans as interested spectators. My impression is, that a good many English *en voyage* (and French and Germans are very often no better) are attracted rather than repelled by disgusting exhibitions, and that if only a spurious halo of propriety were thrown over the scene by the name of religion, they would throng to observe circumcision, or human sacrifice, or even the culinary operations of cannibals. Yet, as to the last, I am perhaps wrong, for in that there would be an element of personal danger. It is then they shrink—it is then they show a surprising keenness of apprehension. "See how they run," when cholera has invaded their hotel, or the waves their steamboat. But they will stand, in seeming approval, while the people of the foreign country in which they are sojourners degrade and deface humanity; they will smile at the performance of horrid cruelties, of which the law would take cognisance at home; they will flock to witness the performance of exercises associated with gross, and to them patent, superstitions; they will do all this, without a sign of disgust or disapproval.

From Persia, Egypt differs most obviously. Egypt Proper is fertile, flat, and well watered by the Nile and its tributaries, and, above all, it is nearer to the civilisation and to the highways of the commerce of Western Europe than are parts of that continent in the east of Russia. But in regard to the "poverty of the poor," or to their oppression in the name of the State, I doubt if there is much advantage on the side of the Egyptian. I was very much reminded of Persian officials when we were passing the ordeal—for it is an ordeal—of getting out of the port of Alexandria. While the Khedive's officers were examining our baggage, half a dozen porters and boatmen cried continually, "Give him something," "Give him a rupee," "Give him half a rupee," "Give him a cup of coffee," while the eyes of the Customs' officer twinkled with hope of the usual bribe. I have heard that a main obstacle to the success of Egyptian railways is the impossibility of preventing the officials from illicit trading in free passages, and I can well believe it. From the Khedive, who emulates the Padishah upon the Bosphorus, in multiplying his palaces at the cost of his miserable subjects and of deluded bondholders, to the murderous deeds of the semi-savages in his service upon the Nile, or in Abyssinia, or in Bulgaria, the Egyptian vice-royalty shows itself more prosperous, but not less marked with extravagance and excess, than the supreme and suzerain power in Constantinople.

CHAPTER XIV.

"From the Levant"—Sunnis and Shi'ahs—Turkish Government and Turkish debt—Fuad and Midhat Pashas—Not a "sick man"—"Best police of the Bosphorus"—Religious sanction for decrees—The Council of State—"Qui est-ce qu'on trompe?"—Murad and Hamid—Error of the West—Precepts of the Cheri—Authority of the Sultan—Non-Mussulman population—Abd-ul-Hamid's Hatt—A foreign garrison—Hatt-y-Houmayoun of 1856—Failure of promises—Fetva of Sheik-ul-Islam—Non-Mussulmans and the army—Firman of December, 1875—Sir Henry Elliot and the Porte—Conscription in Turkey.

A SERIES of letters,* published in 1868, contained our impressions of travel in Greece and in European Turkey. We then visited Thessaly, Roumelia, Constantinople and the Bosphorus, Bulgaria, Roumania, Belgrade, and Croatia. I have no intention of retracing this ground on paper, and my present reference to the affairs of Turkey will only be such as is necessary to exhibit the connexion which exists between the Government of the Sultan and the Mahommedan religion.

I propose to devote the remaining space in this volume to a survey of the general condition of the

* "From the Levant." By Arthur Arnold. Chapman and Hall. 1868.

Mahommedan peoples referred to in the preceding chapters, as affected by the doctrines of the founder of Islam set forth in the Koran. And in this survey the principal place must be given to the political circumstances of Turkey, which is the head-quarters of that larger division of Mahommedans known as Sunnis, as Persia is the head-quarters of the smaller, but still powerful, division known by the name of Shi'ahs.

The prestige of the Caliphate must have been greatly shaken by the catastrophe which ended in the suicide of Abd-ul-Aziz, and by the puppet reign of the unhappy Murad. But these events have called attention to the real position of the Sultan, which, during twenty years of peace, had been somewhat overlooked, possibly because in those years the conquests of the Turks have been, not territorial but financial. The Turkish Government has been the most successful spendthrift of our time. But the day of reckoning arrived, and the Turk could no longer provide the bait with which for twenty years he had been catching a rich provision from Europe. General Ignatieff thought the bubble would have burst at least eighteen months before the declaration of insolvency actually occurred. But when, at last, it broke, this generation saw that which was for most of them a strange sight. They were enlightened as to the basis of the Sultan's power; they saw him regarded as that which is his true character, an acclaimed chief rather than a hereditary sovereign; the head of Islam, with power bestowed and established under the sanctions of the Koran.

If Fuad Pasha [whose disciple, Midhat, is striving for supremacy] had an ideal system of government, it was that which a man far greater than he, but with a mind of similar tendencies, had expounded in *Les Idées Napoléoniennes*. To reconstruct the Caliphate, to reform it into a liberal despotism seated upon the heads of a dumb democracy—this was the thought of the great Minister with whose death is supposed to have departed the glory of the reign of Abd-ul-Aziz. The revolution which cast that wretched Sultan from an eminence of power, awful in its solitude and responsibility to those who can conceive its full extent and authority, to a condition of restraint and imprisonment which rendered life unendurable, was proclaimed as a reversion to the policy of Fuad Pasha. Midhat Pasha was hailed as the political heir of the ex-medical student of Paris. Mahmoud Pasha, with his Russian leanings, was pushed away into outer darkness; in Besika Bay, England had congregated the largest fleet of ironclads that had ever been brought together under one flag; she was hailed as the friend, the inalienable ally of Turkey, which the new Ministers were prepared to show was not a "sick man," or, if sick, that, as Fuad himself said, "Turkey had no organic malady."

Then, in those tumultuous days when the power of Abd-ul-Aziz was passing away, were perpetrated the atrocities, the tearful and bloody record of which Europe has written upon pages that for all time will stand as a dreadful memorial of Turkish misrule. These are, it is now understood, wild fruits which grow by the way-side of the Mahommedan system. Never since 1868, when he became acquainted with the country, has the present writer consciously neglected an opportunity of denouncing the Turkish rule, of showing that the Turkish Empire has organic disease, and that her incurable malady grows ever more deadly as she is forced by new arterial connexions closer and more closely into the light of the political ideas and civilisation of Western Europe. It is not difficult to reduce the pleas for the maintenance of the Turkish Empire to that one plea of expediency, upon which, indeed, the greatest master of Turkish policy, Fuad Pasha, was content to rest its claim when he said, "We are the best police of the Bosphorus," nor to show that the validity of this plea is a reproachful testimony to the greed, and jealousy, and want of true civilisation on the part of the Great Powers of Europe.

The Turkish power is a Mahommedan theocracy. No law is popularly accepted as valid unless it has religious sanction. The Statute Book must run with the Koran. The neglect on the part of the Turkish Power in regard to the fulfilment of the pledges inscribed in the Hatt-y-Houmayoun of 1856, of the due performance of which the other Powers then felt themselves assured, does not vex the mind of a genuine Turk. Those promises were but wind—we will not, as Mr. Gladstone said, call them "air." The obligation to fulfil them was not to be found within the pages of the Koran. They were not, they have never been, endorsed with the *fetva* of the Sheik-ul-Islam. They had not the sanction of the Church. The *fetva* of the Sheik-ul-Islam—which is nought if it does not imply the consent of the whole body of Mussulman clergy — was needed before any could engage in the dethronement of Abd-ul-Aziz. It was needed to put an end to the three months' existence of Murad with the names of Sultan and of Padishah.

In the first chapter of this work, in regard to the Capitulations of 1675, we have seen that the outward manifestation of this theocratic basis can be suppressed. No Grand Vizier offering a Treaty to England, would now style his master "Emperor and Conqueror of the Earth with the assistance of the Omnipotent and the especial grace of God, the Prince of Emperors and the Dispenser of Crowns." Even in the Treaty of 1856 there is no trace of divine authority about the attributes of the Sultan. He is simply styled "Emperor of the Ottomans." This was the work of A'ali and Fuad, the great exemplars of the present time. It is not a final condemnation of the Turkish Power to say that it is theocratic, for the possession of that quality and sanction has been the pretence of all Powers, and is still the reputed basis of most of the Powers of Europe. In his own dominions, the Tsar is just as much the "Shadow of God," as the Sultan. We must look to the ethics of the religion which is the ground upon which such authority is claimed. Mere forms of speech can be changed, and the language of Paris put into the mouth of the Padishah. When a great utterance was composed for Abd-ul-Aziz, the Napoleonic was the most approved form of composition. Had I been blind, I could have fancied myself at the Tuileries on the 10th of May, 1868, when amid hopes not less extravagant than those which encircled the first days of poor Murad's elevation, his ill-fated predecessor, announced the establishment of the Council of State and the High Court of Justice. He, the successor of Sultans whose pretensions to divine direction had not been less declared than those of the infallible Pope; he who was in fact the Pope of the Sunni Mahommedans, confessed that something was wrong, something rotten in his State, "because," said the master of greedy pashas, "if the principles and laws already established had answered to the exigences of our country and our people, we ought to have found ourselves to-day in the same rank as the most civilised and best administered States of Europe." With this naïve admission of failure, and "with a view to promote the rights of his subjects," Abd-ul-Aziz, the reformer, whose praise was then hymned in leading articles nowhere more loudly than in England, pronounced the establishment of the Council of State, "whose members are taken from all classes of our subjects without exception." "Another body," he continued, "instituted under the name of the High Court of Justice, has been charged to assure justice to our subjects in that which concerns the security of their persons, their honour, and their property."

No Christian could speak more fairly. To those who know something of the Turkish system all this was "words," and nothing more. "Qui est-ce qu'on trompe?"* said Prince Gortschakoff to Lord Augustus Loftus concerning Turkish reports. But they did deceive England, for one reason—because we have always had a large party, composed of men of both sides in politics, who did not wish for an exposition of the true condition of Turkey, who were willing to be deceived, and to deceive others. These were the bondholders, who, whatever happened, feared

---

* Correspondence respecting the Affairs of Turkey, No. 58.

to speak ill of Turkey, lest in doing so the value of their property should be depreciated. With regard to the Turkish Empire, the bondholders have always been optimists, and they have had a very powerful influence upon public opinion. Men talked and wrote of Abd-ul-Aziz, as they talked and wrote, for a few days, of Murad, and assumed then, as they were ready to assume in the case of Murad, and as they are now ready—though they are, it must be admitted, less confident, in the case of Abd-ul-Hamid — to assume, that a man whose youth has been passed under suppression and surveillance; to whom education has been denied as dangerous; upon whom comparative continence and frugality have been enforced, would, when he acquired unlimited power and wealth—when he could indulge unchecked the favourite weaknesses of the Prophet—be a lover of liberty and law, a wise and liberal statesman, the husband of one wife, the master of no slaves, and in his private expenditure the delight of anxious bondholders. It has been the inveterate error of the West to suppose that in Turkey figs grow from thistles—that beautiful women are produced by a life in rooms from which the glorious eye of the heavens, as well as the sight of man, is excluded; by walking out of doors in veils, which prevent every breath of fresh air; in shoes and upon stones, which render exercise a torture, and graceful carriage an impossibility; by a life of inanity, ignorance, and indulgence in unwholesome food. The error is not uncommon, nor its cause recondite. We have glanced at the self-delusion of the interested; but there are others who have made this error. Their mistake is akin to that of the dramatists of the Restoration, who, Lord Macaulay says, knew not that "drapery is more alluring than exposure." The mystery of the East has been their delusion, and this mystery, if it is faced closely and fairly, especially if it is regarded during moments when, in the political struggle, its veil is disarranged, is, as we shall see, a cover for evils which prefer darkness rather than light in social life—a despotism, with slavery for a domestic institution, and upon the throne of European Turkey, a misrepresentation founded upon force, upheld by oppression of those who are its subjects, and by the jealousies of the Powers which are entitled its protectors.

The language of the present Sultan curiously resembles that I have quoted from the proclamation of Abd-ul-Aziz. Abd-ul-Hamid declared that,[*] "the critical condition of the Empire arises from a bad application of the laws, based upon the precepts of the Cheri [a codification of the laws of the Koran], and hence have resulted financial discredit, defective working of the tribunals, and the non-development

---

Daily' News Report of Imperial Hatt, Sept. 1876.

of trade, manufactures, and agriculture. To remedy these evils, a Special Council will be charged to guarantee the exact execution of existing laws, or those measures which may be promulgated in accordance with the Cheri. The Council will also superintend the Budget. Public functions will be entrusted to capable persons, who will be held responsible, and will no longer be dismissed without cause."

The same remedy, a "Council," is proposed, but there is a more frank admission in the Hatt of 1876, that the Government of Turkey is founded upon the precepts of the Koran. The Turkish Government has ceased to represent itself to foreign powers as theocratic, but regarding its subjects, this is its truest title. When, in 1856, the Sultan appeared, as we have seen, to throw off in deference to his Christian protectors of the Latin and Anglican Churches, the assumption of divine authority, it was in fact asserted, though in language purely mundane. He was styled "Emperor of the Ottomans," that is, of the Othmans—of the followers of the conqueror whose sword Abd-ul-Hamid has girded on in the mosque of Ey-yub, the leader, in fact, of three millions out of twelve millions of people in Europe, supreme ruler by no other right than that of possession, having no consent or true allegiance from the vast majority of the people of European Turkey, being, in fact, successor of Mahommed in the Caliphate, and of Othman in the Empire. Two facts I may mention which exhibit the true character of the Sultan's rule most clearly; the Mahommedan is to the Christian population in European Turkey as one to three; but the non-Mahommedan people are excluded from the army by which the Sultan's power is maintained. I have quoted the language in which the Council of State was announced. In its formation, the Council was a scandal, and in existence it has been the means of further enriching the oppressors of the country. The non-Mussulman population being as three to one, A'ali Pasha, the idol of the Softas, composed a Council, which indeed exhibited this proportion, but with the figures reversed—three-fourths of its members being Mussulmans.

When Murad was put on the throne, the same farce was played, but the language was less grandiloquent. The Grand Vizier addressed himself, viâ Murad [the Hatt was addressed to "my illustrious Vizier"], in phrases adapted from the failure of 1868.* " The domestic and foreign difficulties of the Government have brought about, in public opinion, a want of confidence which, by disturbing the sense of security in every way, has entailed very material losses. It is necessary to put an end to this state of things, and to find a remedy for it; it is

---

* Imperial Hatt, dated June 1, 1876.

necessary to adopt a line of conduct which shall ensure the welfare, as well as the material and moral prosperity of all our subjects. The realisation of these aspirations depends upon the establishment, upon a really sound basis, of the principles of Government administration, and this consummation is the ever-present object of my care." .... " All our subjects, without exception, shall enjoy full and complete liberty .... and in order to carry out this project .... and with a view to this most essential result, it is both important and necessary that the Council of State .... should be reorganised." Abd-ul-Hamid has said, or implied, at least as much, and we are thus brought to the position in which Statesmen, such as Fuad and Midhat Pashas find themselves when, after entering into promises in the French of Paris, they are surrounded with realities in the Arabic of Stamboul. They can make Hatts, of course, but if these surpass the sanctions of the Koran, they must rest in the pigeon-holes of the Sublime Porte.

The Government of Turkey is unquestionably Mahommedan, and the course of this survey leads us now to inquire what are the inalienable essentials of Mahommedanism? what is its capacity for change, for reinterpretation, in accordance with modern ideas? The position of the Turkish Government, thus representing only one-fourth of the people in the European Empire, and claiming sovereignty over other millions in Servia and Roumania, who have successfully repudiated any direct interference on the part of the Sultan with their internal affairs, is that of a foreign garrison, the soldiery having no connexion with the mass of the people. This Government and garrison cohere by force of religious ties. Both are Mahommedan. It was long ago admitted by powerful friends of Turkey, that is to say, by the Governments of England, France, and Italy, that the only safe path for the Empire in the future lay in the abandonment of this exclusive mode of Government; and it was A'ali Pasha who, in the famous Hatt-y-Houmayoun of 1856, promised the overthrow of the Mahommedan system. To make this assurance more certain, he consented, on behalf of his master, that the contracting Powers of 1856 should be made parties to the execution of this Hatt, by a special reference to it in the ninth Article of the Treaty. Of the thirty-five Articles of this Hatt-y-Houmayoun, the most interesting and, from my point of view, the most important articles have, as Mr. Butler Johnstone, a friend to the Turkish Power, writes, "remained dead letters." I will take his remarks upon this neglect, because there can be no doubt that he does not overstate the case. Referring to the promises of the Hatt-y-Houmayoun, Mr. Butler Johnstone says:—

"(a) There were to be mixed tribunals of justice, codification of the law, translations of the codes into the different languages of the Empire, settled modes of procedure: this has been translated, as we have seen, into mock courts, unpaid judges, arbitrary procedure; and corrupt decisions. (b) Farming the revenue was to be abolished, and a sounder fiscal system established: nothing of the kind has been done. (c) A solemn undertaking was entered into to grapple with the evil of corruption: at present the whole administration is corrupt. (d) Banks were to be established to assist agriculture and come to the aid of commerce: nothing of the sort has been thought of. (e) Roads, canals, and railroads were to be pushed forward with vigour, so as to open up the resources of the country: the absence of roads and canals has prevented the relief of a famished population; and as to railroads, the only important line finished was a cloak for a most notorious scandal. (f) Foreign capital was to be invited and encouraged by every means, so as to develope the great resources of the country: such vexatious obstructions have been placed in the way of foreign capital that it has shunned the country; and men of integrity like Scott Russell and T. Brassey have had all their offers rejected. Unless the pashas catch a glimpse of backshish, foreign enterprise is an abomination in their eyes. (g) Christians were to be admitted into the army on the principles of general equality: nothing of the sort has taken place."

These promises, made by Abd-ul-Medjid, are in all important points identical with those made by Abd-ul-Aziz; they were implied in the Hatt of Murad, from which I have quoted, and they were understood to be adopted by Abd-ul-Hamid. Midhat Pasha is, no doubt, prepared, if he gets opportunity, to follow Fuad and A'ali in the political dishonesty of manufacturing Imperial edicts, made for show and not for use, which cannot have operation in the Turkish Empire, because no law is there held valid which has not the *fetva* of the Sheik-ul-Islam and the general assent of the clergy. I shall contend that these promises are made without regard to the basis of Turkish law — the Koran; that they cannot be executed without a complete surrender of Mahommedan principles, involving, ultimately, an overthrow of the Mahommedan Empire.

A Mahommedan Government could not perform the promises of the Hatt of 1856 without ceasing to be Mahommedan; because Mahommedanism, as a religious system, does not admit the followers of other creeds to administrative co-operation upon terms of equality. The Turkish Government promised codification of law, and independent tribunals of European pattern. How is it possible to put the laws of the Koran into a code acceptable to Christians? The

Turkish Government promised to admit the whole population to the military service on the principle of equality. But this is equivalent to making the army three-fourths non-Mussulman, a situation in which Mahommedan supremacy in the Government could not endure for twenty-four hours. By a monstrous euphemism, the exclusion of the non-Mussulman population from the army is charged to them as "exemption," and they are made to pay about five shillings per man to establish their own degradation. The Christian peasants may, in some parts, be too ignorant to comprehend that in this exclusion their oppression is established. Yet the true character of the tax is very evident from the fact that it has been imposed, not only upon able-bodied men, but in respect of male infants from their birth, and old men long past military service.* This was one of the grievances of the Bulgarians, and by a Firman of last December, the Porte was pledged not to levy the tax upon infants and old men. But this promise, like all the promises of the Turkish Government, was worthless, and Sir Henry Elliot reported to Lord Derby that "unless the Turkish Government were to abandon a large proportion of the revenue derived from the tax, it became necessary greatly to raise the amount to be paid by each individual of an age to

---

Correspondence, No. 33.

serve."* The Government, therefore, with no remonstrance from Sir Henry Elliot, declined to give the tax the appearance even of an exemption charge; and the British Ambassador has reported that this demand, even of an instalment of justice, has led to a discussion of the liability of Christians to military service; for which he has said, "some of them, and especially the Bulgarians, are showing themselves disposed to ask. They are aware that the conscription would, in many respects, press more heavily upon them than the exemption tax; but they know, likewise, that no Firmans or regulations will do so much to bring about a real equality between Mussulman and Christian."† That which, of course, these poor people have not hitherto realised is that a conscription, fairly conducted among the population of Turkey in Europe, could only end in the substitution of Christian for Mahommedan supremacy in the Empire.

Abd-ul-Aziz was Sultan when despatch No. 33 was written; he was in his grave when Sir Henry Elliot returned to the subject on the 8th June. His Excellency has always shown himself more solicitous for the preservation of the Turkish Empire than for the just administration of the Sultan's power; and, accordingly, though regarding the exclusion of the non-Mussulman people from the army as "the one

---

Correspondence, No. 33.   † Id.

great badge of distinction existing between the two races," admitting that "the Christians have become aware that until it is swept away their nominal equality with the Mussulmans cannot be complete and real;" he urges that "it is not necessary that the conscription should at once be put in force among the Christian population; but the military schools should at once be opened to them, and they might be received either as volunteers or as substitutes for Mussulmans drawn as conscripts." Of course the Christians would resist a conscription which sought to make them tools of the misgoverning rule to which they are subject, and from which they have at all times suffered grievous wrongs. They are unequal and unable to appreciate the ultimate results of such a measure in the subversion of the Mahommedan Power.

CHAPTER XV.

Islam in Persia—Mahommedans of India—Ali of the Shi'ahs—Abu-Bekr, successor of Mahommed—Imāms of the Shi'ahs—Reza and Mehdee—Religion in the East—Mahommed as a soldier—War with infidels—Christianity of Middle Ages—Stretching the Koran —Mahommed's marriage law—Status of Mahommedan women— Women and civilisation—Special privilege of Mahommed—Mormonism and Mahommedanism—Consequences of polygamy— Protection of polygamy—Mahommed and Ayesha—Scandal silenced by the Koran—Mahommed's domestic difficulty—Law for men and women — Women in Mahommed's heaven — The Mahommedan Paradise—Mahommed and the Jews—Birth of Christ in the Koran—Miracles of Christ—English loaning to Islam—Mahommedanism and Christianity—Christians of the East—Moslem intemperance—Wine and the Koran—Superiority of Christianity.

LET us now glance at the peculiarities of Persian Mahommedanism, which should have special interest for Englishmen, inasmuch as the dissent of the Persians shows the difference which exists in that large body of our Indian fellow-subjects, amounting to about 40,000,000, whose Mahommedanism is so often referred to as a matter which should rule our policy in Turkey, and as a danger to our Empire in India.

Islam in India is divided into Shi'ahs and Sunnis, a distinction which separates the Mahommedans of

Persia, who are Shi'ahs, from the Mahommedans of Turkey, who are Sunnis. In the Christian world, the Greek and Latin Churches exhibit a similar point of union, and a somewhat similar difference. Both are united in Christ; yet in the world, and in the practice of the religion which they allege to be that of Christ, the Greek and the Roman Churches live as theological enemies. As a rule, theological rancour increases between religious bodies in proportion as their tenets approximate; and, accordingly, in Constantinople we find that the bitterest sectarian enmities exist between the Armenian Catholics and the Armenian Orthodox, their difference seeming to outside observers to be merely "that twixt tweedledum and tweedledee." In the Mahommedan Church, some animosity divides Shi'ahs and Sunnis, separating Persian and Turk—the Shi'ah of northern, from the Sunni of central and southern, India. There are villages in Eastern Persia, and in Affghanistan, inhabited by a mixed population of Shi'ahs and Sunnis, and in some of these, in order to prevent disturbance, the Shi'ahs are confined to one side of a road, while the other side is exclusively devoted to Sunnis.

When Mahommed fought the "Battles of God," Ali, his brave son-in-law, husband of the Prophet's only surviving daughter, Fatima, was ever in the thickest of the fight. He was the Ajax of the heroes of Medina in the warfare against Mecca. If there was single combat to be done, Ali was the man who stepped forward to slay the champion of idolatrous Arabia; it was the flashing vengeance of Ali's scimitar which brought back the tide of battle when it had ebbed away from the standard of the Prophet. But Ali was not the immediate successor of Mahommed in governing the Church-militant of Medina. Among the earliest of the followers of the Prophet, among the companions of his flight—that "Hegira," from which all Mahommedan people date their time, as all Europe, outside Turkey, does from the birth of Christ—was one Abu-Bekr, upon whom it is said Mahommed called, in the agonies of death, to take his place in the mosque of Medina.

In a corner of the courtyard of this mosque stood the Prophet's home, including the apartments of his nine wives. It was in the room of his favourite wife, the beautiful and vivacious Ayesha, that he lay dying, when, according to Sunni belief, he summoned Abu-Bekr to the pulpit, and was held by this act to have indicated a preference as to his successor in the position of ruler or Caliph. After the Prophet's death, Abu-Bekr was acclaimed to this position—the spiritual and temporal headship of Islam. From that time to these days of the unhappy Abd-ul-Aziz, and Murad, and Hamid, the person acclaimed Caliph upon the death or deposition of his predecessor, has been accepted by the Sunni Mahommedans as their chief. For ages this great title has remained with the descendants of Othman; and from him the Turks have acquired the name of Ottomans, or Osmanli. But this restriction to the line of Othman is an accident—a convenience; the line has become sacred by unbroken descent of the Caliphate; but that is all. Turks have become accustomed to hereditary descent of the superior power; but this form of succession is no fundamental principle of their system; and though théir ruler is head of the Church and State, he is, as we have seen, liable to deposition by the authority of the Church. It was the *fetva* of the Sheik-ul-Islam which confirmed Hussein Avni and Midhat Pashas in their resolve to dethrone Abd-ul-Aziz. With the Sunni Mahommedans, the Sultan represents the power of the Prophet.

With the Shi'ahs it is otherwise. To the Shi'ahs of Persia, the Shah is nothing but a supreme magistrate, whose office it is to govern in accordance with, and by the light of, the words of the Koran. With them, Imāms, that is, the full inheritors of the office of Mahommed, are too sublime to walk the earth in these degenerate days. Abu-Bekr was no Caliph of theirs; they repudiate him, and with him the title by which nearly all of his successors have reigned. To Ali, and to the descendants of Ali, especially to his son, the son of Fatima—to Houssein, murdered at Kerbela, is their homage given?* They acknowledge but twelve Imāms; and it is long since they have seen the last of these holy impersonations. The first three Imāms of the Shi'ahs were Ali and his two sons, Hassan and Houssein. The eighth was the very holy Réza, whose shrine at Meshed is always crowded; the twelfth and last, known by the name of Mehdee, was born A.D. 868, and, according to Shi'ah belief, was taken from the sight of men when he was only nine years old. Mehdee is the invisible Imām of the Shi'ahs; he is to return to earth some day, bearing with him the complete and perfect Koran, which, in the Shi'ah doctrine, was entrusted to the hands of Ali. For the Shi'ahs, the humanity of religion, the link between God and man, is found in Ali, and to a greater extent in Houssein; probably because the latter died a violent death.

Returning now to the general subject, I would say that observation of Mussulman authority in Europe, Asia, and Africa, has convinced me of the truth of the following opinion, penned by a distinguished upholder of Mahommedan rule in Turkey:—"Religion in the East," he most truly says, "has not the restricted meaning which it has with us. Everything with them [the Mahommedan peoples] is religious. All those questions which with us would be termed matters of politics, are with the Mahommedans matters of religion. Mahommedanism is, in fact, a religion, a code, and a civil polity, or, rather, these three things are different aspects of the same idea." Therefore, in order to master the internal springs of the Turkish system, we must go to the Koran.

Englishmen have been taken to the Koran by blind guides. Attempts like that of Mr. Bosworth Smith in his "Mohammed and Mohammedanism" have been made to varnish the Koran with modern and unnatural colouring. Ill-judged and inaccurate as I shall show these to have been, such attempts are not, perhaps, surprising. It is the widely spreading revolt against certain dogmas attributed to Christianity which has led to this shallow delight in the Koran, of which the central doctrine is that of the unity of God. The Mahommedan service of the grand mosque, still known to Europe by its Christian name, Santa Sophia, is in its outward aspect lofty and sublime; it is ennobled by a comparison with the mean mummeries of the altars of Seville, or with the farthing tapers and picture-kissings of Moscow. But that outward form of worship is not Mahommedanism; and these things—the wooden dolls of Spain, "Our Ladies" of Montserrat and Atocha, and of this place and that—dolls endowed with revenues and with sacristans for keepers of their wardrobes; the adored pictures of Moscow, devoid of beauty and of the charm of high and authentic antiquity—nor are these things Christianity.

We shall, however, be better able to appreciate the

error of these apologists of Mahommedanism when we have glanced at the leading doctrines of Mahommed. The Prophet of Islam was a soldier, the Napoleon of his age. If the great Corsican had lived twelve hundred years before his time, it is not improbable that *Les Idées Napoléoniennes* would have taken the form of the Suras of the Koran. The sword of Mahommed was never long in its scabbard. He dictated a chapter of the Koran while his cheek streamed with blood from a wound sustained in the battle of Ohud. The Koran encourages Islam to war with the infidel in these words :*—

"Fight on, therefore, till there be no temptation to idolatry, and the religion be God's."

"Fight for the religion of God against those who fight against you. Kill them wherever ye find them; and turn them out of that whereof they have dispossessed you; for temptation to idolatry is more grievous than slaughter."

"War is enjoined you against the infidel; but this is hateful unto you. Yet perchance ye hate a thing which is better for you; and perchance ye love a thing which is worse for you; but God knoweth and ye know not."

"When ye encounter the unbelievers, strike off their heads, until ye have made a great slaughter

⁎⁎ Sale's "Al Koran."

among them. ..... And, as to those who fight in defence of God's true religion, God will not suffer their works to perish; he will guide them, and dispose their heart aright; and he will lead them into Paradise, of which he hath told them. Oh! true believers, if ye assist God by fighting for his religion, he will assist you against your enemies, and will set your feet fast; but, as for the infidels, let them perish. .... This shall come to pass, for that God is the patron of the true believers; and for that the infidels have no protector."

Of course there is not in ordinary times an active desire to indulge in a crusade against overwhelming odds. The supreme teaching of utility is too strong for that. But every Moslem knows that the defeat of heresy by the sword is a cardinal point of Mahommed's teaching; and that Mahommed's Paradise is promised to those who fall in such conflict. It is no refutation of this to allege that the Christianity of the Middle Ages was no better, and to quote the Papal Legate who put the edge of the Roman Catholic sword to all throats with the words: "Kill all, God will know his own." Yet the error which is latent in this line of argument has to be exposed. It seems to some Englishmen to be a discovery, at once interesting and startling, that all systems of religion, those established before Christ as well as that of Mahommed, are inseparably related. They find, not only ideas, but dogmas transmitted; they learn to infer that Christianity is not the Alpha and Omega of religion. Standing in regard to the orthodox interpretation of their own sacred books somewhat in the attitude of "the poor cat i' the adage," "letting I dare not wait upon I would," they are overjoyed with the delicious *soupçon* of irrefragable heterodoxy thus imparted, and in their rapture fail to grasp the utilitarian chain which would lead them, link by link, to an invaluable test in this comparison.

They are not too careful how they deal with their own Bible when "the insuperable dogmatic character" of the Koran is in question. The Member for Canterbury, who, I presume, is with Lord Beaconsfield upon the side of the angels in the matter of Evolution, has argued that "the inspired character of the Christian sacred books has not prevented progress in religion in Europe, and for this reason—viz., that the inspired writings are sufficiently elastic in expression to admit of progressive developments and interpretations; otherwise religious thought, and with it civilisation, would have been strangled in the Christian world. And so it is with the Koran."

These desperate friends of Mahommedan power are blind to facts as well as tendencies. Stretch the doctrines of the Koran to the length they desire, and the religion of Mahommed is gone; strain them politically so as to establish a true equality of

Mahommedan and non-Mahommedan population, and the Empire of Othman must pass away. Of course, doctrines of the Koran may be amended by a revised interpretation—that is, some of them. Women need not be condemned to suffer ill-health from want of fresh air because the Koran tells them "to discover not their ornaments,"—to conceal their charms from all but certain persons. Upon this matter, directly affecting the whole population, there are several interpretations now in sight among Mahommedans. The Persians include the eyes, the Turks do not; and the opinion of high society in Constantinople has ceased, in fact, to include any part of the face, the only difference from European custom being that, whereas the veils of English ladies fall from the head-dress, and are not always worn, those of the belles of Stamboul, not less diaphanous, but indispensable, mount from the chin to the nose.

The Koran says, "Take in marriage such women as please you—two, three, or four, and not more;" but the faithful may enter into temporary connubial arrangements with any number "of those women" whom they have "acquired" as "slaves." It will be said that there is nothing in these words to prevent the spread of monogamy, which is already the established rule of life with many Turks. Nothing whatever; indeed, we find these words in the Koran: "If ye fear ye cannot act equitably towards so many, marry one only, or the slaves which ye shall have acquired." Moreover, it is obvious that time tends to encourage the decline of polygamy. The men of Constantinople who have but óne wife have not lost confidence in the teaching of the Koran. They are coming to European ways, because by increasing the individuality of women, civilisation has surrounded polygamy with embarrassments. Some of them say they prefer to have but one wife because of the better enjoyment of her society, and the avoidance of jealousies and difficulty in regard to children. Others admit that expense sways their mind; the ladies of Stamboul have acquired by association tastes which are very costly: a liking for jewelled watches, for Paris fashions in dress, in carriages, in furniture. Each one of Mahommed's nine wives had but a mud-built shed, all grouped in one corner of the ground surrounding the mosque at Medina. Ayesha alone would have ruined him if, with his means, the Prophet had humoured her extravagances in modern Stamboul.

Wherever Mahommedanism touches a higher civilisation, the woman at once gains individuality, the veil becomes more transparent, and polygamy is less common. Why? Because the progress of civilisation is synonymous with the advance of individuality, and individuality is both troublesome and costly in the persons of dependents. "There is nothing in the religion of Islam," said a writer of the highest authority in a recent article upon "the Situation viewed from Constantinople," "which can fairly be called adverse to civilisation." I shall abundantly expose the falsity of this proposition; but if the writer had said, "There is nothing in the religion of Islam which can withstand civilisation," I should have agreed with him. The thinly-veiled beauty of Constantinople has requirements unthought of by the secluded Persian lady, and thus the Turk is guided to the equitable law of monogamy. I will even admit that, in adopting this rule, the Moslem does not repudiate the sanctions of the Koran, and that, after a life spent in fidelity to one wife, he does not regard with scorn or contempt the "specially revealed" privileges of Mahommed in regard to polygamy. Yet it is hard to feel aught but disgust for Christian writers who degrade themselves by penning apologies for the rampant lust of Mahommed. He slaughtered a Jewish tribe, and selected a wife from those he had made widows. He coveted Zeinab, the wife of Zeid, his adopted son, and could not rest until he had compelled a divorce between Zeinab and Zeid, so that he might take Zeinab for himself. It was this last outrage which led Mahommed to perpetrate in the Koran his greatest offence. The lowest depths of historical imposture seem to contain nothing so foul as the deliberate admixture of special licence for himself, in regard to polygamy, with sacred principles of justice in the Koran. Surely I have made a larger concession than truth will admit, in saying that the practice of monogamy, which the apologists of the Turk rightly declare to be extending in Turkey, is consistent with reverence for the man who, because he wished to take for himself the wife of another, and could not gain possession of her as a slave, put these words into the mouth of the Mahommedan God :—

"O Prophet, we have allowed thee thy wives, unto whom thou hast given their dower, and also the slaves which thy right hand possesseth of the booty which God hath granted thee, and the daughters of thy uncles, and the daughters of thy aunts, both on thy father's side and on thy mother's side, who have fled with thee from Mecca, and any other believing woman, if she give herself unto the Prophet, in case the Prophet desireth to take her to wife. This is a peculiar privilege granted unto thee above the rest of true believers. . . . . Thou mayst postpone the turn of such of thy wives as thou shalt please. God, knoweth whatever is in your hearts, and God is knowing and gracious."*

* Sale's "Al Koran."

Joe Smith and Brigham Young have not been without success in their humbler way, and in more rational times, but it may fairly be doubted if they would have had as large a following had their sacred books contained special privileges of this sort for the leaders of Mormonism.

Polygamy, which implies the unnatural appropriation of women by the rich of the male sex, is responsible for much of the vice of Eastern nations. The worst side, the lustful inspiration of the Koran, is nowhere more strikingly exhibited than in the laws relating to adultery and fornication. Against the traffic in the latter vice the Koran is most severe, and in throwing down the house which I observed in ruins in Kashan, the Governor had only fulfilled the duties of a true Mussulman. The Koran says:— "If any of your women are guilty, produce four witnesses from among you against them, and if they bear witness against them, imprison them in separate apartments till death release them, or God affordeth them a way to escape." In the days of Mahommed, women were imprisoned under this law till they died, and their death was often brought about by starvation, or some other cruel means. Later, this practice was mitigated by the Sonna, and while their male partners in crime were of course free, unmarried women guilty of unchastity were scourged with a hundred stripes, and married women were stoned.

Women slaves, being held less accountable for their vices, received half the penalty to which free women were subject, and as stoning could not be done by halves, flogging was their punishment.

The polygamous households of Mahommed and his followers were protected by these laws; but for the crime of men against women the Koran has no punishment. "Compel not," says the Prophet, in the 24th Sura, "your maid servants to prostitute themselves, if they be willing to live chastely, that ye may seek the casual advantage of this present life; but whoever will compel them thereto, verily God will be gracious and merciful unto such women after their compulsion." This particular passage in a book held sacred by millions of mankind, was the "revealed" reply of Mahommed to the complaint of a woman, a slave in the household of Abd'allah Ebn Obba, who had six female slaves, on each of whom he laid a tax, and obliged them to pay it by the proceeds of an unchaste life. This suggestive rule of the Koran is still in operation, and we have had an opportunity of learning upon official authority how it works in Turkey. "A custom prevails here," Mr. Consul Abbott reported, "to exempt from military conscription a Mussulman young man who elopes with a Christian girl, and whom he converts to his faith. This being a meritorious act for his religion, it entitles him as a reward, to be freed from military service."* Mr. Abbott's expression "elopes with," is an obvious euphemism for "abducts."

A difficulty which occurred in the household of Mahommed, and which nearly caused the cruel death of Ayesha, the most beautiful and engaging of his wives, led to the issue of a Sura specially "sent down from heaven," which did inflict some punishment upon men in their relations with women, the inspiration being obviously the jealousy of Mahommed. In the sixth year of the Hegira, when Mahommed was beginning his career of conquest, he undertook a military expedition against the tribe of Mostalek, and on the march he was accompanied by his young wife Ayesha, who rode upon a camel, screened from all eyes in a curtained structure, fastened upon the back of the animal. One night, when the forces of the Prophet were returning to Medina, Ayesha ordered the driver to stop her camel. The animal was stopped, and made to kneel. In the darkness Ayesha retired a little way into the desert. In returning, according to her own account, she discovered that she had lost a necklace of onyxes, a gift from her husband, the Prophet. She therefore retraced her steps, looking carefully for the lost treasure. If a well-trained camel is placed upon its knees, it is not difficult to step from the harness into a carriage, or

---

* Consular Reports on the Condition of Christians in Turkey.

howdah, upon the animal's back. The driver supposed, after some minutes had elapsed, that Ayesha was again in her place, and taking this for certain, led the camel onwards.

When Ayesha regained the track, she found the camel gone, and sat herself down by the wayside, thinking, so she said, that search would soon be made for her. She fell asleep, and in the early dawn of morning was awaked by one Safwan, who trembled as he recognised the favourite wife of the Prophet. He awoke her. Ayesha said, by softly murmuring twice in her uncovered ear the words: "We are God's, and unto Him we must return." Ayesha's first instinct was to shroud herself from this man with her veil. She then allowed Safwan to set her upon his camel, and to lead her towards the army, in the rear of which Safwan had been one of the most distant stragglers. They overtook the forces of Mahommed when the soldiers were resting about the hour of noon. Immediately there was a great cry of scandal in the household of the Prophet, and Abd'allah Ebn Obba spread through the camp a charge of planned adultery with Safwan against Ayesha.

Mahommed was a terribly jealous husband; moreover he was thirty years older than this vivacious girl. His jealousy increased as he advanced in years; and, on one occasion, when the hand of a companion was thought to have touched that of

Ayesha, the Prophet felt so much uneasiness that he was not comforted until he had settled the present and future of his wives by a revelation from heaven. And accordingly, in the 33rd Sura we read:—" O true believers, enter not the houses of the Prophet, unless it be permitted you to eat meat with him, without waiting his convenient time: but when ye are invited, then enter. . . . . And when ye ask of the Prophet's wives what ye have occasion for, ask it of them from behind a curtain. This will be more pure for your hearts, and for their hearts. Neither is it fit for you to give any uneasiness to the apostle of God, or to marry his wives after him for ever; for this would be a grievous thing in the sight of God."*

When Ayesha returned, seated upon Safwan's camel, she won Mahommed's belief in her protestations of innocence. But the Prophet found that evil tongues were not stopped from speaking against the woman who, after the death of Khadijah, had the strongest and most enduring hold upon his affections. He resorted therefore, as was usual with him in any personal difficulty, to revelation; and in a Sura which, as I have before said, was introduced as specially "sent down from heaven," he promulgated a new law for the punishment of Ayesha's enemies. "Those," says the Koran, in the 24th Sura, "who accuse

---

Sale's "Al Koran."

women, and produce not four witnesses of the fact, scourge them with fourscore stripes, and never more receive their testimony, for such are infamous prevaricators. .... As to the party among you who have published the falsehood concerning Ayesha .... every man of them shall be punished according to the injustice of which he hath been guilty." And according to this *ex post facto* law, those who spread the scandal — Abd'ullah Ebn Obba, Zeid Ebn Refaa, Hassan Ebn Thabet, Mesta Ebn Othatha, and Hanna Bint Jabash—all received fourscore stripes, except Abd'ullah, who was too considerable a person to be beaten, even by the authority of the Koran. On this occasion Mahommed propounded by way of the Koran, one of the very few laws which pretend to be equitable in the relations of polygamous husband and wife. "They," he dictated in the same Sura, "who shall accuse their wives of adultery, and shall have no witnesses thereof besides themselves; the testimony which shall be required of one of them shall be, that he swear four times by God that he speaketh the truth, and the fifth time that he imprecate the curse of God on him if he be a liar. And it shall avert the punishment from the wife, if she swear four times by God that he is a liar; and if the fifth time she imprecate the wrath of God on her if he speaketh the truth."*

---

* Sale's "Al Koran."

Islam is adverse to civilisation; the Koran is not "sufficiently elastic in expression to admit of progressive developments and interpretations," because it is a religion essentially opposed to the progress of humanity. It is a religion of force and of sex. "The true servants of God," says the Koran concerning the Mahommedan heaven, will be rewarded with "delicious fruits, and the virgins of paradise withholding their countenance from any other than their spouses, having large black eyes, and skin like the eggs of an ostrich." The coarse materialism of this, and many other passages almost similar in words, together with other passages I have quoted bearing upon the relations of Islam with infidels, sustain Mr. Gladstone's description of the Turks, of whom, in his eloquent pamphlet, he says:—"For the guide of this life they had a relentless fatalism; for its reward hereafter a sensual paradise."

This unspiritual, sexual language of the Koran has been dealt with by an English apologist in a very shallow argument. The writer of "Mohammed and Mohammedanism" clearly knows nothing whatever of Oriental people. He would probably be surprised as well as shocked to find that among the superior classes the conversation is of this character, even in the presence of women and children. It is a hard fact, that no higher ideal of supernatural life is given in the Koran, and the grossness of the picture is, we are told, explained by Mahommedans to be merely "Oriental imagery." This might seem plausible at a distance, if the programme of Mahommed's heaven included entertainments for women—if for them there was something more than bare admission. They are not even translated into the "black-eyed virgins," who are to share the fruits and the couches of paradise; for, says the Koran, "We have created the damsels of paradise by a peculiar creation."

It is not my purpose to contrast one religion with another. I am not engaged in the defence of Christianity, nor in the needless work of vindicating its superiority to Islam; yet it is with a feeling of offence that I find in the work above mentioned the heaven of Mahommed contrasted with the heaven of Christ, "where they neither marry nor are given in marriage;" and the sensual hereafter of Mahommed condoned with the absurd apology, that "a polygamous people could hardly have pictured to themselves a heaven without polgyamy." The *raison d'être* of women on earth, in the eyes of Mahommedans, has been translated so faithfully and truly into their heaven, as to lead many to suppose that the Koran allows no future life to women. But evidently the denial of a share of paradise to women was not the idea of the dictator of the Koran. He constructed heaven as he observed the earth, and has therefore, not without show of reason, been held to have denied the immortality of women, while extolling that of men. If all the Turcophiles in the world tug together at the words of the Koran, they cannot be expanded or reasonably interpreted so as to exhibit an equality of divine favour to men and women.

When Mahommed grew strong he became the relentless persecutor, the cruel exterminator of the Jewish tribes in the neighbourhood of Medina. But the early Suras of the Koran suggest that there was a time when he laboured to stand well with the Jews and with those of them who had become Christians, or who honoured Jesus Christ as a great prophet. Mahommed relieved the Jews from the crime of Christ's crucifixion. He caused this to be written in the Koran: "They have said, 'Verily we have slain Jesus, the Son of Mary, the apostle of God,' yet they slew him not, neither crucified him, but he was represented by one in his likeness. They did not really kill him, but God took him up to himself, and God is mighty and wise."* Christianity was becoming a considerable power in the time of Mahommed; and so far as he understood the doctrines of Christ, he adopted them. But it never occurred to Mahommed that Jesus Christ was God. He acknowledged the birth of Christ as miraculous. The version of the birth of Christ given in the Koran is said to

Sale's "Al Koran."

have been obtained from the writings of the Apostle Barnabas. It is very curious:—" We sent our spirit Gabriel unto her, and he appeared unto her in the shape of a perfect man. He said, 'Verily I am the messenger of thy Lord, and am sent to give thee a holy son.' The pains of childbirth came upon her near the trunk of an old palm-tree. She said, 'Would to God I had died before this, and had become a thing forgotten and lost in oblivion!' And a voice called to her: 'Be not grieved now that God hath provided a rivulet under thee; and do thou shake the body of the palm-tree, and it shall let fall ripe dates upon thee, and eat and drink and calm thy mind.' And when she brought the child to her own people, and they said, 'Thou hast done a strange thing,' she made signs to the child to answer them; and they said, 'How shall we speak to him, who is an infant in the cradle?' Whereupon the child said, Verily I am the servant of God; he hath given me the book of the Gospel, and hath appointed me a prophet. And he hath made me blessed wheresoever I shall be, and hath commanded me to observe prayer and to give alms so long as I shall live. And he hath made me dutiful towards my mother, and hath not made me proud nor unhappy. And peace be on me the day whereon I was born, and the day whereon I shall die, and the day whereon I shall be raised to life.' This was Jesus, the son of Mary." And again:—

"Verily Christ Jesus, the son of Mary, is the Apostle of God, and his word which he conveyed into Mary, and a spirit proceeding from him." "God" speaks again and again in the Koran of the "evident miracles" which he permitted Jesus to work; but the Koran never leans to the doctrine that Christ is God. "They are infidels who say, 'Verily God is Christ, the son of Mary.'" "And when God shall say unto Jesus at the last day, 'O Jesus, son of Mary, hast thou said unto men, Take me and my mother for two gods beside God?' He shall answer, 'I have not spoken unto them any other than what thou didst command me—namely, Worship God, my Lord and your Lord.'"*

An English school leans to Islam because it is monotheistic; they touch gently on its faults for the sake of its assertion of the unity of God. Perhaps we should have fewer exhibitions of this sort if it were generally known that, while denying the Godhead of Christ, the Koran accepts his miraculous conception and birth; and, denying that he was crucified, holds to his miracles, and declares that those miracles were an exhibition of divine powers. We must recognise the fact that to write upon the history and the influence of religions, one upon another, in a way to be of permanent value, something more is

---

* Sale's "Al Koran."

requisite than is displayed by any of the apologists of Mahommedanism whom we have met with. When one of these writes of an "elastic" Bible, and of "stretching" the Koran, towards what line is it that these sacred books are to be strained? Religion, it seems, is to be made to fit in with civilisation.

If we want to understand whether there is anything in Islam opposed to this union with civilisation, we must know what we mean by one and by the other. We have now seen something of the doctrines of Islam. What, then, is civilisation? If it were merely buying ironclads, laying down telegraph wires, borrowing money upon worthless paper, building with glass and iron, or arming men with breach-loaders, I should say, "Islam has done all these things." But I take civilisation to be, in its briefest meaning, the extension of civil rights—the co-existence of the supremacy of law with the liberty of individuals to develop and employ their faculties for their own utmost happiness and advantage.

The sum of success in this endeavour is ever increasing. We know more truly than we can know any other thing that

"Through the ages one increasing purpose runs;"

and we have in this fact, in the increasing individuality of mankind, in what we call progress or civilisation, a test by which to judge the doctrines of religion, whether they be transient or eternal. Of the facts which the history of the world has furnished, no one is more patent than the fact and the method of human progress, in which many religions have been and will be submerged. Mankind is outgrowing, or has outgrown, the practices of slavery and polygamy which are sanctioned by the Koran, and which did not seem hateful in the days of Christ. The experiences of life lead to the laws of life, which are necessarily more and more concerned with the rights of individuals. Of the Book of Mahommed, nothing is left, in the light of the present civilisation, but the idea of God, supreme, omnipotent, impersonal. It is not so with the words of Christ. His standard—that of the brotherhood of mankind—is the banner of the time to come, and gives the largest prospect of progress which eyes can see upon the horizon of humanity.

The Christians of Turkey are often dishonest, not seldom drunken; and though not inferior to the people of Russia in political capacity, are in this respect far beneath the level of any other European people. But theirs are vices and deficiencies such as ages of oppression by a foreign soldiery (the Turks are such to them) would produce anywhere. They have had no instruction—no consolation, except from priests as ignorant as themselves. The extolled virtues of the Turk are those which have ever been exhibited by conquerors in the plenitude of supremacy above millions who toil to make their wealth; such as a foreigner would have seen in the Anglo-Normans eight hundred years ago.

In Mahommedan countries, where there is no interference by civilised powers, we have seen that a convert to Christianity forfeits his property upon application to the Sheik-ul-Islam by the next of kin. In the present year, an Armenian Christian of rank postponed his visit to a royal personage on account of wet weather. I asked him what connexion the humidity of the atmosphere had with his intention, and he said that non-Mussulmans were not welcome, the tradition from the times when they were forbidden to walk the streets in wet weather—in order that Islam might avoid the superior power of contamination which their garments acquired by moisture—being not yet quite forgotten. It is not true that the non-Mussulman population has a monopoly of intemperance. I have never seen people drink ardent spirits in such large quantities as some Mahommedans of station whom I have met with in travel. A Moslem Prince lately asked me why I drank wine. "It does not make you drunk. *I* take arrack," he added. English doctors in the East are frequently summoned to cases of delirium tremens, but

<blockquote>Offence's gilded hand doth shove by justice.</blockquote>

The rich Moslem drinks privately, the non-Mussulman publicly. The Moslem drinks at night, the non-Mussulman at all times. Perhaps a majority of Mahommedans would refuse to drink intoxicating liquor; though in a troop of servants I have never seen more than a respectable minority of this mind, and it is possible—indeed it is probable—that of the poor, many believe the Koran to be as inexorable as our Good Templars. The belief is common throughout Europe that the use of intoxicating liquors is forbidden in the Koran. The author of "Mohammed and Mohammedanism" falls into this error. He says that Mahommed absolutely prohibited gambling and intoxicating liquors. The Prophet did nothing of the sort in the Koran. The words of the Moslem Bible are these:—"They will ask thee concerning wine and lots (*al meiser*). Answer, In both there is great sin, and also some things of use unto men; but their sinfulness is greater than their use."* I should suppose that even Mr. Bass would go as far as this. It is, however, the belief of pious Moslems that when Omar demanded from the Prophet direction more definite, in order that a better condition might be maintained among the then encompassed army of Islam, Mahommed did in some terms forbid gambling and the drinking of intoxicating liquors; but this prohibition was never

---

* Sale's "Al Koran."

made part of the Koran. In Mahommed's paradise we find the apotheosis of Bacchus. Youths in perpetual bloom are to attend the happy "with goblets, and beakers, and cups of flowing wine; their heads shall not ache by drinking the same, neither shall their reason be disturbed." The "black-eyed damsels" are again introduced, and the promise is given to the men in paradise:—" They shall not hear vain discourse, or charge of sin, but only the salutation, 'Peace! peace!'" As to gambling, Mahommedans play cards upon the sands of the desert, as well as upon the decks of ships, and on the carpets and mats of their homes.

But I have made ill use of the present opportunity if I have induced upon the mind of the reader an impression very favourable to the Christians of Turkey and Persia. For this much I am always prepared to contend: they do possess, and their masters do not possess, a religion which admits of progressive developments and interpretations. The progress of humanity may for all time be illumined by the morals of the Gospel of Christ. It is nothing to show that Mahommedanism is more successful in proselytising Eastern peoples than the harshly dogmatic, un-Christian "Christianity" of some dogmatic preachers. We may develop and interpret Christ's teaching as universal, for all sorts and conditions of men, and without distinction of sex. The purest doctrines of liberty entered the world by the mouth of Christ. Mahommedanism is a democracy for men, and not for all men, but only for such as are not slaves; and with these last and lowest, the whole sex of women is indirectly placed. The religion of Islam is opposed to progress, and must decline with the irresistible advance of civilisation.

THE END.

www.ingramcontent.com/pod-product-compliance
Lightning Source LLC
Chambersburg PA
CBHW030729230426
43667CB00007B/644